A Jew Who Defeated Nazism

Dedicated to Yvonne Klemperer, who has so generously shared her memories, and encouraged and enabled this telling of her uncle's story.

A Jew Who Defeated Nazism

Herbert Sulzbach's Peace,
Reconciliation and a New Germany

Ainslie Hepburn

Pen & Sword
MILITARY
AN IMPRINT OF PEN & SWORD BOOKS LTD.
YORKSHIRE – PHILADELPHIA

First published in Great Britain in 2022 by
PEN AND SWORD MILITARY
An imprint of
Pen & Sword Books Limited
Yorkshire – Philadelphia

Copyright © Ainslie Hepburn, 2022

ISBN 978 1 52679 322 5

The right of Ainslie Hepburn to be identified as Author of this work has been asserted by her in accordance with the Copyright, Designs and Patents Act 1988.

A CIP catalogue record for this book is available from the British Library.

All rights reserved. No part of this book may be reproduced or transmitted in any form or by any means, electronic or mechanical including photocopying, recording or by any information storage and retrieval system, without permission from the Publisher in writing.

Typeset in Times New Roman 11.5/14 by
SJmagic DESIGN SERVICES, India.
Printed and bound in the UK by CPI Group (UK) Ltd.

Pen & Sword Books Limited incorporates the imprints of Atlas, Archaeology, Aviation, Discovery, Family History, Fiction, History, Maritime, Military, Military Classics, Politics, Select, Transport, True Crime, Air World, Frontline Publishing, Leo Cooper, Remember When, Seaforth Publishing, The Praetorian Press, Wharncliffe Local History, Wharncliffe Transport, Wharncliffe True Crime and White Owl.

For a complete list of Pen & Sword titles please contact
PEN & SWORD BOOKS LIMITED
47 Church Street, Barnsley, South Yorkshire S70 2AS, United Kingdom
E-mail: enquiries@pen-and-sword.co.uk
Website: www.pen-and-sword.co.uk

Or

PEN AND SWORD BOOKS
1950 Lawrence Rd, Havertown, PA 19083, USA
E-mail: Uspen-and-sword@casematepublishers.com
Website: www.penandswordbooks.com

Contents

Introduction vi
How Herbert Sulzbach changed the lives of thousands of people:
his commitment to Anglo-German reconciliation

PART I **(1894 – 1944) Two Countries, Two Faiths, Two Wars**

Chapter 1 Frankfurt. A World of a Bygone Age 2

Chapter 2 Neubabelsberg. Starting Again 22

Chapter 3 London, Basel, Onchan. Flight and Exile 38

Chapter 4 'Somewhere in England' 63

PART II **(1945 – 1951) Turning Men's Lives Round**

Chapter 5 Comrie. Confronting Nazism 80

Chapter 6 Featherstone Park. Trust, Confidence and Humanity 98

Chapter 7 Berlin. City of Ghosts 117

Chapter 8 'Somewhere in Europe' 135

PART III **(1951 – 1985) Friendship and Reconciliation**

Chapter 9 German Embassy, London. Building Bridges 144

Chapter 10 Düsseldorf, Germany. Staying Friends 166

Chapter 11 Everywhere. Reconciliation 180

Acknowledgements 191

Bibliography 201

Index 208

Introduction

How Herbert Sulzbach changed the lives of thousands of people: his commitment to Anglo-German reconciliation

Herbert Sulzbach was not the head of a political party, nor an agitator within a powerful organisation, nor someone with massive influence over those in authority, when he successfully changed the lives of thousands of people at a critical time in world history. Rather, he was a middle-aged refugee who somewhat reluctantly became involved with those who had once oppressed him. Leaving his fear and loathing on one side (and eventually casting them aside completely), he embarked on an extraordinary personal commitment to individuals. With dedication, idealism, and considerable personal charisma, he worked amongst German prisoners of war (PoWs) – some of them very senior Nazis – at the end of the Second World War, offering them a different view of patriotism, democracy and common humanity. His passion and lifework became the fostering of understanding and friendship between people, Anglo-German reconciliation, and the creation of a strong and united Europe. As a result, most of these German officers were eventually repatriated to help to build a new and democratic society in their homeland. For that reason, the PoW camp where Sulzbach worked became what some have called 'the kindergarten of the new German democracy'. Almost forty years afterwards, a Member of the British Parliament (MP), Sir Bernard Braine, remarked to him:

> I have talked with men who once believed fanatically in Hitler but whose hearts and minds you changed. Your name will always rank high among those who at a crucial period in history helped the German people to rediscover themselves and to build a just and free society.

INTRODUCTION

Herbert Sulzbach was born into a secular Jewish family in Frankfurt am Main at the end of the nineteenth century, and he grew up with great riches and an assured place in the high society circles in which his wealthy family moved. As a young man, he fought for Germany in the First World War and was decorated for his courage. During the years between the two world wars, he maintained his affluent lifestyle, directing a small commercial business near Berlin whilst enjoying the artistic and hedonist social life of the city. All this changed during the 1930s when the National Socialists came to power. As a Jew, he was stripped of many of his rights, his business was compulsorily purchased, and in 1936 he fled as a refugee to Britain.

In Britain, Sulzbach had no money, prestige or even employment to ease his way. Shortly after war was declared between Britain and Germany in 1939, he and his wife had their 'friendly alien' refugee status officially reinforced, but this was of no help to them the following May when they and many other Jews were interned as 'enemy aliens'. When he was released a few months later, Sulzbach was allowed to enlist in the British Army and fought willingly for Britain throughout the rest of the war.

As the journalist and broadcaster Ludovic Kennedy said to him several years later, after he and Sulzbach had worked together on radio and television programmes:

> You are quite unique; there is no one anywhere in the world remotely like you. To have fought for the Kaiser in one war and worn the uniform of King George in the next is amazing enough; but to have distributed your love and loyalties that both Germans and British can, without jealousy, claim you for their own, and that you can feel equally at home with both of us – that surely is genius.

For over three years from January 1945, Herbert Sulzbach worked as an interpreter at camps for German PoWs in Britain. During the first year he was at a 'black camp' in Scotland where he encountered young, passionately idealistic Nazi soldiers who had experienced no social environment other than National Socialism. It was a daunting task to try to implement the official British 're-education' policy, but within weeks Sulzbach was gaining some grudging respect amongst the men with his one-to-one encounters, his experiments in forming 'cells' of prisoners who were beginning to appreciate some of his points of view, and his determination to provide facts and proof of Nazi lies. Significant success was achieved as a result of his hard work and energy, personal charm, and profound belief in the goodness of people – whatever the horrors of the past. Those in authority were quick to see the extraordinary results that his work had amongst the young prisoners, and at the beginning of 1946 Sulzbach was transferred to a PoW camp for German officers at Featherstone Park, near Haltwhistle in Northumberland.

Here, in a camp for 4,000 prisoners, he worked in an astonishing variety of ways to enable the men to face the recent past, understand the present, and commit to a better future for themselves and their destroyed country. This was no easy undertaking and there were many who recognised that much of his success came from Sulzbach's own character and personality. A filmmaker, Bridget Winter, who worked with him years later to record the work of the camp, said of him:

> Herbert Sulzbach is deeply interested in the lives of everybody he meets, friend or foe. That is undoubtedly why he achieved such remarkable results in his work at Featherstone Park, and why foes became friends, and Anglo-German ties were so quickly re-established and strengthened after the war. Diplomatic, gentle, sympathetic and caring, he saturates himself with friendship and is instinctively understanding of all viewpoints.

It was not lost on the German prisoners that their mentor was a Jewish man who had lost members of his family and many friends in the war that they had led, and they were usually considerably humbled and inspired by his attitude towards them. In the 1970s, when Herbert Sulzbach worked to promote Anglo-German reconciliation through radio programmes, he met the journalist and broadcaster Angela Rippon, who recognised that:

> Herbert's simple but dedicated belief in the necessity of mankind to forgive and forget and live together in harmony is infectious. His generosity of spirit is an inspiration.

INTRODUCTION

The PoWs expressed similar sentiments, and when the gates of the camp closed in May 1948 many of the returning officers took up high-profile jobs in local and national government in Germany, in the press, and in the law – taking with them what they themselves called 'the Sulzbach spirit'. They kept in touch with each other and also with Herbert Sulzbach, who received thousands of letters from them over the years. In the early 1960s, as a new Cold War threatened, they formed the Featherstone Park Association and honoured Sulzbach as their president. The association aimed to promote understanding, friendship and reconciliation between Britain and Germany, and it continued with this work until most of the members were too elderly and infirm to attend its meetings – but by that time their ideals had been enthusiastically adopted by a younger generation.

After the closure of Featherstone Park PoW camp, and at the age of 57, Herbert Sulzbach joined the staff of the new German Embassy in London as a member of its Cultural Department. The embassy faced considerable hostility in the post-war tensions in London, and during the 1960s and 70s Sulzbach's work was largely directed towards gaining credibility for the new democratic Germany, and for creating links between people and communities. He worked directly with individuals and groups and also made many friends with people who worked in the press, radio and television in order to highlight and promote ideas of Anglo-German friendship and reconciliation. It became his life's mission to make reconciliation not only possible but endurable.

Herbert Sulzbach retired from the embassy after thirty years working there, at the age of 87. He lived another few years but the work of the embassy, and his friendships with his remaining PoW friends, stayed at the centre of his life. When Sulzbach died, the ambassador at the time, Baron Rüdiger von Wechmar, observed that his legacy of reconciliation for all German and British people was:

> The spirit of forgiving, the strong sense of freedom (and a critical eye for everything that could infringe upon it), as well as the recognition that our common European culture and basic beliefs find us together in defending peace and justice.

PART I

(1894 – 1944)
Two Countries, Two Faiths, Two Wars

Chapter 1

Frankfurt. A World of a Bygone Age

Number 57 Friedrichstrasse was an imposing and handsome four-storey villa, set behind tall ornate railings in a prosperous street in Frankfurt am Main. Solidly built, with large windows, the mansion stood in spacious grounds with a landscaped garden of mature trees, wide lawns, and a narrow iron footbridge straddling a small stream. Inside, the typically heavily furnished rooms were capacious but unpretentious, with the Persian carpets, family portraits, pianos and books of a successful banker's family.

Friedrichstrasse is still a leafy avenue lined with similar large houses in extensive grounds. In 1892 Herbert Sulzbach's parents, Emil and Julie, had joined the flow of other well-to-do families – many of them liberal Jews, like themselves – who built houses and settled in what was to become a very affluent area in the western part of Frankfurt. Their neighbours were mostly rich bankers, lawyers and jewellers.

Further along the road, on the corner with Freiherr-vom-Stein-Strasse, a small but grand synagogue with a domed central building in an Egyptian-Assyrian style was built during 1908/10 to minister to this growing Jewish community. Not that the Sulzbach family frequented the synagogue: they were what the Nazis would later term 'Jews by race' rather than 'Jews by faith' and saw themselves as fully assimilated into *haute-bourgeoisie* German society. For them, at the beginning of the twentieth century, there was no distinction between being German and being Jewish.

Emil and Julie Sulzbach commissioned Franz von Hoven, an independent architect who was active in the city's artist society, to build their villa. They moved into the new home with their two young children Ernst, aged 5, and Lili, who was not yet 3, along with several members of household staff. It was here that Herbert Sulzbach was born at 4.15 am on Thursday 8 February 1894.

FRANKFURT. A WORLD OF A BYGONE AGE

In common with other families of his time and class, he was looked after by a nurse whose name was Dora. His parents kept a fond and careful watch on him, making sure that he was vaccinated and noting his developmental milestones. 'He is very sweet, well-behaved and trusting. He is still blond and blue-eyed and has a bright complexion. Only when Dora leaves the room does he yell miserably,' his father wrote shortly before Herbert's first birthday. There was a good bond between the three children, although in early childhood Herbert was perhaps closer to his sister.

It was a gilded childhood, spent not only in a large and comfortable house with a glorious garden, but also in a safe and secure community – and a seemingly safe and secure world. Many years later, Herbert remembered this time as 'the normal carefree years of childhood, but there was also an apparently carefree Europe. We were ruled by the Kaiser and England was ruled by Edward VII.'

The month of May was always a particularly happy time for Herbert during his childhood, signalling as it did the start of summer and increased opportunities to be outdoors. It began with the May Day festivities when he would often go with his school friends on trips to the nearby Taunus hills, or on the Rhine, or into the mountains. As he grew older, he joined his father in the deer hunt on 1 May and relished this time in the adult world, getting up at four in the morning – always 'a glorious morning' – to drive into the nearby Odenwald forest in the stalking car.

In the summer there were lizards and butterflies in the garden. Even on school days he would get up early and by 5 am would be ready to go for bike rides with his friends in the woods, where they saw thousands of anemones and marvelled at the birdsong. Summertime also meant tennis at school with Herr Pless, and rowing in boats with Herr Scherk.

In about 1904 Councillor Kleyer personally drove to deliver one of the first Adler cars from his factory to Herbert's father at home. The family chauffeur, Herr Blank, usually took the wheel on car outings, and was also handy with his tools on those occasions when the car broke down in the middle of the forest, or in the snow. Herbert was delighted to be able to go on frequent trips with his mother and friends into the nearby forests – the Odenwald, Spessart and Westerwald.

Herbert's father had his birthday on 7 May, and there were particularly big celebrations for his fiftieth birthday in 1905, when Herbert was 11 years old. This included a serenade by the band of the 81st Frankfurt

Regiment, who marched to the house to sing for him at seven o'clock in the morning.

Summer was heralded by swallows circling over the garden. On Wednesday afternoons two Italian organ-grinders played to the Sulzbach children in the garden and were rewarded with ten pfennigs. Every year the family spent several weeks of the summer on holiday, often by the sea. Zandvoort, in Holland, was a popular destination for wealthy Germans and the Sulzbachs usually met friends there. For Herbert, in his early teens, these included two of the princes of Hesse, Max and Friedrich Wilhelm von Hessen (the Kaiser's nephews), who from 1906 were also his school mates. (Both of them were killed in the First World War.)

One day in 1903, Herbert – aged 9 – saw a steamship out at sea from Zandvoort and asked where it was going. 'To England,' his father replied. Four years later Herbert made his first visit to England – with his parents to see his sister who was at a finishing school in Eastbourne. He was astonished by some of the differences that he encountered:

> I will not forget the impression made on me by the contrast of the German notices *Verboten* [Forbidden] with the sign that I saw in an Eastbourne park: "Ladies and gentlemen will not, others must not, touch these flowers."

Swimming was a popular activity in the summer and when they were in Frankfurt Herbert went with his brother to swim in the River Main. The Mosler Swimming Institute opened every springtime at the Nizza – a park on the northern bank of the river. The institute was built as a temporary structure on wooden pontoons, which were taken down in the autumn. After a swim, Herbert and Ernst would buy pretzels from the traders on the bank. The two boys became closer as they grew older and had a great deal of fun together – buying Shrove Tuesday jokes together from the shop 'Sennelaub' in the Kornmarkt, for example.

There were also the delights of the Grüneburgpark, only a few minutes' walk from Friedrichstrasse. Owned by the neighbouring Rothschild family, the park had been remodelled by the landscape architect Heinrich Siesmayer into an English style garden – and was a favourite haunt for Herbert and his friends for collecting chestnuts.

Siesmayer had also designed the adjacent Palmengarten and when the lake there froze over in the winter the whole Sulzbach family would go skating. As a child, Herbert always looked out for the boots with fourteen and nineteen on the buckles – his lucky numbers, he thought at the time. (In adult life, he superstitiously held on to these as his lucky numbers in games such as roulette.)

Herbert's paternal grandfather, Rudolf Sulzbach, lived not far away, at Bockenheimer Anlage 53 in the centre of Frankfurt. His opulent mansion stood opposite the new Opera House, overlooking the Opernplatz – a huge public square which was well suited to large parades. His near neighbour, at Opernplatz 2, was the court photographer J.B. Ciolina, who took many of the Sulzbach family studio photographs. It was from Grandfather Rudolf's house that the extended Sulzbach family watched the Kaiser's birthday parade every 27 January. It was always a day off school so Herbert's teachers attended in their uniforms, parading with the local 81st and 63rd Companies. Afterwards, the grandchildren were allowed special biscuits from the confectioner Büfschle.

Since 1872 Rudolf Sulzbach had been a member of the Frankfurt chamber of commerce and also president of the board of directors of the stock exchange. He was appointed as an honorary member of the chamber of commerce and supported an endless number of philanthropic ventures. He had refused the offer of a hereditary title but was still willing to participate in the *haute-bourgeoisie* society of Frankfurt and enjoyed the occasional game of *trente et quarante* with King Edward VII at Baden-Baden.

Rudolf Sulzbach died in 1904, when Herbert was 10 years old. He left thirty-two million Gold Marks. 'He was one of the kindest and richest men in Germany,' remembered his grandson. In memory of their father, Emil and Karl established a foundation of 100,000 marks for the education and training of talented young businessmen and for the benefit of those in need of help. On the day of his funeral, commerce in Frankfurt came to a halt to allow the kilometre-long funeral procession through, and Caesar Seligmann gave the funeral address.

Herbert revered his grandfather and adored and admired his father. Emil Sulzbach had been a partner in the family banking firm, Gebrüder Sulzbach, from the age of 24. But a few weeks before Herbert was born, he resigned from the business in order to devote himself to music. Rudolf Sulzbach arranged for one of his oldest colleagues, Hermann Köhler, to become a partner in Emil's place.

Emil was then 38 years old and an accomplished pianist, having studied under Wilhelm Lutz and Iwan Knorr. He was also a composer of songs that were known in several European countries. In January 1891, the *Manchester Guardian* had reported on:

> Mr Theinhardt's concerts at the Concert Hall for the propagation of contemporary music. Song, *Der Ungenannten* (with English horn obligato) by Emil Sulzbach.

He inspired a great love of music in all his children. Lili was a pianist and Herbert took violin lessons under Hermann Keiper. Frequent musical events were held either at the Sulzbach home, or at concert halls in the town, or at the Frankfurt Konservatorium. The Konservatorium was founded in 1878 as a school for music and the arts for all age groups. In the late nineteenth century, with teachers like Clara Schumann on the faculty, it became internationally well-known. Emil Sulzbach was chair of the governors from 1904 until 1923.

Like many other Jewish businessmen in Frankfurt, Emil was actively involved in science, the arts, and various social institutions in the city and was generous in his patronage. He was on the board of directors of the widows' and orphans' fund of the opera house, provided funds for student musicians, and was on the board of directors of the Senckenbergianum, Frankfurt's natural history museum. The Sulzbach family also provided financial backing for the Palmengarten.

Herbert said of Emil:

> I have often described my father as the most modest millionaire. He lived only for others, spending millions for music and poor musicians, helping thousands without ever mentioning his name.

Emil Sulzbach died in a sanatorium in Bad Homburg on 25 May 1932. At precisely the same time on that day, a concert on a local radio station included 'four songs with orchestra accompaniment (Emil Sulzbach)'. The conductor was Hans Rosbaud and the soloist was Anita Franz (soprano). As Herbert later said:

> When my father died, he was listening to the radio at the moment when one of his songs – *Es ist der Erden schönste*

Zeit – was sung. One of the Frankfurt papers reported this as, "he heard his song and died".

Emil's 'last wishes' indicate his deep involvement with musicians, poets and writers, as well as concern for his family. His passing was recorded in many national and local papers with honour and respect for an unassuming, thoughtful and artistic man.

After his death, the city council honoured Emil Sulzbach with the naming of a street in Frankfurt in gratitude for his charitable works (although this was delayed for many years as the National Socialists came to power shortly afterwards and revoked the council's decision).

The Sulzbach wealth came from the family bank. Historically, the only sources of income open to Jews had been the retail trade, the business of lending money, and pawnshops. There had been laws prohibiting Jews from engaging in agriculture and in the professions, but there was no prohibition against the taking of interest. So, Jews, almost out of necessity, had become bankers.

On 5 April 1856 Rudolf Sulzbach and his older brother Siegmund had founded the private bank S. Sulzbach, which became particularly involved in the financing of new industries – electrical engineering, chemistry, and transport. Ten years later, after the death of their father, the bank was renamed Gebrüder Sulzbach. When Siegmund Sulzbach died in December 1876, Rudolf Sulzbach became the senior partner.

He involved the Bank of Brussels and the German Bank of London in his interests and floated foreign railway share certificates on the Frankfurt stock exchange. The bank helped finance the Brunswick State Railway Company (Braunschweigische Landes-Eisenbahn-Gesellschaft), which opened up the agricultural areas around Brunswick, particularly for the transportation of potash, which was mined there. It had interests in the railways being built in Turkey and Russia, and contributed to the consortium responsible for the building of the Saint Gotthard railway in Lucerne, to the Oregon committees of the Philadelphia and Reading railways, the Southern Pacific and California railways, and the Chicago-Milwaukee railway companies, as well as to railway building in Brazil and Canada.

In its financing of new industries, Gebrüder Sulzbach, together with Jacob Landau from Berlin, raised the capital that enabled Emil Rathenau to acquire the licensing rights from Thomas Edison for his German Edison company. The first international electricity exhibition was organised in Frankfurt in 1891. In the 1890s the bank was involved in the financing of numerous companies, which initiated the founding of the Allgemeine Elektricitäts-Gesellschaft (AEG), as well as financing the aluminium company Neuhausen Alusuisse.

Rudolf's two sons both joined the banking house as partners – Emil in 1879, and Karl in 1883. In March 1914 a young lawyer, Heinrich Kirchholtes, married Karl Sulzbach's daughter and was subsequently admitted as a partner in the bank in 1919. Their marriage would become significant for the future of the bank twenty years later, since Heinrich was not Jewish.

The Sulzbachs' success was due partly to their pioneering spirit, hard work, and willingness to take risks. But all prosperous Jewish businessmen in Germany had benefited from the opportunities offered by the religious tolerance of the German Enlightenment, and it was this philosophy of thought that was also the basis of the education system of the time.

The unbiased search for truth of the Enlightenment – the worlds of Lessing, Schiller, Goethe, Kant and Mendelssohn – was at the heart of the education on offer at the Goethe Gymnasium in Frankfurt, which Herbert Sulzbach attended from 1904 until 1913. Whilst he was not a brilliant scholar, his Enlightenment education remained important to him throughout his life. In later years it came to represent the 'true Germany' for him.

In 1904, when Herbert first started at school, of the 441 pupils at the Goethe Gymnasium, 125 were Jewish. He enjoyed the company of his fellow pupils but was not very interested in academic study. His favourite subjects were languages and he consistently received good marks in French and English, but science subjects, Latin and Greek (as well as handwriting) were 'poor'. Attendance at Jewish religion classes was voluntary, and numbers were low until a new Rabbi revised the syllabus and took over the teaching. The students' interest was renewed, but even so, religious instruction did not appeal much to Herbert.

A few years after starting at the Goethe Gymnasium, Herbert began to be tutored at home by a young man, Bernhard Löffler, who was ten years older than him. Throughout his childhood and youth, Herbert was also taught at home by an English governess from Berkshire, Gertrude Stone ('Nini'), who was part of the household. She gave him lessons in the school room at home and in many ways became a mother substitute for Herbert as his own mother (whom he adored) seems to have been somewhat distant, in the manner of their time and class. In June 1913, when he was 19 years old, Herbert wrote in his diary:

FRANKFURT. A WORLD OF A BYGONE AGE

> I think with pleasure of the times after our meals when I used to sit with Nini keeping an eye, telling her things, and cursing about Homer, history and French.

A few months earlier, at the end of 1912, he had used his diary to record: 'the engagement of the blissfully happy Lili; the victory of love.' This was two months before his own nineteenth birthday, and he was frequently inclined to be romantic and rather sentimental. The list at the end of this diary showing his conquests of the local girls is quite long, and his romances had become increasingly important to him over the previous couple of years. From a scholastic point of view, the time spent in romantic involvements was not giving him much academic success, and he was glad of Dr Löffler as a confidante. At about the same time as Lili's engagement he wrote of an evening when his tutor:

> ...came to supper with me and Nini. It was lovely; we just made music. He is so nice, that I shall remember it for a long time. We talk about everything. I told him first about Lili's engagement, and about Hester, Martha, Agnes, Mimi, Marthe, and Mieze. We talked together until eight o'clock struck, and I still had to finish off some homework quickly.

Emil Sulzbach had returned a few days earlier from a music festival in Vienna to an emotional household, held 'an audience' with Georg von Boxberger, Lili's fiancé, so 'everything is regularized, and the engagement can be announced.' The following December days were cold and the lake in the Palmengarten froze over. Herbert sent a message to Mieze (his current romantic attachment) and at eight o'clock on 12 December 1912 they went, together with Herbert's parents – and Lili and Georg – on to the ice. 'We were given a warm reception.'

Lili and Georg (who was not Jewish) were married in Frankfurt on 18 January 1913, and two days later Herbert's written *Abitur* exam began. He heard a month later that he had failed. His diary that evening was not cheerful:

> A car took me back to the house where Papa, Mama and the terrible Nini would be sad. The parents were nice and consoling. Nini cried. Everyone, including me, was of the opinion that there was nothing more to be done about the

business. My story caused general regret and I was gloomy throughout the seventeenth and eighteenth. My thoughts stayed with Mieze. Oh, how often had I written in my diary, "Will my *Abitur* be damaged?"

On 2 March 1913 Herbert met Friedl Schneider, whom he called Bob, who began to replace Mieze Kindervatter in his affections.

Since he didn't plan to go to university, and a place in the family bank was assured, his job prospects were not affected by his failing the *Abitur*. But the planned celebratory six-month trip abroad was downsized to a shorter visit with his tutor to Italy, North Africa and Sicily. Meanwhile, Mieze was going to finishing schools in Switzerland and then England for the following year and Miss Stone was going to Kissinger to help Lili prepare her new home.

Herbert and Dr Löffler set out on their trip on 23 March 1913 and were accompanied for the first few days by Herbert's parents, who were themselves travelling on to Rijeka and then Abbazia and Vienna. Their first stop was at the Hotel Excelsior in Trieste, from where they visited Miramare, Pula, and Brijuni.

After saying goodbye to Herbert's parents, the two young men travelled on the Simplon express to Venice, where they went by gondola to the Hotel Royal Danieli on the Grand Canal. There was a festive reunion as they met with Fritz and Dora Lechmann, who were living at the hotel. The Sulzbachs and Lechmanns had often met at Zandvoort during Herbert's childhood summer holidays.

They stayed in Venice for two days before continuing on to Genoa for a further two days. On 2 April they left by sea on the *Derfflinger* for Algeria, arriving several hours late after a violent night-time storm at sea. Their stay in Algiers lasted for ten days and they had a wonderful time. By day, they explored the local sights, including being transported on one excursion 'on two really obstinate Yemen animals.' Herbert was kept busy recording everything in letters home to his parents and in his diary. It was a hectic lifestyle:

> Then in the evening we went with the hotel waiter to the town, first to the casino and then to the gaming rooms to play roulette, where I won 21 – 28 francs, and then lost them all again. On the twelfth was a ball to which we were invited, which went on until early morning.

They were about to leave Algiers when they discovered that they had run out of money. They had spent thousands of francs – mainly shopping for carpets and pictures, buying champagne, and losing at roulette. Unable to draw out any more, they sent a quick cable to Herbert's father for extra funds and were then able to journey on via Constantine and El Kantara to Biskra, where they stayed for a fortnight.

Somewhere in the desert between Touggart and El Oued they caught two fenek foxes, which they fed with snakes and lizards in their hotel rooms. They planned to present the foxes to Frankfurt Zoo on their return. Their travels then took them via Timgad and Constantine to Tunis. They stayed there for a week before spending a further week in Palermo, Sicily. A further fortnight of travelling, with a week spent in Taormina, brought them back home – via Catania and Syracuse.

As well as living the high society life in the splendid hotels where they stayed, Herbert and Dr Löffler visited many ancient monuments and experienced breath-taking adventures on their travels, which they documented in long letters back to Herbert's parents. Herbert appreciated the value of this journey and remembered it for the rest of his life. In his diary he wrote, 'we have had months of a fine, independent life, in which we have both learnt, seen and experienced a great deal, so that now we will apply ourselves to our jobs with double enthusiasm,' and before returning home, he wrote two letters. One was to his parents, thanking them for making the journey possible, and the other was to Miss Stone, 'to thank her for all the trouble that she took for my sake during my years at school.'

He was indeed extremely grateful to his parents, recording his feelings, as usual, in his diary:

> And now we are going home, back to work, and on towards the seriousness of life. What an amazing youth it has been because of my beloved parents. I have had everything, and I thank them with the greatest possible gratitude. Now my upbringing is completed, and I step out of youth and into life.

Herbert and Dr Löffler arrived back in Frankfurt on 9 June 1913. The following day Herbert's parents took the two desert foxes to the Frankfurt Zoo where the animals were enthusiastically received. Settling back again after his trip, Herbert began to adjust to his new life of early adulthood.

Since Lili now had her own home, there were rearrangements in the house in Friedrichstrasse. Herbert enjoyed taking over her bedroom – 'which has much more space' – and 'sorting it out' as his own. His old school room was to become 'a real gentleman's smoking room, with club chairs, space for books, lovely wallpaper and linoleum, a smoking set and cupboard – with nothing of the old schoolroom left behind.'

He started work as a trainee at the family bank a week after his return, on 17 June 1913, and was soon plunged into a busy time of half year accounts. He reckoned that he was getting used to the work well, although he regretted that he needed to work harder at his punctuality. Meanwhile, he was enjoying his friendship with Friedl and saw her most days. His working day finished at 6 pm and they would afterwards meet at the Bristol Hotel, or go for walks in the forest, or out for jaunts in the prized new family car.

That October Lili gave birth to a son, Herbert Franz Rudolf von Boxberger. A few weeks later the baby was christened at the Sulzbach home by Pastor Willy Veit. As well as Lili and Georg with baby Herbert, both sets of their parents attended the mid-morning celebration together with Herbert, Miss Stone, Frau Blank (the chauffeur's wife), and Lili's maid. Herbert found it a moving and solemn occasion.

He was cheerful and optimistic at the end of 1913 and in his diary on the last day of the year he wrote (with more hope than prophetic foresight):

> A new year begins, which will only bring happier things, and the old one is behind us. 1913 was for me a year of happiness, with contentedness at the side of Mieze and of Friedl, with travel in foreign lands, and with my new job. I would like 1914 to pass as smoothly as the old year and for all my relatives to have an even more wonderful year.

In March 1914, he enjoyed meeting with some of his former school friends at a reunion in the 'Kaiserkelb'. It was little more than a year since they had all left school but there would never be another such event: by the same time the following year many of these young men had been killed in war.

Herbert was becoming increasingly disenchanted with his work at the family bank and wanted a change. He was undecided between starting an apprenticeship in commerce in Hamburg or joining the military. He talked about his plans with a family friend, Dr Bückner, during some weekend visits at the Sulzbach hunting lodge during May and June 1914.

The hunting lodge, the *Jagdhaus*, was the family's much-loved country retreat where the men were happy hunting, and where they all enjoyed entertaining. Emil Sulzbach had had the lodge built in 1912 in the Spessart, a low mountain range in southern Hesse, not far from Frankfurt. There were always weekend visitors – family friends, fellow hunters, and people from the world of music – especially during the summer months. That summer, 1914, Herbert frequently made the journey by train and bike to join his parents at the *Jagdhaus*. One weekend they entertained the singer Delia Rheinhardt; on another they saw roe deer and big game; and there was always walking in the mountains.

On one of these weekend walks he finally took the advice of Dr Bückner and resolved to start military service in the cavalry. During July he was accepted by the 2nd Bavarian Field Artillery Regiment at Würtzburg and expected to start as a recruit on 1 October. But European politics overtook his plans. On 28 June, shortly before Herbert attended the military selection proceedings, Archduke Franz Ferdinand of Austria and his wife were murdered in Sarajevo. Over the next few weeks, events moved swiftly, and Herbert tracked them in his diary:

> 23 July [1914]. Austria's ultimatum to Serbia. World War depends on Serbia's refusal.

> 25 July 1914. Serbia's refusal. Excitement and enthusiasm. All eyes now turn towards Russia; will she support Serbia? The whole week has been stress and agitation.

The weather was hot, sultry and heavy in Frankfurt on 31 July as the Kaiser announced 'the imminent danger of war' and Austria mobilised. Herbert was excited by the heightened atmosphere around him, especially when Germany mobilised troops the following day:

> There is no possible description of the magnificent enthusiasm and superb mood during the week since the Serbian-Austrian declaration of war.

Two days later, Lili's husband went to Wilhelmshafen to report for duty as a captain in the medical corps on SMS *Ariadne*, while Herbert hoped to enrol with the 63rd Artillery Regiment at Frankfurt. Everywhere there was immense activity, patriotic fervour – and tears from the girls. All the menservants from the Sulzbach household – 'Berthold, Heinz and everyone, everyone, – ach, so many' – joined up.

All Herbert's friends had volunteered and seemed to have disappeared. Lili, aged 24 and alone with a 10-month-old baby, returned to her parents' house. The family was concerned about Ernst, who was in London and would need a few days to be able to get home. Frankfurt was, according to Herbert, 'sorrowful and solemn, and full of patriotism.' An officer was quartered with the Sulzbachs, their prized Adler car was requisitioned to go to the Front at Metz, and a curfew was imposed from eleven o'clock. Miss Stone had earlier returned to England after her many years with the family, and Herbert's father had bought her a boarding house in Bayswater to provide her with some security.

In the evening of 4 August 1914 England declared war on Germany. Three days later the Sulzbachs received a telegram from Ernst to say that he had travelled as far as Hamburg and was on his way to Frankfurt. When he arrived, he enlisted in the Strasbourg Hussars.

Herbert enlisted on 8 August with the local 63rd Regiment and two days later he was fitted with his drill uniform, as were many of his friends who were in the same battery. His friend Martha gave him a lucky penny. The new recruits were allowed out into town, which Herbert found amusing since they didn't even know how to salute. He went with Friedl to have their photograph taken at a studio in the Rossmarkt. While they were out, he was startled when the crowds parted to allow a young cavalry officer through, with his horse leading a train of forage wagons.

He spent his last evening, 29 August, at home with Lili and his parents. Then the appalling news came that SMS *Ariadne* had been sunk. The following day they were profoundly shocked and deeply distressed to learn that Georg was dead. Lili was inconsolable and found it almost impossible to say goodbye to her younger brother in his uniform. Herbert's parents were also extremely upset so it was a sad and difficult leave-taking.

During the First World War Herbert fought as a gunner, displaying enthusiasm, courage and cheerfulness in nearly all of the main battles on the Western Front. Throughout the war years, he retained an imperturbable belief that he and his fellow German soldiers were fighting for a just cause. As well as fighting in battle, he periodically attended training sessions as heavier and more complex guns were built and new tactics developed. His first garrison was in Belgium and throughout the autumn and winter of the first year of the war he fought at battles around Lille, and in Flanders and Armentières.

The war was not over by Christmas, as some had predicted. He began 1915 in Champagne, and during the four weeks in which he fought at the first Battle of Champagne he and his colleagues withstood wave after wave of attack by Allied soldiers. Herbert's guns were firing shells day and night – an experience he remembered in grim detail for the whole of his life. As an old man, he described how:

> The French tried to break through our line and didn't succeed, but it was one of the most unpleasant experiences for us young soldiers. We were twenty years old. We had the first casualties, the first dead, the first dead horses, first dead comrades. They were terrible weeks. The horses got stuck in the mud, and many of the horses had just to be left in the mud. We couldn't get them out; they died in the mud.

Herbert's fluency in French was useful during the war, particularly when acquiring billets and provisions. Sometimes he stayed for several weeks in the same area and made friends with the local people. Whenever he returned to such an area, he made a point of visiting those who had been kind to him. After the Battle of the Champagne, in early 1915, he and his fellow soldiers were withdrawn for several weeks to a quiet little village called Les Petites Armoires. The friendships that he made there with the French population were kept for many years. 'People there were really kind to us; there were no bad feelings. They gave us milk, and eggs and butter,' he remembered.

It was an extraordinary situation for the French people living in the countryside as well as for the young German soldiers. It gave the kind-hearted, courageous and generous young Herbert reason for thought and consideration. In his dealings with the local people, and with the French prisoners that he met, he 'realised for the first time that hatred didn't really exist. We started to love this French soil, and the French people. Suddenly we felt pity for the whole country, and we started to like the country we were fighting. I think that was the feeling of all of us.' It was a strange experience for him of the possibilities of reconciliation even in a time of war.

After this peaceful interlude at Les Petites Armoires, Herbert was next involved in the static trench warfare in the countryside around Roye and Noyon, and also in Picardy. He was about 20 kilometres south of the battles of the Somme at the end of 1916 and was back near Noyon in the spring of 1917. 'My well-beloved Noyon', he called the town, and from time to time – as an officer by then – he enjoyed the comforts of the German HQ in Noyon's former *Hotel Arnette de la Charlonny*.

Although Herbert had been aware of a brief spontaneous truce at various points along the Front at Christmastime 1914, he had not been part of this. But he remembered a different occasion in 1916 as the Battle of the Somme raged within hearing. As a musician and lover of music, it affected him deeply.

Although he could hear the guns and the noise of the battles on the Somme, his area was relatively peaceful with only sporadic shooting. The opposing trenches were only about 30 yards from each other, so he could see and hear the French soldiers. On one splendid and quiet summer night, a Frenchman began to sing – 'a wonderful tenor singing Rigoletto.' The German soldiers stood in their trenches to watch and listen, not daring or wanting to shoot. When the singing came to an end, they applauded, and out of the night the French soldier called back, '*merci*' (thank you).

During 1917 Herbert Sulzbach served in the battles on the Siegfried Front, at the twin battles Aisne-Champagne. By then, he belonged to an *Eingreif* division, a special task force liable to be thrown into the thick of an emergency at short notice. He took part in the huge battles in 1918 on the Avre, and near Montdidier and Noyon, as well as the German offensive in the spring of 1918. For him, 'the greatest event with the most excitement' was the preparation for the great German breakthrough on 21 March 1918. Planning for the attack was meticulous and the German soldiers were well-rehearsed.

Herbert's regiment belonged to the 18th Army under General von Hutier, opposite Britain's General Gough's 5th Army. Herbert was in St Quentin itself, with his guns amongst the already-destroyed houses, as 21 March approached. The action that he witnessed that day – the sights, the sounds, the smells – stayed with him for ever. The battle started at 4.40 am with the enormous noise of a barrage of gunfire from the

Germans. Five thousand guns firing at the same time made the giving of verbal orders impossible: orders were whistled. The gunners continued firing for five hours, at the end of which the whole area was filled with thick smoke as well as the spring mists.

As he pursued the French a few days later Herbert tripped over a copy of General Pétain's order. He was deeply impressed by what he read, particularly the words, 'Hold fast your ground. Keep steady; reinforcements are coming. This is battle. Soldiers of the Marne, of the Yser, and of Verdun, I appeal to you. The future of France is at stake.'

He began to appreciate that the French were fighting for what he described as 'a sacred cause'. As he remembered later, in another war, 'the respect that I had always had for the courage and heroism of the French became admiration – although I was then her enemy.' He kept the order that he had found.

Then came July 1918, which he recorded as 'the most decisive day that the end was coming.' Allied forces, including American troops, attacked the Germans – who didn't expect to be defeated. But they were overwhelmed by the numbers of troops and tanks directed at them by American, French and British forces. When a retreat was ordered, Herbert was only a few kilometres away from the opposing forces. On the evening of 18/19 July, he was adjutant in charge of three batteries. On that momentous night, he managed to lead the withdrawal of all three batteries without any loss of man or horse.

From then on, Herbert and his men were fighting defence battles and retreating into the very places from where they had previously advanced. Eventually, on 11 November 1918, 24-year-old First Lieutenant Sulzbach wrote in his diary:

> The order arrived this morning: "*Von 12 Uhr Mittags an ruhen die Waffe*" ["Hostilities will cease at 12 o'clock"].'

It was a very bitter moment. Herbert and his fellow soldiers had anticipated the end of the war as victors, as 'the most splendid event of our lives', but instead found themselves surrendering, 'humbled, our souls torn and bleeding.'

Their defeat was shattering, sudden, and inexplicable to the men in the German Army. Despite a subsequent widespread drop in morale, Herbert tried to remain positive and never lost faith in his generals. He was scathing when he saw military discipline weaken and proudly led his unit's march back to Germany in an orderly manner. He had survived the four years of war with only very minor illnesses and injuries and was a respected officer. One soldier remembered hearing others speak of him with admiration:

> I heard his name for the first time in the autumn of 1917, in a bunker at the River Aisne near Laon, when officers spoke about something extraordinary that – again – he had achieved. *"Dieser Sulzbach"* ["that Sulzbach"], they marvelled in disbelief.

Herbert had fought with courage, patriotism and optimism. Many of his former school friends did not survive the war, but new friendships forged in battle and trench warfare remained strong and durable. He was awarded the Iron Cross Second Class in 1916 at the Battle of the Somme, and the Iron Cross First Class for what he did between 18 July and 1 August 1918 during the Second Battle of the Marne. But the defeat of Germany saddened him to the depth of his soul. He received his army discharge papers at Frankfurt on 6 December 1918. He was very depressed about the 'humiliating conditions of unconditional surrender', and always maintained that 'it was the last knightly war between enemies' – and that Germany didn't deserve Versailles.

Back in civilian life in Frankfurt, Herbert hoped to pick up the life that he had left behind four years previously. A week after his army discharge, he bounced back into the social round by accepting an invitation to the twentieth birthday party of Margot Rocholl that was being given by her stepfather, Professor Salomons. Herbert had known Margot throughout his childhood. Her older brother, also Herbert, had attended school at the Goethe Gymnasium in the year below Sulzbach and had been particularly well-known as a keen tennis player amongst his school friends. He had been killed in 1916 fighting on the Eastern Front at Gostinari in Romania. Margot and Herbert Rocholl's father, Wilhelm Rocholl, had been a protestant lawyer and had died young when his two children were still toddlers. Their mother, born Meta Eichengrün, was Jewish and had later married Professor Salomons.

Petite and pretty, with enormous dark eyes, Margot was four years younger than Herbert Sulzbach. Her gaiety, charm and sense of fun completely captivated him – especially after all his recent grim experiences of war – and they became engaged on 15 March 1919. He was the first amongst his former classmates to decide to marry, and his 'joyful happiness with Margot is indescribable.'

Their marriage service was held on Tuesday 27 May 1919 at St Paul's protestant Church, Frankfurt, with twenty to twenty-five people attending. Sixty to seventy friends and family members were invited to an afternoon reception and tea at Margot's family home, Westendstrasse 25. It was a happy occasion where 'everyone seemed happy with our happiness.'

Margot and Herbert departed for a three-month honeymoon. First, they went by train to Berlin to visit relatives and then moved on to Westerland. Herbert's diary for his honeymoon records much swimming in the sea, and many hours spent playing roulette in the casino. Over sixty years later, he told a friend that these weeks had actually been *'mehr Roulette als Bett*!' ['more roulette than bed']. Despite being on his honeymoon, Herbert kept in touch with the confusing and worrying political changes of post-war Germany, recording in his diary accounts of revolutionary activity, and his concerns of imminent civil war:

1 July 1919. Transport strike in Berlin.

5 July 1919. There is a rail strike in Frankfurt. The transport strike in Berlin has been going on for almost 8 days!

At the end of their honeymoon Margot and Herbert returned to Frankfurt and went to live with her parents at their large villa in Westendstrasse, only a short walk from Herbert's parents' house and in the same prosperous area of the city. Shortly afterwards Herbert became unwell, feeling anxious and jittery, and went for a six week stay at a sanatorium at St Blaise. Perhaps the intensity of his experiences over the previous few years was having an effect.

While he was away, he received 'a glorious telegram' from Margot, announcing that she was expecting a baby. 'Long live the young father.' Margot was 21 years old when Dorothee Martha Madalaine Ellinor Sulzbach (they called her Dodo) was born on 25 May 1920 in the Vaterland Hospital in Frankfurt. Herbert visited his wife every day and found her and the baby to be 'very sweet, simply charming and beautiful'. When they left hospital ten days after the birth, it was to return to a 'house full of flowers and gifts.'

Dodo was born at a time of political turbulence in Frankfurt. The year 1920 had begun with city-wide strikes by revolutionaries, whilst other members of the community were fervently patriotic in the Wilhelmian tradition. It was a time of contrasts: whilst the trams often failed to run, coal was scarce, and the trains were on strike, the New Year of 1920 was celebrated loudly in the 'Frankfurthof'. Herbert was there and recorded in his diary that, 'Thunderous applause rang out in the middle of the night when everybody sang in the New Year with *"Deutschland uber alles"* ["Germany above everything"]. It is an omen for these dreadful times to be naturally proud!'

By the beginning of April 1920, French troops were occupying Frankfurt as a result of the French government claiming that Germany had broken certain articles of the Versailles treaty. The people of Frankfurt became increasingly hostile as the occupiers positioned machine-guns at the post office. Tension mounted and before the situation could be diffused the guns were brought into play, and some civilians were killed and injured. There was general confusion, distrust, and anxiety for the future.

A few weeks after his daughter's birth, Herbert got on his bike to visit his parents at their *Jagdhaus*, particularly to talk about his future employment prospects with his father. Returning to work at the family bank was still not an attractive proposition and had become even less so now that he missed the excitement, responsibility and leadership opportunities that the war had given him. He also had a wife and child to support.

By the end of their discussion, Emil Sulzbach had agreed to finance the purchase of a directorship of a fancy paper business for Herbert. Margot's stepfather was in agreement with the plan and negotiations went ahead for the purchase of a small factory in Neubabelsberg, on the outskirts of Berlin, near Potsdam. The process was hampered by political tension, inflation and increasing economic uncertainty, which was having a considerable impact on the Sulzbach family fortune and very much depressed Herbert's father.

Eventually Herbert and his father, as well as Professor Salomons, put up the necessary money for the purchase of a factory in Schillerstrasse, Neubabelsberg (now Otto Erich Strasse). Discussions of detail continued throughout the autumn of 1920, during which time Herbert found accommodation for the family in the leafy Grunewald area between Berlin and Neubabelsberg.

At the beginning of November Dorothee was baptised in Frankfurt at Margot's parents' house. A week later, on 12 November 1920, Margot and Herbert left Frankfurt with their baby and her nurse, Ellinor, to start a new life in Neubabelsberg. They were happy and excited, but also a little apprehensive. As Herbert was well aware:

> The greatest period in our lives with the move to Berlin has come. There are many conflicting feelings and much gratitude. We are leaving parents and memories of youth and are feeling very sentimental. A new life is beginning, and for the first time it is our – Margot's and mine – own life.

Chapter 2

Neubabelsberg. Starting Again

It was a crazy time to be experimenting with fresh ventures, as the 1920s opened up in Germany, but – as usual – Herbert Sulzbach was upbeat. He knew that this undertaking would be 'a hazardous business' in the current political and economic climate but he remained optimistic. He recognised the 'steep learning curve and colossal amount of work' that would be required, especially in the first year of his new business, but he relished the challenge. In particular, he felt that he had acquired once again some status and authority that he had lost when the war ended. He was also glad to be self-sufficient and less reliant on his and Margot's parents.

Up until then both Herbert and Margot had lived very close to both of their families in Frankfurt and there were concerns that moving away from this support with a young baby might be too stressful. But Herbert was confident that their marriage was 'SO happy and ideal' that this would remain so 'WITHOUT local influence!'

In October 1920 Herbert attended the three-day International Trade Fair in Frankfurt, networking, socialising and gaining his first insights into his new business. The fair was very well visited, and Herbert judged it to have been a success.

He went to work in his new factory for the first time on 15 November 1920 and delighted in having his own office. He was very much looking forward to running his own business and was enthusiastic and fascinated about the printing process when the new machinery started up a few weeks later and the first fancy papers were produced. He found it all 'magnificently technical'.

Sulzbach's factory lay near the Griebnitz See, one of the lakes to the north-east of Potsdam, which was itself about 24 kilometres south-west of Berlin. It was an affluent area where since the end of the nineteenth century the wealthy people from Berlin had been building large villas on the shores of the lake. Nearby was the industrial town of Nowawes, which was well served by the railway line that had been built about seventy years earlier and went directly to Berlin.

Berlin was a city of modern technology, and industries were attracted by its pioneering water, gas and electrical systems. Sulzbach's small fancy paper factory was in Schillerstrasse, numbers 9 – 15. Next door was a net factory.

A few months later, on 8 February 1921 – his twenty-seventh birthday – Herbert rented a flat in a large mansion at Taubertstrasse 5 in Grunewald, on the edge of Berlin. The apartment covered the top two floors of the house, with a bedroom, nursery, kitchen and dining room above a hall and a drawing room with a grand piano. Both he and Margot were delighted with the flat, but Herbert's diary hinted at some of the tensions that were beginning to build in their marriage. On his return from negotiating the renting of the flat he found a note from Margot: 'Today I promise that I will never be nasty to you again, but only be loving and respectful, and you will always be a loving and beloved husband.'

They moved in to Taubertstrasse a month later, soon after attending the Leipzig Trade Fair together. On the same day as the trade fair opened, the London Conference was held to discuss Germany's post-war reparations. Sulzbach cut out a short article from a German newspaper that described the conference's opening church service, at which the Archbishop of Canterbury had preached from the biblical text, 'I tell you truly, you will not be let out until you have paid the last farthing.'

Sulzbach was outraged and commented that it seemed as though war had been declared against Germany all over again. Along with many of his compatriots, he felt 'defenceless rage, terrible fury!' He remained extremely proud of his own distinguished war service and was angry with those Germans who demonstrated their anger with strikes and revolutionary activities. Continuing civil unrest was also affecting business and on the same day that Herbert and Margot moved into their new home he conceded that the situation at his factory was 'not completely carefree' and that he needed more business capital.

A couple of months later he returned to Frankfurt to discuss these business worries with his father. By then Emil Sulzbach had even more serious concerns of his own. Apart from the devastating effect of the deterioration of the national economy on his own financial affairs, and his subsequent clinical depression, he had recently been told that his wife was very ill. He shared none of this with Herbert – who was concerned and upset by his father's apparent aloofness – but an operation a few weeks later confirmed that Herbert's mother had intestinal cancer.

All these pressures took their toll on Herbert and Margot's marriage and Margot's moody behaviour became even more pronounced. Herbert was alarmed that her 'nastiness and irritability' had become worse. He was extremely saddened that 'every word from her seems said to torment.' He felt crushed by this sadness, by his financial and business concerns, by the scarcity of goods, and by the anxiety over his beloved mother's serious ill-health.

A fortnight later, Herbert and Margot sat down to discuss their marriage, and agreed to bring it to an end. It was a wretchedly painful time for Herbert, who couldn't help comparing the carefree pre-war period with the subsequent war and revolutionary events. He felt bitterly that he had 'had no youth, from nineteen years until today, so that now I am twenty-seven years old, and my life and my youth have been one rush.' He was worried by so many aspects of his everyday life and also regretted the humiliation of the end of the war and of his marriage.

Herbert continued to live at the flat at Taubertstrasse that they had entered only a few months previously with such high hopes, and Margot went with 1-year-old Dorothee to live with a relative a few streets away at Lynarstrasse 4. Herbert remained in close contact with them both and tried to support his wife, especially when she was sad and disturbed towards the end of the year when her grandmother died. Margot was a complex and often unhappy person, despite her apparent gaiety, and many years later her daughter said of her, 'she didn't have a happy life, but it was mostly her own fault, as she was so difficult to get on with, and so intolerant.'

Although life became more peaceful for Herbert, he missed Margot. Much later, he recognised that very soon after the end of a traumatic war he had married quickly, had a child quickly, and had just as quickly divorced – and had perhaps been less mature than he had thought. However, at the time he was only conscious of his loss. 'In this last year I have lost too much – physical, psychological, and material.'

It was clear that Sulzbach's business could not be saved in its current form, and urgent talks for liquidation began. On 10 August 1921 the Deutsche Zentral-Boden-Kredit AG became the new owner, although

NEUBABELSBERG. STARTING AGAIN

Sulzbach remained part of the new company. Thankfully, things then began to pick up at the factory and valuable orders started to come in.

But Herbert's summing up of 1921 was melancholy:

> With the changes in my dealings with Margot, and with the business, things are now somewhat better. I love her despite everything, but there is no inner stability, no support for one another. I need and long for love, warmth, sincerity.

Whatever he wrote in his diary after that entry was perhaps too distressing because several pages were very carefully cut out.

It was freezing in Germany at the beginning of 1922, with temperatures of minus 20 degrees and never more than minus 16. Rail strikes began throughout the country and Sulzbach, along with many other people, was unable to get to work. On 3 February he organised cars to enable his employees to travel to the factory. Two days later a general strike of the city workers meant that no trams ran. Lighting, gas and other services were discontinued, with only some telephones functioning. Sulzbach saw it as 'a catastrophic state of affairs which could destroy the whole economy'.

His birthday fell a few days afterwards, but nobody remembered it. Margot was ill and neither of his parents could send a telegram. He had no letters or presents and found it to be 'a depressing birthday that I would prefer to forget.'

A couple of months later he returned to Frankfurt with Margot for the Easter weekend. They saw their families and many of their friends and were both much happier in familiar surroundings – going to parties and dances with people they had known all their lives. Herbert was glad to have had 'a harmonious Easter with Margot, a nice memory to have.' The following week they spent what they agreed to be their last day together as a couple.

Shortly afterwards, back in Berlin, Herbert met with his Frankfurt friend Schwarzschild at the Café Telschow, near the Zoo, and amongst the crowd of friends and acquaintances there he met Beate Scherk. She was to become the great enduring love of his life and the day that they met – 26 April – was a date that was celebrated by them both for the next sixty years. Beate kept a clear memory of that day, of how she had been in town with her sister Ruth, but then they had become separated. After briefly meeting a friend, Martin Gumpert, on the street, she continued to Café Telschow where Herbert Sulzbach was with his friends. She remembered being embarrassed because she had somehow marked her green suit. Twenty years later she would write to Herbert, 'How wonderful to hear that you cherish having met me.'

Beate's childhood had been spent in Berlin where she attended a private school before training in radiography at the celebrated Lette-Verein Photographic School in Berlin. She completed her training just as war was declared and worked as an X-ray nurse in a military hospital in Berlin. In 1919 she decided to change her career and became an actress.

Three days after their first meeting, Herbert and Beate spent the evening 'dancing and enjoying ourselves' together at the Boston Club in Berlin, and a few days later they were both with Beate's friends at the Blue Bird, a legendary Russian emigré cabaret in Berlin's Goltzstrasse. Herbert was already smitten, not only by Beate but also by her social milieu and her friends.

By the time that Beate met Herbert, she had performed in several plays by the Expressionist playwrights Walter Hasenclever, Ernst Toller and Berthold Brecht. She was working at the Residenztheater and the Tribüne theatre in Berlin, under the direction of Max Reinhardt, and had also taken parts in various films – which at that time were silent and only produced in black and white.

Beate was glamorous, stylish and creative. Her friends included Walter Hasenclever, the painter Oskar Kokoschka, the actor Ernst Deutsch – and her uncle was the musical composer and conductor Otto Klemperer. She was the epitome of the 'new woman' of 1920s Berlin – slender, with short hair, she smoked and was part of the new sexual revolution of the time. Two years younger than Herbert, she came from an upper-class Jewish family and was wealthy enough to be able to pursue her independence.

Herbert felt exhilarated, accepted and happy with Beate and her friends. A few days after their evening at the Blue Bird he wrote hopefully in his diary:

> I cannot find words to describe this fantastic woman. Can I have found THE woman who will remain the highest of them all – intelligent, wise, thoughtful and loving? I sincerely hope that a good and lasting friendship will develop.

A week after this, on 13 May 1922, Herbert and Beate looked for a flat for him in Berlin and their lives became so busy and happy that entries in

NEUBABELSBERG. STARTING AGAIN

his diary ceased for the rest of that year. In June they went away together for a few days to Bremen. They went by plane and Herbert, who was infatuated with flying as well as with Beate, remembered the occasion for many years. 'You ate peanuts at the front of the aircraft, and I sat at the back!'

In August they were on holiday in Westerland and on 16 September 1922 Herbert's divorce from Margot was confirmed in Berlin, at Landegericht III. He had accepted guilt for the breakdown of the marriage and bore the costs of the lawsuit.

On 11 January 1923 French and Belgian troops occupied the Ruhr, in the North Rhine-Westphalia area of Germany. The governments of France and Belgium had lost patience with the slow rate of reparation payments from Germany as defined in the Versailles Treaty and had also become distrustful of the Germans' motives. The Ruhr was Germany's major industrial region, producing eighty percent of its coal, iron and steel, but after this occupation by foreign troops production practically came to a standstill – mainly because the German government was encouraging passive resistance by the workers and civil servants.

Faced with a dramatic decline in tax revenues when the industries closed down, the German government began to print more and more money in order to meet its reparations obligations. Prices then escalated and by the summer of 1923 there was a crisis of inflation in Germany. Everything became worthless, and food became both a currency and an obsession.

Herbert Sulzbach was furious at the occupation of the Ruhr. As a patriotic soldier he was deeply offended by the military invasion, and as a businessman he was considerably affected by the subsequent spiralling inflation. When Beate received a letter from an aunt in America who was of the opinion that the Germans deserved this treatment by the French, and had behaved just like it themselves in 1914, he decided to reply to her himself. After giving detailed explanations of his own viewpoint, he added, 'the Allies will regret it'. Much later, he would wish that he had never written that letter.

On 19 June 1923 Herbert Sulzbach and Beate Scherk were married in Berlin. Beate moved out of the home that she had shared with her widowed mother and her sister and moved into a flat with Herbert at Prinzregentenstrasse 80, Berlin.

Throughout the 1920s Beate continued to work as an actress, retaining her maiden name for her work, and Herbert's factory benefited from Germany's improving economic stability. He travelled frequently for business, building up an extensive network of contacts in France, Britain, Holland and Belgium. He and Beate had a large circle of friends, Jewish and non-Jewish, from many different professions, and it was an energetic, joyous and creative time for them both.

They numbered amongst their friends several of the avant-garde artists who made Berlin famous as a cultural centre. The young intellectuals involved in the Expressionist movement in Germany took some of their inspiration from the new Freudian and Jungian psychology of the period, which particularly fascinated Beate. These new ways of trying to understand the human mind – of reaching some elusive truth – challenged Expressionist writers and other artists to find new ways of expressing latent states of mind. She thrived in these circumstances, and Herbert was delighted to be included in the heady artistic environment.

In 1926 Herbert surprised the two French families with whom he had been friendly when he had been billeted with them during the war, by opening up a correspondence. In their letters they exchanged personal and family news, and his French correspondents seem to have accepted him as a friendly fellow human being rather than their former enemy. It is clear from Sulzbach's own war diaries that he looked for the humanity in all individuals, regardless of any limitations such as nationality.

In his letters Herbert wrote of his respect for the French people's 'nobility' and thanked them again for 'all the good that you did for us; you were and are our good friends.' While hoping that the French and Germans would never again be at war, he expressed his pleasure that 'the political situation between France and Germany is working towards a reconciliation between our two peoples.'

Madame Dubois wrote back that there was never a day when they did not 'talk about you and Monsieur Reinhardt, as well as Monsieur Riese.' She was glad that Sulzbach had written in French as an earlier letter that she had received from Reinhardt had been written in German. It was impossible to read the handwriting, she knew no German, and nobody in the vicinity could translate. Sulzbach continued corresponding with his French friends until early 1938, when the European political situation took further dramatic turns and brought contact to an end.

The events of the 1914/1918 war remained vivid for Herbert Sulzbach throughout his life. When he visited London on business in November 1926 he was impressed when he left his hotel on the Strand

NEUBABELSBERG. STARTING AGAIN

in the morning of Armistice Day to see all the traffic in London come to a halt, everyone stand still, and all the men remove their hats for the two minutes silence at eleven o'clock.

Despite having the concern of his business, and a great deal of travel connected with it, Herbert and Beate enjoyed long, expensive and idyllic holidays during the 1920s. In 1927 they went to Lugano and Genoa for about six weeks in the spring, although during the autumn of that year Herbert was in a sanatorium in the small mountain resort of Arosa with suspected tuberculosis, which proved to be an inaccurate diagnosis.

In March and April 1928, they went on a long holiday in their much-loved Adler-Triumph car. Beate's sister, Ruth, accompanied them and together they visited Paris, Marseilles, Cannes, Turin, Genoa, Monte Carlo and Lugano over a five-week excursion. There were also shorter trips that summer to Bremen, Magdeburg, and Grundsee.

The following March (1929) Sulzbach prepared for the Leipzig Trade Fair. By then, his company, 'Butag', had merged with the 'Uffel' factory in Leipzig and was known as 'Butag-Uffel AG, Neubabelsberg'. He was quoted in one newspaper as saying:

> The spring trade fairs will be even more lively than last autumn's, and we believe that visitor numbers will be high. The present shortage of money will affect the domestic trade, but we are optimistic about overseas buyers.

Then a few months later, on 24 October 1929, the Wall Street stock market crashed. When American banks called in their loans, the economic situation in Germany suddenly worsened dramatically, bringing serious political tensions. Millions of people were thrown out of work, and thousands of small businesses were forced to cease trading.

When Sulzbach wrote to his French friends just after Christmas 1929, he was despondent because 'life in Germany is full of cares.' He considered the economic situation – lack of money, the closure of factories and farms, high unemployment – to be a direct result of 'that terrible war. After eleven years, we are now seeing the results.'

The following year, Hitler's party increased its votes tenfold, which Sulzbach saw as 'catastrophic'. He was grateful to his loyal workforce at the factory for maintaining a profitable business. A photograph taken in May 1923 shows a group of six very cheerful young members of his staff, who seven years later – on 15 November 1930 – sent him a celebratory letter on parchment to offer their 'warmest congratulations' on the anniversary of ten years of his directorship. They signed themselves as 'your always devoted employees.'

Herbert was helpful, caring and compassionate in his dealings with his small workforce. Later in the 1930s, one of them needed to leave the factory to look after her terminally ill mother. After her mother's death this ex-employee replied to Herbert's letter of condolence, expressing her gratitude for his concern and material help. 'You are still the dear good, ready-to-help Herbert Sulzbach.'

The 1930s began sadly. In September 1931 Herbert commented particularly on the large numbers of unemployed and on anti-Semitic fights taking place in central Berlin, on the Kurfürstendamm. 'The times are terrible.' He recognised that the 'crises, collapses and useless conferences' meant that the national economy was 'on a precipice' and by early February 1932, he was reporting 'huge worries in my factory.' Uncertain about what he could do to play any part in stopping the escalating riots and civil unrest, Herbert joined the League for Human Rights and attended meetings regularly.

A few weeks later, on the evening of 25 May 1932, he was summoned to Frankfurt with his brother and sister, but they arrived too late to see their father alive. Emil Sulzbach had died earlier that day in a sanatorium in Bad Homburg. At the funeral, which was held in Frankfurt, the address was given by the Director of the Konservatorium, Bernhard Sekles. The local newspaper devoted considerable space to the occasion, describing Emil Sulzbach as 'a man of "the old school", with a noble disposition. He understood that through a kindly and generous nature, one would gain many friends.' Herbert had always been very close to his father and shared many of his characteristics.

Emil had written to his older son, Ernst, three years previously of 'these miserable days of sickness'. Herbert was always glad that his father was spared knowing of Hitler's large share of votes in the elections held two months after Emil's death, as well as of the continuing and worsening difficulties for Jews in Germany. Hitler became Chancellor of Germany on 30 January 1933.

Two weeks afterwards, on 16 February, Herbert received an announcement from Frankfurt City Chambers to tell him that his father would be honoured by having a street in the city named after him, but the National Socialists moved immediately to block this suggestion. Dr Landmann, the Jewish mayor of Frankfurt since 1924, had been required to leave his post and the new Nazi lord mayor cancelled the naming of the street because Herbert's father was Jewish. (But 'Emil Sulzbach Strasse' eventually came into being in 1945.)

Less than one month after Hitler came to power, the Reichstag was in flames. Herbert noted the frequent killings, the prohibition of reliable newspapers, and the heightened fear everywhere. A few weeks later, on 1 April 1933, Jewish shops were boycotted for the day and SA guards stood with placards in front of all Jewish shops to intimidate prospective buyers. Then at midnight on 10 May 1933, in Germany's university towns, there was a ceremonial burning of books banned by the Nazis as being morally decadent. In Berlin, on the Opernplatz in the centre of the university area, the books that students threw on to the flames included those by Walter Hasenclever, Beate and Herbert's great friend.

That summer, Herbert was in no doubt that totalitarianism had come to Germany. All Jews had been removed from public office and countless Jews had already emigrated. 'It is a completely different Germany,' he wrote. 'We no longer go out in the evening.' In September of that year, Goebbels took over the Chamber of Culture and excluded Jews from film, theatre, music, fine arts, literature and journalism. Beate had recently been engaged to work under Fritz Feld, but her post never materialised after this exclusion. Walter Hasenclever fled to France, Beate's doctor emigrated, and Beate and Ruth's elder sister, Ida, emigrated with her family to South America. Other friends went to Palestine. Oskar Kokoschka left Austria for Prague and then London, and many other artists and actors emigrated.

Herbert was still allowed to direct his factory, but since Beate could no longer work in the theatre she turned to writing. They and their friends constantly discussed emigration. It was a massive and complicated decision. A great deal of courage was needed, as was money to pay the extortionate taxes demanded by the Nazis.

Despite their worries, early in 1934 Herbert and his friends went skiing (as they usually did in the winter) for several weeks in Ruhpolding, but he was called back to Frankfurt when his mother died on 11 February. He attended her funeral with Beate and Dorothee, and they stayed in Frankfurt for several weeks. In the autumn of that year Herbert and Beate holidayed in the Black Forest with their car and returned to Frankfurt to visit his parents' grave, which had by then had its simple headstone engraved with the names of both Emil and Julie.

On 19 August 1934 a referendum was held in Germany on merging the posts of chancellor and president after the death of President von Hindenburg. Eighty-eight percent of Germans voted positively, allowing Hitler to assume both offices.

Herbert and Beate continued to search for different means of employment. During 1934 Beate began to write a dramatisation of a novel by Julian Green, although it was never published, and Herbert collected his wartime diaries together for publication. *Zwei lebende Mauern* (*Two Living Walls*) was published the following year by the Berlin publishers Bernard and Graefe and received enthusiastic reviews even from Nazi journals and newspapers. He did not discover until almost forty years later that his book of patriotism, courage and invincibility during the 1914/1918 war had become recommended reading for leaders of Hitler Youth patrols.

In July 1934 a government decree awarded all front-line soldiers from the war an Iron Cross medal, and Herbert duly received his in Berlin the following February. Despite all the mounting restrictions on Jews, Herbert was able to renew his international driving licence in February 1935 and set off with Beate and her sister for a six-week holiday in Italy and Sicily by car. They visited many of their favourite locations and had a happy, enjoyable, and apparently carefree time away, but as they returned to Germany they were confronted by the 'Jews not wanted' ('*Juden unerwünscht*') signs hung up for all to see in every village through which they passed.

A month later Sulzbach was in England for business purposes and also to extend his personal contacts in case of emigration. One person he visited was his old governess, Miss Stone, who was now married and living as Mrs Booker in Steventon, Buckinghamshire.

The situation for Jews in Germany continued to deteriorate but Herbert had never been an especially cautious person. Even in 1932, before Hitler had become chancellor, he had written a controversial letter to one of the mainstream Berlin papers, using some strong language about Hitler. His letter had not been published, but he had received an anonymous reply from a member of the newspaper's staff, which threatened that he had 'already been noted for extra treatment.'

Beate became increasingly concerned about their personal safety. One day Herbert met his wartime friend, Hans Ado von Seebach, on the Behrenstrasse in Berlin. 'You must get out,' von Seebach advised urgently. 'Go to England when you can.'

In January 1936 Sulzbach went to London to consult with his business associates there. He arranged with his agent for the establishment of a paper factory in Slough, which would give Herbert employment once they had emigrated and meanwhile might also facilitate obtaining visas. He and the agent, Henry Sanders, visited the proposed factory, which was of a similar size to the one in Neubabelsberg.

The following month Herbert was back in Berlin to host a farewell supper for his brother, Ernst, and his wife, who were emigrating to Mexico. Herbert then returned to London for a fortnight of more business talks and arrangements. Beate was very supportive and encouraging of all that he was trying to do, and wrote to him saying, 'I have never before been so glad to begin a new life, even though I don't know how it will work out.'

It was agreed that Beate's sister, Ruth, would emigrate with them. Meanwhile she went to live at Herbert and Beate's flat, as company and reassurance for Beate during Herbert's trips away. The restrictions placed on Jews, as well as Beate and Ruth's considerable anxiety about potential trouble, meant that they now rarely left their flat. 'Today is wonderful weather,' Beate wrote to Herbert. 'I did not go out, but in the end, I went with just Ruth and the old people to Josty's.'

Nowadays there were very few artists and intellectuals still living in Berlin, so the Café Josty was no longer the vibrant, popular meeting place that it had been ten years earlier. Beate and Ruth's mother had decided not to emigrate with them. Her neighbour, and the family's great friend, Grete Diener – who was not Jewish – had undertaken to try to take care of and protect her. It was now far more difficult for Frau Scherk to let out rooms in her house to tenants – as she had previously done for aspiring young actresses. Many years later, Herbert and Beate heard from one of these tenants, Sybille Schmitz, who had first arrived in Berlin in 1927, aged 18 years old. She wrote:

> I would so much like to see you again, and talk about the old times, when a small beginner at the Reinhardt [Deutsches Theater in Berlin] came to Mother Scherk and rented the smallest room that she had. I still remember how Beate gave interior design advice to Mother Scherk. The beloved good Mother Scherk, who took such care of me.

A JEW WHO DEFEATED NAZISM

In May 1936 Herbert's English business agent, Henry Sanders, visited Berlin. Herbert, Beate and Ruth offered him hospitality and showed him around Neubabelsberg and the surrounding area – inviting him for picnics, walks and boating trips with them in the forests nearby. In July 1936 Sulzbach applied for an exit visa and told his friends and business associates of his intentions to emigrate. Some of them were surprised. A typical response came from the director of another paper factory in Berlin:

> This application for an exit visa will not be granted; you are just doing it for a laugh! I am absolutely astonished about your plans and my best wishes go with you. To be quite frank, it would be nicer for me from a personal and a business point of view if you would stay with us.

Sulzbach asked some of his business contacts to help him with the mass of paperwork needed for emigration. Herr Julius Blüth, from Eisenbach, gave his testimonial:

> I can testify that the above-named company has manufactured its product with good taste, skilful adaptation to the needs of consumer stock, and impeccable technical performance. The company Herbert Sulzbach & Co. has enjoyed the very best reputation amongst experts.

Huge barriers were placed in front of those Jews who decided to emigrate – even though the National Socialist government wanted them to leave the country – and many countries around the world limited immigration during the depression of the 1930s. In Germany, the Nazis restricted the amount of money and the goods that emigrants could take with them. Jews came to anticipate the plunder of their properties and businesses by officials – as well as the need for bribery to make negotiations possible. The 'Reich Flight Tax' ('*Reichsfluchtsteuer*') was a massive tax on those who left and could impoverish all but the most wealthy.

Their bank accounts were also blocked. Emigrants were not allowed to take remaining money abroad but had to put it in 'blocked accounts' in German Marks for the supposed use of prospective emigrants.

NEUBABELSBERG. STARTING AGAIN

They could draw on these accounts themselves to buy foreign currency – at extremely unfavourable exchange rates.

The Olympic Games were held in Berlin in August 1936 and all the 'Jews not wanted' signs disappeared for a few weeks. Henry Sanders was back in Berlin that month and in December Sulzbach went to London again for further negotiations about his English factory. He was beginning to experience serious difficulties with Sanders and wrote with much anxiety to Beate about his concerns over his agent's trustworthiness. He also became increasingly worried that during his time away from Berlin, Beate and Ruth were frequently being telephoned by the Gestapo, who seemed to know the content of his letters home and who were sometimes distinctly menacing towards his wife.

Beate tried to reassure him, writing to him:

> I had hardly sat down at the machine to write to you, when your very nervous letter arrived. All is well here. Nobody has called us. It is good to know how things stand with Sanders, and we must accept it, and keep up with the times.

Herbert returned to Berlin in time for Christmas and at the end of that month, on 30 December 1936, he was forced by the Nazis to sell his factory – at a derisory rate – and leave Neubabelsberg. The new owners planned to use his factory as premises for a colour film company for the nearby Babelsberg studios. Sulzbach wrote to his staff to tell them the news and received the following reply from one employee:

> So, is it thus definitely all over? We now only have the memory. I should not be melancholy, but perhaps sometimes I will sit down, and recreate the pictures which I have of the merry birthdays of 'Butag-Uffel' and the outing to Werder – of taking snaps on the steamer of Herr Sulzbach, who was my boss.

In January 1937 Sulzbach was back in Slough and London. Then he and Beate took a fortnight's holiday in April to their favourite Italian haunts – Genoa, Venice, Lugano – and went to the Berlin Hoppegarten races in early May. Later in May Herbert finally and officially emigrated to England with his daughter, Dorothee, who was then aged just 17.

He found that the factory in Slough was already failing, and it was declared bankrupt at Marble Arch, London, on 30 May 1937. The firm was liquidated on 18 September 1937 and Herbert was very depressed as a result. In August he heard that the Frankfurt family bank, Gebrüder Sulzbach, which had been founded by his great-grandfather, was being compulsorily 'Aryanized' – a move that had been anticipated by the owners of the bank. By then Walter Sulzbach, Herbert's cousin, had retired as a partner and was living in America. The sole proprietor became Heinrich Kirchholtes, who was not Jewish but was married to Gertrud (Walter's sister and Herbert Sulzbach's cousin), so the bank still retained the family connection. On 1 January 1938 'Gebrüder Sulzbach' became 'Bankhaus Heinrich Kirchholtes'.

During the summer of 1937, while Herbert was in London, Beate's younger sister had a disconcerting and chilling experience that only increased their wish to leave Germany. When some valuables were stolen from her home Ruth reported it to the police who then questioned her. She was articulate and helpful to a particular officer who reported this to his superior. The senior official then suggested that 'someone' could make good use of such a skilful young woman. Ruth was young, attractive, and blonde – and perhaps to Nazi eyes she looked Aryan, although both her parents were Jewish.

It was suggested to her that she could help the Gestapo by going to a certain place, such as a café, and if a Jew sat down nearby she could catch his eye, speak to him, and go off with him somewhere. The next day, when she reported back, she would have earned herself 500 Reichsmarks and another Jew would have been captured for flouting the Nuremberg laws. Ruth was appalled. It became imperative to leave.

Herbert returned again to Berlin in August 1937 to expedite the arrangements for his wife and sister-in-law's emigration and the transportation of some of their furniture and belongings, which they would be allowed to take out of Germany since they had paid the required taxes. He found Beate and Ruth extremely nervous about his presence in Berlin, as well as about continuing threats from the Gestapo – so he rushed back to London as soon as he could.

Herbert went backwards and forwards between London and Berlin several times during 1938 to organise the complicated emigration process, and was very conscious of the danger every time. Since he had himself already emigrated, he could have been in serious trouble each time that he attempted to re-enter Germany. In February there was a second farewell for Ernst who had returned from Mexico and was emigrating again – this time to Sweden.

Herbert Sulzbach's final visit to Berlin was in May 1938. He travelled via Bremerhaven and prepared to emigrate with Beate and Ruth. Their farewell party was held, at the insistence of a friendly policeman who was a Nazi party member, in a local pub. The policeman, Ott, who had already helped them by falsifying Beate's passport, attended wearing a huge swastika in his buttonhole and was joined by the inspector of taxes.

Herbert, Beate and Ruth left Berlin on 14 May and took emotional and distressing farewells from Herbert's sister, Lili, and from Frau Scherk. They spent their last day in Germany, 18 May 1938, in Hamburg and ate at a charming grill bar, amongst German officers in elegant uniform. Between Hamburg and Cuxhaven, they and their belongings were subjected to an unpleasant search by obnoxious officials. These humiliating searches, when Gestapo agents were known to demand bribes of all sorts at the very last moment of departure, were part and parcel of the Jewish emigrant experience. On 19 May they sailed on the *New York* from Cuxhaven to Southampton, arriving in the evening of 20 May.

Kristallnacht took place six months later, on the night of 9/10 November 1938. Immediately afterwards Herbert received a brief note from a good non-Jewish friend, Otto Reise, whom he had known since his school days in Frankfurt, and who had himself emigrated to Switzerland to escape the horrors of National Socialism. Otto wrote simply: 'Laughter passes one by. There remains only sorrow and shame.'

Herbert's friends in France also wrote to him in sadness and with hopeful encouragement: 'You are still young and skilful and in particular very intelligent. One must never lose hope in life.'

More than two years earlier, when planning their emigration, Beate had told Herbert, 'Of course I am willing to make the final undertaking. I am completely calm about any obstacles.'

As she arrived in England and sat in the boat's tender that took them from the *New York* across the stretch of water to the quay at Southampton, she looked steadily into the lens of Herbert's camera as they both, with Ruth, set about making yet another new beginning.

Chapter 3

London, Basel, Onchan. Flight and Exile

Herbert, Beate and Ruth went from Southampton to an affluent residential area in north-west London where many other Jewish refugees had already chosen to settle. Beate and Ruth lived with their Aunt Mary Klemperer and Herbert stayed in a nearby boarding house while they searched for more permanent accommodation together and tried to find means of earning some money.

Ever since the success of his 1914/1918 war diaries in Germany, Herbert had been trying to get them published in Britain and in America. His American contacts found the material interesting but 'too dated', and English publishers in 1938 were too aware of the likelihood of another war with Germany to consider the timing appropriate for publication. He was forced to look for a different occupation.

Herbert left his wife and sister-in-law with their aunt and travelled to Basel in Switzerland where he was in touch with many friends who were committed to fighting Nazism. With some of them he planned to write booklets and pamphlets that would tell people about the reality of the tyrannical leaders of Nazism and their regime. In late September 1938, he debated his ideas with a writer friend, Wilhelm Herzog:

> You talked yesterday of your plans to publish a booklet in three languages – short, with slogans about the crimes of the leaders of the Third Reich. But there could be another one in all the languages of the world, to enlighten the people – not the leaders – about this murderous Reich. And also, the same thing just in German – a pamphlet for the German people to disabuse them of their rulers in case there is a war.

Sulzbach had also been trying – since the beginning of 1938 – to negotiate the conceding of various patents for the benefit of Britain. One involved the chemical industry, and another was an invention for cartouches for guns, which Herbert had been asked by the German inventor to offer to England. He was constantly working with other businessmen, as well as with academics and writers (all of whom were refugees from Nazism and who expected war with Germany). They wanted to do all that they could to fight National Socialism, and even as late as February 1939 Herbert was claiming that if his offer of patents were accepted:

> It would be extraordinary how much England could gain just now in the rearmament race!

However, he – like many different envoys from Germany at this time – was unsuccessful in promoting his ideas and beliefs within influential circles in Western Europe, despite using all his many contacts.

Herbert was still in Switzerland when talks were held between Germany, Italy, Britain and France over the fate of Czechoslovakia, and he was appalled to see Czechoslovakia being abandoned. After the Munich agreement had been signed in the early hours of 30 September 1938, he recorded in his diary how he was:

> ...stirred by all the scenes of joy and enthusiasm in Munich, Paris, London and Rome. But the slandered and mocked President Beneš of Czechoslovakia is the friend of democracy! Honourable words have been forgotten by the elderly Chamberlain. In 1934 Hitler said that he had no ambitions over Austria. In 1935, he said that he had never had any thoughts of annexing Austria nor any kind of territorial wishes in Europe. Now he makes even more promises and the statesmen of democracy believe him yet again! They forget that Hitler has broken his word thousands of times, because it is only a means to an end.

Herbert spent a lot of time over the following days in correspondence – writing first to those he admired and supported. To President Beneš he wrote:

> I hope to convince you that millions of people are full of admiration, respect, and sympathy for you and the entire Czech people, who have given extraordinary proof of

their honour and dignity. We join with you in contempt, indignation and boundless sorrow for what has taken place in Munich.

To Duff Cooper, a member of parliament who had resigned his post in Chamberlain's Cabinet immediately after the Munich agreement had been announced, he wrote:

> Please accept my sincerest congratulations for your courageous, brave and reasonable step. Only people like you will be able to save England's name and honour.

He was offended by a suggestion in France that Neville Chamberlain should be honoured with the gift of a villa. To the editor of *Paris Soir*, he wrote (under the name of Paul Herbst-Bach):

> Do you not think that it would be more humane – and more in accordance with the wishes of the people – to organise a subscription in favour of the Czech refugees who have been driven out of their country, rather than for Mr Chamberlain who offers his friendship to a man who is threatening everybody? The gift of a villa intended for Mr Chamberlain would more appropriately be addressed to Mr Beneš, who has contributed more to peace by his impressive resignation and his enormous sacrifice.

Under the name of Herbert Paul, he wrote briefly to Neville Chamberlain: 'Please never forget that the motto of the new German right is: "Right is what is useful for Germany. Wrong is what does damage to Germany."

Herbert was astounded that British and French politicians seemed to fail to understand what Hitler was planning and doing. As he saw it, Hitler's objectives had already been explained by the man himself.

'If Chamberlain has never read anything from *Mein Kampf*, is there no one in the Foreign Office who knows Hitler's ideology?' he wrote in his diary.

Harold Nicolson also regretted that so few British politicians were familiar with *Mein Kampf*. While he recognised 'the purity of the Prime

Minister's intentions', he was sorry that there appeared to be a serious lack of understanding of the true nature of the Nazi movement within British governing circles.

Herbert Sulzbach used the name 'Christophe Hellier', and an address in Zofingen, and also the pseudonym 'A. Lecomte' from Neuchatel, to write to Gunter d'Alquen, the chief editor of the *Das Schwarzen Korps*, which was the SS weekly and Goebbels' mouthpiece. The paper had issued a sarcastic 'obituary' to Czechoslovakia, which had enraged Herbert – who replied with an equally sarcastic letter:

> What heroic courage is proved through your filthy Goebbels' propaganda of the heroic German victory that has been gained! You have proved yourselves to be just as magnanimous, generous, and chivalrous against Czechoslovakia as you once were against the "hostile" Jewish "superior strength" and against Austria. No people in the world can ever attain your heroic courage!
>
> When will people wake up and realise that this country is only ruled by beasts in the form of men? Mind you, WHEN they once wake up, no pity will be shown to the leaders – to all the murderers, blackmailers and sadists who have lied to them. If only you and your seduced people knew WHAT people think of them! It is not hatred, because hatred includes a certain respect – it is boundless, unending contempt for everything that appears and is ordered in Germany.

Almost nine years later, in July 1947, Gunter d'Alquen became a prisoner of war of the British and found himself at Featherstone Park camp where Herbert Sulzbach was the interpreter officer. It was with some satisfaction that Sulzbach resurrected his copy of this letter to show to the former editor. Although d'Alquen was moved to a camp for more serious war criminals six weeks after his arrival, Sulzbach talked with him frequently during that time and d'Alquen made a special point of seeing him to say goodbye. On that day, clicking his heels and bowing, d'Alquen conceded:

> Herr Sulzbach, I only wanted to say that you have freed me from certain prejudices.

Only a few weeks after the offensive against Czechoslovakia, on the night of 10 November 1938, the pogrom of *Kristallnacht* took place. Synagogues and Jewish-owned stores and buildings throughout Nazi Germany and Austria were ransacked and set alight, and many Jewish people were arrested, treated violently or murdered. Afterwards Herbert wrote to the editor of the *Daily Telegraph and Morning Post*, speculating that:

> These Germans would never have dared to do such atrocious things if they had not been made strong and powerful by Mr Chamberlain's policies. The British ambassador should be recalled. What happens in Germany is not an internal matter.
> The view of the Swiss people is that the pogroms followed Munich because Germany now considers itself master of the world. The last bit of British credit could be saved if England were to say: Germany can no longer exist for us until it returns to civilised manners.

The editor chose not to publish his letter.

At the end of November Herbert returned to London to see his family but was back in Basel in the New Year of 1939, continuing to campaign tirelessly and energetically for positive and united action against the evils of Nazism. Writing to Henri de Kérillis, a French journalist and politician who was strongly hostile to appeasement of Germany, he asked:

> How can we bring together all those men like yourself – Duff Cooper, Churchill, Herbert Morrison, Eden, and all the Duff Coopers of Italy, Spain and many other countries before it is too late? It seems to me that all good Europeans, true friends of peace, should come together.

And to Duff Cooper himself he fretted that:

> Whilst the Nazi propaganda is organised in the most precise German manner down to every detail, the people fighting Nazism are as DISorganised as possible! Don't you think

that something ought and COULD be done to produce organised propaganda for the truth? If we can manage to UNITE those who fight for human rights, humanism, and freedom – and can increase their activity – there is some hope that the poison can be successfully contradicted.

On 15 March 1939 Germany invaded and occupied the rest of Czechoslovakia – as it had the Sudetenland six months previously. From that day, Britain changed its policy towards Hitler and accepted the apparent inevitability of war with Germany. Herbert noted in his diary that:

> Here in Basel everyone is as agitated as they were six months ago by what has taken place in the old Czechoslovakia. Can the same happen here tomorrow? So many people are now trying to get away from Prague. The whole of the Czechoslovak Republic is occupied – right from the German borders – with Gestapo, SA and SS. Nobody can get out! Nobody!
>
> And now Hitler sits in Prague, so in a few more days there will be the GERMANISATION OF EUROPE! Who can uphold the law? In a matter of days, whole countries are vanishing from the maps. The French and English are now beginning to see that Hitler will sooner or later get started in the west. The question that the French ask is, "When will it be our turn?", and it begins to dawn on Poland and Hungary that it could be their turn next.

In April 1939 Herbert wrote to Duff Cooper on behalf of the many German-speaking refugees he knew: 'I live in London and would be glad if I could render service to England, helping to organise a Foreign Legion of German and Austrian refugees.'

He admired Duff Cooper and respected his policies. As he wrote to the *Daily Telegraph and Morning Post*:

> I was impressed by your excellent leading article suggesting Mr Churchill's return to the Cabinet. But in my opinion, there is another man who should also return: Mr Duff Cooper.

No one is more feared in Germany than him, and in every German newspaper his name is mentioned first.

In June 1939 Herbert returned to London via Paris, and joined Beate and Ruth at the 'beautiful new flat' that they had found in Belsize Park. Living nearby were many of their friends – the Jacobys, the Haas family, an old school friend Paul Wolff, and 'the ever-helpful Mr Ehrlich'. Grateful to Herbert's grandfather for his help in setting up a banking business many years earlier, Mr Ehrlich generously provided much-needed funds for the Sulzbachs almost throughout the war.

On 1 September 1939 – the day that German forces invaded Poland – Herbert went to Waterloo Station, where British soldiers were already mobilising and taking leave of their families. He felt 'helpless and overwhelmed' as he thought back to the previous war when he had fought 'on the other side': 'Should all that repeat itself? Have people learnt nothing? Were twelve million soldiers killed in four years for nothing?'

In the underground train to Waterloo:

> The carriages were crammed with soldiers in khaki and near me an English soldier in his forties sat on his kit-bag, with his medals from the 1914/18 war pinned to his chest. I would have liked to have shaken him by the hand and asked his forgiveness, that a quarter of a century ago I had perhaps had to shoot at him. I saw in the British soldier of 1939 a comrade, who had once been my enemy in 1914.

Two days later, 3 September 1939, Britain declared war on Germany. Beate always remembered that day – which was also her forty-third birthday:

> I shall never forget the day when I sat in front of the radio in Ruth and Kathleen's room and heard Chamberlain's voice, "Now we are at war with Germany". Kathleen screaming hysterically, Ruth and me going down to pack a suitcase, me on the street trying to get a cab. At that same moment we heard the first, but false, alarm. "Can they have come so quickly?" we thought, and sheltered first in the Ministry of Health, then in the cinema. And then there was the charming

man, who took the shoulder of Ruth, who was trembling, and said, "Take it easy." "We will try to", I said.

Within a week, Herbert had volunteered for service with the British Army. He received a standard reply saying that his letter had been passed on to the relevant department.

He also wrote to the King of Belgium, in a vain attempt that he could influence the Nazi leadership:

> Your Majesty, more than any other person in the world, is respected in Nazi Germany. Intervention on your part would be considered as objective and loyal by all the countries at war.

On 25 October 1939 Herbert and Beate were required to appear before a tribunal that endorsed their 'friendly alien' status. Even so, they were finding it impossible to find any paid work. As Herbert wrote to a friend in Brussels:

> It gives me pleasure to try to help the legitimate cause, and unfortunately I have no other employment. I feel very depressed and am rarely not melancholy. If you think too much about the times that are past it sends you mad. We have let three of the rooms in our flat and with this – plus a few pounds that an old friend of my grandfather gives me – we can just keep going. But it is quite sad to be so dependent on the kindness of others.

During the spring of 1940 the increasingly tense wartime atmosphere encouraged the anti-alien xenophobia that was appearing in the British popular press. Jewish organisations were anxious to protect the refugees and advised them against speaking German too loudly in the street or showing German-language newspapers. In the accelerating and ugly mood that all aliens should be interned in the interests of national security, Herbert had a short correspondence in a national newspaper with a man who had supported internment:

> The aliens – as far as they are refugees from Nazi oppression – are honest in their only and deepest wish:

to help England in her struggle, so that humanity, justice and freedom may conquer Nazi barbarism. Who can have a greater hatred of Nazis than us, and who knows their devilish manners better?

Having received no positive reply from the British military authorities, Herbert volunteered in April to serve with the Norwegian forces. In his frustration that the refugees from Germany were not being encouraged or allowed to contribute to Britain's war effort, Herbert wrote to a member of parliament, Captain J. McEwen:

> How can anybody make use of the knowledge that we refugees have of Nazism and – amongst those who have been soldiers – of their military services? I am working wherever I can for this country and really want to help to overthrow Nazism. Cannot the government make use of our services?

On 10 May 1940 he wrote offering his military services to the Dutch and Swiss Legations, and to the Belgian and French Embassies, in London. He also wrote to Neville Chamberlain:

> I would only like to serve the Allies, to help in this struggle – against the devils in Germany, and for humanity, freedom and justice. Perhaps you would be able to help in making use of so much effort, goodwill and faith that is lying in the refugees.

He also remained extremely concerned about the lack of activity in positively countering German propaganda, writing one day to a friend in the Ministry of Information:

> Since this morning the German radio stations *Hamburg-Bremen* have been trying to convince the Belgians to lay down their arms, telling them that England and France are those who destroy their country, and that the Germans come for protection. What appears to me to be so very urgent – and I cannot understand why it has not yet been done – is

that British and French radio stations should act as quickly as possible to check this dangerous German propaganda by talking to the Belgians in French. As Brussels is silent perhaps this should be done on the Brussels wave-length.

On the very day that Herbert Sulzbach wrote this letter, 15 May 1940, German forces overran Holland before moving on to Brussels.

The following day Herbert's daughter married an Englishman, George Smith, at the Methodist Kingsway Hall in London. Dorothee was a few days short of her twentieth birthday and her husband was 21 years old. George was a pacifist and a member of the Peace Pledge Union, which was a vociferous anti-war and pro-appeasement movement.

During that same month, May 1940, as France fell to the Germans, public opinion in Britain became hysterical that the rapid subjugation of the Low Countries and France might be due either to a spy network amongst the aliens or to the activities of anyone thought to be pro-Nazi. Peace Pledge Union members came into the second category, so on 24 May 1940 four police officers searched George and Dorothee's flat and also demanded the names and addresses of their next of kin.

Consequently, the next day the police arrived to search Herbert and Beate's flat. As Herbert explained a few weeks later in a letter to the Under-Secretary of State at the Home Office:

> Had I wished, I could have had plenty of time to destroy any correspondence which might have appeared compromising. The officers were extremely courteous and took with them a great number of files which they promised to return soon. I received them back two days later and Inspector Davis told me that he would like to keep one file and a few letters: one referring to my Dutch shares and one copy of an English letter written by me in 1923 to an aunt of my then fiancée in USA.

This was the copy of the letter that Herbert had written in his fury at the French invasion of the Ruhr in January 1923, which had ended with the words, 'the Allies will regret it'. His comments and opinions from almost twenty years previously were used against him when he and Beate were summoned before the Regional Advisory Committee at Bow Street police station on 31 May 1940.

A JEW WHO DEFEATED NAZISM

The judge was unfriendly and impatient. Unwilling to listen to any of Herbert's replies to his questions, he merely remarked that the 1923 letter 'proved' that his ideas were the same as Hitler's. 'You are a Nazi', he said.

> I found it difficult to reply to this offensive remark. I tried to make him understand that I am a refugee from Nazi oppression and that I could prove my pro-British attitude with dozens of examples. The judge was just uninterested to hear.

At 12 o'clock that day they were given the verdict: they were both to be interned – separately.

Beate was taken to Holloway Prison and Herbert was imprisoned in Bow Street police station for a few days before being taken to Kempton Park. Neither of them knew where the other was until several weeks later and their leave-taking was awful. Herbert felt desperately concerned for Beate, as well as wretched for himself.

At the same time as the evacuation of Dunkirk was coming to an end, the new internees at Kempton Park were glad of the beautiful weather. Herbert found friends and acquaintances there, some of whom he had last seen ten years previously, and as a group they determined to stay together if possible.

On 15 June 1940, a fortnight after his appearance before the judge, Herbert was taken with other internees from Kempton Park to Liverpool. He remembered the horrors of: 'marching between fixed bayonets and the civilians turning away or looking at us furiously as if we were convicts.'

From Liverpool they sailed to the Isle of Man, landing at Douglas, and Herbert was among those men who were marched a short distance away to Onchan. Everything there had been only recently and hastily arranged for the internees to be accommodated in the large boarding houses along a few roads of Onchan – Royal Avenue West, Belgravia Road, and Imperial Terrace. A football pitch at the corner of Onchan Park had also been included in the camp. The *Manchester Guardian* had carried a report on the internment camps at Onchan and Douglas a few weeks earlier, at the end of May:

> Onchan, where sixty houses have been commandeered, and one in the centre of Douglas promenade comprising

three dozen large boarding houses, are being surrounded by barbed wire. The tenants of the Onchan houses have to be out by Friday. They have to leave all their furniture, bedding etc. The camps in Douglas and Onchan will accommodate 2,000 each.

The men were allocated to these houses, with about twenty men to a house, and Herbert found that while his house had a few beds in it, with mattresses and blankets, there was no bed linen. One man in their group volunteered to do the cooking, but conditions in the house were primitive. The authorities had given no political screening of the internees, and one member of Herbert's household was soon discovered to be a Nazi.

The Edwardian and late-Victorian boarding houses were all large, with anything from five to sixteen bedrooms, and some had impressive views from the headland over the sea. Barbed wire separated the internees from the beach, and the men were guarded by soldiers from the Pioneer Corps who carried their bayonets. It was the only time in his life that Herbert Sulzbach hated the sea.

'I sometimes stood at the barbed wire, looking down to the blue sea and upwards to the blue sky, and couldn't stop my tears flowing,' he wrote to Beate.

Most of the internees dreaded the possibility of deportation across the sea to Canada or Australia, and they were completely unable to discuss the situation with their families from whom they were separated – especially since the incredibly slow postal service seriously hindered written communication. On 1 July 1940 – two weeks after Herbert had arrived on the Isle of Man – the *Arandora Star* left Liverpool for Canada. On board were German and Italian prisoners of war and internees. The ship did not have an escort and was sunk by a German torpedo in the early hours of the following morning, with great loss of life.

On 3 July Herbert wrote to his camp officer, Lieutenant Shaw, who had shown great understanding of their circumstances:

> All those of us who are married tremble at the thought that we may be deported at any time and separated from our wives and children for ever. I, like many of us, have not heard from my wife for almost five weeks, ever since we were interned, and I do not even know where she is.

We would make this appeal even if we were enemy prisoners, but as you know we are refugees from Nazi tyranny, have suffered more than words can say for years, and are not only friends of this country but prepared to fight and die for it.

The married internees also petitioned the Archbishop of York by telegram on 5 July:

We have sent the following telegram today to the Home Office and War Office:
"We 478 married internees of Onchan internment camp Isle of Man implore you to assure us that under all circumstances shall we be transported together with our wives and children to the same destination stop if an emergency should arrive we want to share this emergency together with our dear ones stop please realise that we have lost everything freedom fatherland property stop do not take from us the very last which preserves our will to live stop leave us our wives and children to live or to die with together stop."

Unknown to Herbert, Beate had already arrived on the Isle of Man. She had written frequently to her husband but none of her letters had yet reached him. Holloway Prison had been a terrible experience for her and the other women internees, all of whom had been housed no differently from ordinary prisoners. She was allowed to write two letters a week, neither of which was to exceed twenty-four lines, so she had to choose between keeping in contact either with Herbert or with her sister when there was so much for them all to decide.

With her sister, Beate tried to make arrangements about the subletting of the rooms in their flat in case all the other (Jewish) tenants were interned. Ruth tried to visit Holloway, especially as Beate requested money, food and items of clothing, but there were strict restrictions around visiting arrangements and times – and then a visit was allowed for a mere fifteen minutes. Meanwhile, Ruth organised the flat and tenants, tussled with the local labour exchange for permission to look for a job, and tried with a friend's help to make good their bomb shelter in the garden so that it no longer sank into the mud.

LONDON, BASEL, ONCHAN. FLIGHT AND EXILE

Beate did not know at the time, but while she was in Holloway Prison her former great friend, the playwright Walter Hasenclever, committed suicide in a concentration camp at Les Milles, near Aix-en-Provence in France, on 21 June 1940. Many years later, she reflected on the tragedy of that time:

> The news of his death reminded me of a promise that he had once asked me to make; that I would go to him "when he came to dying", wherever he might be. We had dreamed a dream in which there was no National Socialism, no war, no closed borders. Holloway Prison is a paradise compared with the camp near Avignon: but we were in the same hour behind bars.

Internees at Holloway were allowed into the garden twice a day, which Beate was pleased to do, often admiring the fashionable clothes that some of the other women had chosen to take in their small bag when interned. But she spent much of the day on her bed, conserving her strength and feeling physically very weakened by this ordeal. The bed – a straw mattress on the floor – had become more comfortable after she had followed the advice of a 16-year-old girl, Madi, in the adjacent cell and used her silk petticoat as a pillowcase. They had all been told that they would be going to the Isle of Man, but she had no idea when that would be.

After four weeks in Holloway Prison, Beate arrived at Port St Mary, via Liverpool, where she had spent an uncomfortable night on the floor of a sailors' hostel without a mattress. It was 1 July 1940 and she was taken to *Mallmore*, a large boarding house on the seafront in Port St Mary, where she shared a room with three other women. They were each obliged to share a standard boarding house double bed with another internee. Women internees were housed in boarding houses at Port St Mary and Port Erin, in the south of the Isle of Man. The landladies of these houses were not given notice to leave (as they were in the men's camps) but remained to cater for the internees.

Beate wrote to Herbert:

> Since I have been here, I have felt much better and am looking very well. I am much better off than you for we

can walk and walk without seeing any barbed wire, and my boarding house is right on the beach. I am sitting at the window and looking over the sea and the sun is shining. We starved in Holloway but here the food is good. We have enough to eat and I am sleeping soundly. We even have running hot and cold water!

But what do you think about Canada? Will we have to go there one day? I would prefer not to go but if I must, I should like to arrange to sell our furniture first.

Eventually, on 6 July 1940, Herbert received a telegram from Ruth that told him of Beate's whereabouts. He wrote immediately to his wife:

Beloved, my beloved Beate, I have just received Ruth's telegram that you are there, and ten million stones fell from my heart. Now do nothing but try to be quiet and lie in the sun and be assured that I and we are fighting like lions for our wives.

A few days later, on 10 July 1940, there was a debate on internment in the House of Commons. It was strongly argued by members such as Victor Cazalet, Eleanor Rathbone, and Josiah Wedgwood that the system was wasteful of human resources. Internment was also said to be bringing into disrepute Britain's name as a nation fighting for the values of a liberal civilisation.

Herbert wrote hopefully – and forcefully – to his wife about this intervention:

Peake gave a lovely speech four days ago in the House of Commons for us and against deportation. All of us here are in terrible fear, but many clever and intelligent men are working together for our families. If we have to sign, I would only do it with "together with my wife". I will try to stay in England with you. No, I would NOT like to go. Don't say "yes" to anything without knowing my decision. If you have to sign something, you must write "according to my husband's wishes". Only if we are forced to go, shall we leave England.

LONDON, BASEL, ONCHAN. FLIGHT AND EXILE

Beate's own letter crossed with Herbert's:

> I repeat that I will go – sail with you – whether it is to Canada or Australia. But I doubt that we shall be allowed to sail together, and I fear that you will have to leave first, and I will have to follow. The atmosphere is full of rumours and they say that men are already leaving. I do believe in the final victory for England, even if it may be a longer war. We must have patience and I am strong and can wait. I have been calmer since I knew that you were so near. Yes, we both went through a hard time, but we are young enough to start again!

The slow delivery of mail continued to be a huge problem for the internees, with letters arriving weeks late. Part of the problem was that the post had to go via the censor – in Liverpool – even if it was destined for another internment camp just a few miles away. A July visit from the Bishop of Chichester, who was horrified to see stacks of mail bags awaiting the censor, improved the situation temporarily. But, even so, near the end of August a bemused and angry Beate wrote to Herbert:

> Yesterday, on the 26 August, your letter of 13 July arrived. It had taken forty-five days for a distance of one hour – and other people get mail from the USA in thirteen days!

Herbert complained furiously to the camp commandant about the postal service:

> I enclose a letter of Mrs Sulzbach from 19 July, which was received yesterday, 27 August! This vitally important letter took forty-three days to get here, even though it was written during days of the greatest nervousness. It has been made impossible for us to contact our family in matters of the highest importance, with wives not knowing if their husbands would be forced to leave for Canada or Australia, and not knowing if they would be forced to stay here alone. My wife already had thirty-two days in Holloway prison behind her – in conditions which are almost impossible to relate!

A JEW WHO DEFEATED NAZISM

As well as campaigning for their release and for improvements in internment conditions, Herbert was greatly involved with the cultural life of the camp at Onchan. He had quickly been appreciated as a leader of men, and as an optimist who – despite his personal sadness at the time – always argued convincingly of the defeat of Nazism. In many discussions with his fellow-internees about the war, he talked optimistically and inspirationally of Britain's ability to win the war. He was one of a group of men who were instrumental in setting up and organising a Popular University, and establishing a camp newspaper, the *Onchan Pioneer*.

> Half of all internees were intellectuals from all over Germany and Austria. I was on the committee of the university – languages, mathematics, everything was taught. One chap developed into a pastry cook; we could buy pastries from him. But the spirit of the activities was always excellent.

Herbert Sulzbach lived in House 18 at Onchan camp. Every morning, after a roll call, a large number of men in the camp would make their way expectantly to the poster outside House 18 to find out the latest news and the programme for the day for the 'Popular University'. During the autumn of 1940, the 'university' was central to the intellectual and social life of about sixty percent of the internees who took part in its programme – both as tutors and students.

During their internment, Herbert and Beate met each other twice, each time on organised meetings for married internees – once at Port St Mary and another time at Derby Castle, a large entertainment centre just below the cliffs at Onchan. Both occasions were highly emotional. At their first meeting on 26 July Beate discovered that Herbert was not only upset, stressed and unhappy, but was also suffering from boils on his face. However, her joy was overwhelming:

> I was so excited yesterday, so happy to see you and to speak with you again even if it was all a bit sad. It was such an event, and to experience such an emotional moment in public was rather horrible in spite of our great joy in seeing each other, in embracing each other. I couldn't sleep tonight so I got up and sat near the window when it was dawning. I looked at

the contours of the far hills and watched the sheep that were grazing under my window, even in the night. There seemed to be peace everywhere.

As the internees continued to try to persuade influential people that they should be released, public opinion began to turn in their favour. Two correspondents reminded readers of the letters pages of the *Manchester Guardian* that:

> Most of these foreigners came to England as to a city of refuge, seeking to escape from the atrocious tyranny of Hitlerism, which they detest as much as we do. Many have suffered terrible wrongs under that tyranny before they contrived to escape. Nearly all have lost their property, and all have lost the practice of their work or profession.

And:

> Such a policy [as internment] is clearly indefensible on any grounds of justice. It must be due either to a desire to identify all Germans as Nazis or to a singular lack of imaginative insight into the refugee problem.

On 6 August 1940 the House of Lords debated the internment of aliens, with the Bishop of Chichester – who had just returned from his visit to the Isle of Man – giving a graphic account of the situation and a spirited defence of the internees:

> I want to suggest that there is all the difference in the world between aliens of enemy nationality and refugees from the enemy.
> Do you know, my Lords, that Jews and non-Aryan Christians who have no chance of a home or a life in Germany, who have been brutally expelled from Germany, who are not regarded as Germans at all or as human beings by Hitler, and who cannot possibly be a danger to England, form the great majority of the internees in the aliens' internment camps? These men who suffered at Germany's

> hands long before the war began, what motive have they for helping Germany? Why should we by our treatment of them make the enemies of Germany our enemies?
>
> One of the tragedies of the refugee situation is the waste of talent and ability. In the Isle of Man and at Huyton I was astounded at the quantity as well as the quality of the material available: doctors, professors, scientists, inventors, chemists, industrialists, manufacturers, humanists – all wanting to work for Britain, freedom and justice.

Two weeks after this debate, a recruiting officer from the British Army arrived on the Isle of Man. Internees who were young and fit enough were offered freedom from internment by joining the Auxiliary Military Pioneer Corps. They were told that registering for the Pioneers would also immediately automatically free their wives from internment.

On 19 August 1940 Herbert Sulzbach sent his wife a telegram: 'Registered today Pioneer.'

Beate was delighted:

> I am so glad that you were able to register for the Pioneer Corps even if it will give me new troubles and makes me anxious, but I hope with all my heart that they will appreciate your qualifications for some kind of leading job so that you can feel in your element again – and at least you will feel free!

Towards the end of October Herbert heard that he would soon be released to join the Pioneer Corps. He was allowed 'a few special lines' to Beate:

> I had the news yesterday and was sworn in at Douglas. I leave tomorrow instead of today. I can't tell you how happy I am to become a soldier. Do be happy and quiet with me as life now has a sense again and a lovely aim too!

The evening before he left Onchan, his friends and fellow internees paid him tribute at a special celebration where they presented him with a folder of documents, letters, and drawings that made him very happy and very proud. A signed tribute declared that:

LONDON, BASEL, ONCHAN. FLIGHT AND EXILE

> Our great friend Herbert Sulzbach has shown to 1500 internees on their way from London via Kempton Park to Onchan Isle of Man, in a time of great mental strain, how one man with courage and initiative can help his fellow. By organising some of the most remarkable literary events in our internment camp and by his cheerful personality he has enabled us to carry our fate in a dignified way and even make our internment a human inspiration to every one of us.

The British officer in charge of Onchan camp saw them all off at first light the following morning. Shaking Sulzbach by the hand he delighted him by declaring: 'Once an officer, always an officer.'

On the other side of the barbed wire at last, the new Pioneer recruits were driven in a car past Onchan camp at 7am that morning. 'We waved, they waved, we were free! What a moment!'

The previous night had been stormy and Sulzbach feared the sea crossing. They were delayed leaving Douglas for several hours and eventually arrived in Liverpool that evening in the dark of the blackout, with a half-hour walk to the station – carrying all their luggage. Herbert described events in a letter to Beate:

> At 7.30 the sirens screamed, and we went into a shelter, where hundreds of families were housed with all these children, babies, beds and blankets; the noise and smell were all depressing – but the spirit was wonderful.

When the 'All clear' sounded they made their way to the station and took a train to Bradford, where a van was waiting to take their bags. The men marched to their barracks, where they finally got a meal at 1.30 in the morning.

The following evening Herbert wrote to Beate with a delighted account of his first day in Bradford:

> At 10 o'clock we marched for the first time through a part of Bradford – we were about one company strong and we kept in step! The civilians were watching and smiled at us. We sleep in a hut on fifty beds of wood. Five months ago, we would have grumbled but today it seems lovely.

His wife was very happy for him and anticipated her own imminent freedom:

> This is the first letter to my British soldier-husband. I am so proud of you! And so happy to see your happiness. I had an appointment with our superintendent about my release and she will speak with the commandant for me and then let me know whether we have to wait or whether it would be advisable to make a new application. I was told today that Pioneer wives will attend a new tribunal. All my sadness has passed. I am so happy that you are free.

While he was glad to be free of internment and pleased to be fighting in a British Army unit, Herbert Sulzbach never lost his sense of amazement at the turn of events in his life. As he wrote to Beate:

> I could write volumes looking back on the fate of one single generation. I am sitting in a large room, like an assembly hall of a school. We are in khaki battledress; some are writing, some are playing cards, some are singing. Today I am proud to wear this uniform, but I can't help thinking of a quarter of a century ago. It is unbelievable! I feel myself transferred into what I saw in 1914 through my field glasses "on the other side". I loved something in this nation that I was not aware of – but I loved and admired their quiet heroism. Can you, my darling, understand what makes me thoughtful, happy, pensive?

He attended a church parade and was one of only eighteen men who went to the Church of England service – the others went to the synagogue.

> We sat there as soldiers amongst the civilians. Most of our chaps have gone to town so I am having rather a quiet Sunday afternoon. I and some ten boys are alone, and I am enjoying the quietness – which is the only thing that I am missing here.

Then, three days later, at 7 pm on Wednesday 6 November 1940, their house in London took a direct hit during a German bombing raid. Beate's

LONDON, BASEL, ONCHAN. FLIGHT AND EXILE

sister was sheltering in a nearby underground station and the house was empty so nobody was hurt. Ruth wrote to tell Herbert and Beate what had happened:

> There is no number 58 anymore – it is lying in the garden. The whole long side has gone as far as the drawing room. There is no staircase, no hall. My God, it's a mess! All the silver and the rest of our fur coats are saved. We have lost seven trunks with all kinds of linen, silk curtains, men's suits, and five Persian rugs. We have also lost the kitchen with most of the china, as well as both of the gramophones and all of our records.

Ruth went to stay with Mrs Booker at Steventon, taking the rescued 'church glasses' with her. A few days later she returned to London to deal with the rest of their belongings. Some of the furniture could be lowered through the still-existent drawing room window and was taken to a council holding centre in a house in Hampstead. Ruth reckoned that they had probably saved enough to furnish three rooms in a different flat, and although Herbert's room had been destroyed, she was able to retrieve most of his papers, including his diaries, as well as Beate's drama manuscripts.

It was stressful and exhausting for her, making the necessary arrangements in a London that was constantly being subjected to bombing raids. Ruth was trying not only to keep Herbert (in Bradford) and Beate (on the Isle of Man) informed but also to carry out their different instructions. Mrs Booker had offered to store their belongings in her garage at Steventon, but there would be insufficient space for everything. Ruth had to negotiate removals, with a firm that wanted money (that she didn't have) for precious rationed petrol before they would take goods anywhere. She tried to sell some of their rescued goods but found Herbert rather out of touch with what she was dealing with.

> I laughed at what you wrote: sell the china for £200 or £300! Do you know what it is worth? For the Frankfurt china – all the plates, everything all together – you won't get more than £6. The china is not to the English taste and it has your family monogram. The furniture is not worth a penny.

Again, it is not to the English taste and is much too big. The church glasses are worth £40. As is some of the silver, but not the decorated pieces because they are not English silver. The solicitor has said that you will get the money after the war. Have we got any money NOW to pay a solicitor?

On the Isle of Man, Beate tried to help with some of the necessary formalities. It was all very confusing, as she explained to Herbert:

I went to the Police Station to enquire about claiming compensation. They were not sure but advised me to apply to Hampstead Borough Council NW3 within four weeks after the event. That would be the 4 December, so I hope that you have already applied. I heard that we had to get a form from the local police to fill in, but how can we fill it in if we don't know how much has gone, and whether and how much could still be saved? Who could look for the remnants?

Meanwhile, Herbert was gradually settling into the army. After their initial training at Bradford, his unit was moved to Didcot, not far from Steventon, so he was able to surprise Ruth with a hurried visit on his first free evening there. He found life in Dirnall Camp to be:

…not hard but not too happy; the conditions are depressing. It is a distance of thirty metres to the WC, which are terrible open latrines, and there is mud between the huts to the washhouse where we must wash in the darkness at 7 am. There are sixteen of us in our hut. It is warm inside and we each have a good, soft mattress on a bedframe. At the moment I am sitting on the iron end of my bed, with a bench in front of me and on it a square piece of wood as a table for writing, and a candle! Ten of the boys are here in the hut; one is shaving, one is reading, one is writing, and the others are talking in a strong Viennese accent. But can you imagine how difficult it is to concentrate or to write at all? Our company works outside the camp, loading and unloading goods wagons at the depot. The sixteen in my hut are nice and I am the oldest.

LONDON, BASEL, ONCHAN. FLIGHT AND EXILE

He was still at Didcot at Christmastime, and although he had not been looking forward to the festival, he enjoyed it far more than he had expected. He told Beate:

> *Heilig Abend* passed quietly. At 10.30 pm I left the camp with two friends. We walked along together – three musketeers from 1940 and officers from twenty-five years ago. Much of the walk to the church reminded me of similar nights in the last war: the absolute darkness, walking together in uniform, the atmosphere. The sweet little church was crowded, everyone said their prayers and you know what I was thinking of. It was a strange Christmas Eve and I liked it.

Christmas Day itself was cold and dry, and the men had no duties. Their midday Christmas dinner was a surprise to Herbert. The barrack dining hall had been decorated with coloured streamers and the tables put in three long rows and covered with white tablecloths. The men were served their dinner by the corporals and sergeants and Herbert was amazed at the spread.

> We each had a slice of roast goose, pork and beef, with potatoes and Brussels sprouts – all wonderfully prepared – with beer, and then real plum pudding. So, there I was, amongst these 280 boys, singing "It's a long way to Tipperary". It was the spirit of these couple of hours which I so much admired and loved! The whole situation, and my happiness as a soldier in this army, made me very pensive.

Both Herbert and Beate were disappointed that she was still interned on the Isle of Man at Christmastime. She described to Herbert how they had celebrated:

> Our landlady made us feel more at home by arranging evenings with music and giving us coffee and cake. For our Christmas dinner table, I made some place cards with Madi. I wrote a funny and typical sentence for each person and Madi illustrated the words. Everybody had to find their right place, even though there were no names on the table-cards.

> There were roars of laughter during lunch, so our idea must have been a success. Then I had visitors for coffee, which I enjoyed. So, you need not feel sorry for me. My only sad thought was that you might feel lonely as I didn't know how you were spending Christmas.

Writing to Beate just before the New Year, and looking back over the previous year of 1940, Herbert considered that:

> Tomorrow ends a year which would always be for you and me – even if we were to live to be a thousand years old – always the most fateful and most important year of our common life.

A few weeks later, at the end of January 1941, Beate had some good news which she relayed to Herbert: 'You have got your wish and my release has been ordered. I will see you soon! At last the moment has come that I have waited for for eight months!'

As arranged, she went to Steventon on her release date, Friday 31 January 1941. A few weeks earlier, at Christmastime, Beate had written to Herbert: 'Would you mind my singing again when I am free? I did not sing for seven months.'

He had been appalled: 'Oh, if only I could send these words to the Home Office! Do sing and sing – during all your happy life with me!'

He began to write some ideas for a proposed autobiography.

> Each generation, I believe, is convinced that its lot has been harder, and its experience greater, than that of the previous one. Yet I think that our life bears one of the greatest tragedies that has ever been the burden of any generation.

Chapter 4

'Somewhere in England'

It was amazing to the middle-aged Sulzbach that he was now a member of the British forces. Throughout the Second World War, he remained strongly aware of how very different this experience was compared with his previous service in the Kaiser's army.

Although he was glad of the company of men of his own age in the Pioneer Corps, Sulzbach recognised that his unit included a real medley of German-speaking refugees from the Third Reich – from all backgrounds and walks of life, and with varying degrees of commitment. In his own *Soldier's Service and Pay Book*, details of his place of birth and his parents' nationality had been redacted, his 'trade on enlistment' entered as 'manufacturer', and whatever had once been written for 'religious denomination' had been changed to 'protestant' on a covering piece of paper.

One immediate problem for Herbert and Beate was how they could pay their way on a severely reduced income. Once Sulzbach had joined the British forces, the friend of his grandfather had assumed that he could withdraw all financial help, which seriously concerned Sulzbach, who had no other source of income. A flurry of letters ensued between him and Mr Ehrlich, or his secretary. Sulzbach wrote:

> I am now ruined. I do beg you with all my heart to continue the money that you promised. My wife's allowance is only nineteen shillings and with your help we can at least live. Please do again be the father Ehrlich you were to me before internment and send me your help.

The reply came:

> Mr Ehrlich has guaranteed members of his own family. It was counted on that all, or most of them, would go to

America, but it is no longer possible for them to emigrate, so Mr Ehrlich's list is full. In these circumstances it is rather welcome that one is not burdened for the maintenance of men who are earning their keep in the army.

A worried Sulzbach returned with: 'No, you have no obligation, but you said in January 1938 that you are always there for me,' and he was slightly reassured by the response:

I am instructed by Mr Ehrlich to send you a cheque for one pound ten shillings, enclosed herewith, being fifteen shillings a week, as desired, for two weeks, and to let you know that Mr Ehrlich will allow you fifteen shillings per week for a period of altogether twelve weeks.

So, for a short time there was a reprieve.

In November 1940 Herbert Sulzbach's company went from their Bradford training camp to Dirnall Camp at Didcot, where he was stationed for several months. As Sulzbach described this:

We worked in countless huge army depots and in the evenings, we played cards. The weeks and months were monotonous.

In February 1941, Sulzbach was transferred from 229 Company to 93 Company, which was then sent to a posting near Cirencester. His work alongside Canadian lumberjacks was physically strenuous, but he was able to meet Beate in some of his free time because by then she was living in a furnished room in the town.

Three months later 93 Company moved to Codford in Wiltshire to work alongside the Royal Engineers. They stopped en route near Salisbury, setting up their tents on the county cricket grounds at Bremerton where Sulzbach enjoyed being woken in the morning by the sound of the cuckoo.

Beate remained living in her lodgings in Cirencester, since it had become clear that Herbert would be spending much of his time on the move with his company. Throughout the next four years she had no settled home and relied on a succession of friends and landladies for accommodation in different rented rooms, so that she would never be too far from her husband.

While the work remained laborious, boring and monotonous, Sulzbach was enchanted by the English countryside in which he lived and worked that springtime.

> The landscape was soft, mild and gentle. The meadows were like a yellow carpet, the pear trees were in blossom, and there were delightful cows. There was a small stream with trout and in the mornings the cuckoo called, and the blackbirds sang. It was a concert of birdsong such as we used to hear in our garden in Frankfurt. Everything breathed peace.

The artist Keith Vaughan, a fellow member of the Pioneer Corps, was at Codford at the same time as Sulzbach and has left a visual record of life in the barracks that echoes Sulzbach's experience there. His drawings do not depict a glamorous or heroic view of war; they show men off-duty – smoking, playing cards, reading, or just resting.

Sulzbach became increasingly frustrated and bored with this lack of front-line direct action and in July 1941 he asked to be allowed to serve overseas.

> I hereby certify that I understand the risks (which have been fully explained to me) to which I and my relatives may be exposed by reason of my employment in the British Army outside the United Kingdom. Notwithstanding this, I certify that I am willing to be employed in any Theatre of War.

However, he changed his mind when he realised that he would be sent into action in a Pioneer Company, rather than as part of a fighting British unit.

> My only sister and my wife's mother live in Berlin. I therefore would be grateful if I could not be sent overseas. This does not contradict my attitude to fighting Nazism, but my hope was to join an artillery unit and so be one alien amongst British soldiers. Capture in that case would not involve the risks of being made prisoner in an entirely German unit.

As well as risks to himself in the event of capture, he came to realise that there would also be risks for Lili and Frau Scherk if he were to be found fighting for the British.

'I was in regular correspondence with my sister and mother-in-law until the outbreak of war. Any reprisals would always be on my conscience if anything happened to my relatives,' he wrote to the military authorities.

So instead of serving overseas, Herbert Sulzbach moved with his company when it transferred to Donniford Camp at Liddymore, near Watchet in Somerset. The work was less exhausting and Sulzbach was glad to be by the sea.

> The sea crashed as it did in my youth in Zandvoort, or as it did in Heligoland, or Genoa, or in De Panne and brought back countless memories. That eternal crashing of the sea is like infinity.

They were there only a short while before being moved to 'a beautiful wooded camp not far from Plymouth' at the end of the month. Two weeks later he visited the city, which had been heavily bombed six months previously. He was shocked at his first sight of a ruined British town.

> I had a lift out of the camp with Deloch, a charming married navy officer. In Plymouth there was wreckage everywhere. The emptiness was weird – there were so few people for this large city. There were more and more ruins the closer you got to the centre. It was spooky to see a wooden board advertising 'Bed and Breakfast' at a small house standing between neighbouring ruined buildings: an invitation to bed and breakfast next to the dead! I saw just one single shop amongst the ruins. It was like the horrors of 1918, and in the centre, it was as though an earthquake had destroyed it.

From Plymouth, 93 Company was moved further along the coast to Salcombe in South Devon, but within a fortnight Sulzbach was hurriedly admitted to a small military medical centre at nearby Kingsbridge. Although in considerable abdominal pain, thought to be from a problem with his liver, Herbert Sulzbach was overwhelmed by an encounter on his first day there, which he described in his diary:

'SOMEWHERE IN ENGLAND'

This little military field hospital has its own unique atmosphere: there is not the usual strictness, but a friendly (and very good) military doctor, kind nurses, and a pleasant room with five patients. From my bed I have a wonderful view through the window to the hill, which is still in its summery green, although the trees on the summit sparkle in a hundred varieties of green, yellow and red.

All five of us were admitted on the same day. Conversation began towards evening and moved from company and regiment talk to more personal matters. The young men seemed interested in my fate and I told them about Germany, which I loved, and Nazism, which I hated. They had little idea about any of it. Then we got to talking about the last war. It was strange for these boys to be in the same room as a former German officer from 1914, who is today one of them. The boy opposite me had lost his father in the last war. He had fallen in Flanders in 1918, and the father of my neighbour had died ten years ago as a result of his injuries from 1917. We became silent and it was painful for me to think that perhaps I had been guilty.

Then the boy whose father had been killed in 1918 said to me, "It's amazing that in 1914 you were fighting our fathers and today you are a comrade of their sons. What an extraordinary life!" And he fell asleep. He had spoken my own thoughts, and had expressed them without the slightest bitterness, but quite simply as to an old friend. What grand characters they are, these young men and the entire English people! How proud we can be to wear their uniform!

Within a few days, Sulzbach was moved to the much larger Stoke Military Hospital at Moretonhampstead, where he was to stay for several months. In this former hotel (where Ribbentrop had once stayed) Sulzbach shared a room with just one other patient. His supposed liver or gall bladder problem turned out to be the effects of an enlarged and infected appendix, which was removed by 'my wonderful surgeon, Major Nicholson' on 30 December 1941. Sulzbach did not enjoy this surgical experience and was still feeling queasy a week later.

Two or three weeks later he was taken by ambulance to Bystock Court, an Edwardian mansion near Exmouth that was being used as a convalescent home for servicemen. He had been looking forward to going there.

'Bystock should be fantastic!' he wrote to Beate. 'It is a millionaire's estate for a hundred men with splendid rooms and amazing food. In the afternoons you can go to the cinemas in Exmouth for free!'

He stayed at Bystock Court from mid-January 1942 until the middle of March, by which time he had been away from his company for almost five months. He enjoyed his quiet and restorative days there with good care from the medical and nursing staff – and with plenty of time to read. During his time at Bystock, Sulzbach read books by the military historian Basil Liddell-Hart and started a correspondence with the author that lasted until Liddell-Hart's death in 1970.

By the middle of March 1942 Beate had arranged to make a more settled home in Surrey with some old friends of the Sulzbach family. Nellie and Frederic Kaula had rented *The Plain House*, in Walpole Avenue, Chipstead, from Herbert and Lois Gatliff, and at the Kaulas' invitation Beate lived with them there until July 1944. *The Plain House* became a beloved and relatively luxurious oasis and refuge from the war for both Herbert and Beate. She moved there on 18 March 1942 and he visited whenever he was on leave. At about the same time, he received his first letter since the outbreak of war from his brother, Ernst, in Stockholm.

In April 1942 Sulzbach was considered medically fit enough to rejoin his company, which was then in Falmouth, Cornwall. His fitness level, which had been graded A1 before his illness, was downgraded to a C rating and his duties were appropriately rescheduled. He was pleased to be back with his company and enjoyed the warm spring weather by the sea.

'After lunch today there was not much to do,' he told Beate in a letter, 'so I lay on the beach with the others and roasted in the sun. There was a blue sky, the blue sea, murmuring waves, and a tangy smell. The beach was full of children and women – and soldiers. The children paddled in the water, and some people were bathing (on 17 April!). But the entrance to the beach was through wire emplacements, and out at sea were eleven minesweepers keeping a good distance from each other. Each ship had its small balloon above it – like the kites of the children on the beach.

'SOMEWHERE IN ENGLAND'

And near us was an infantry company reinforcing the barbed wire. As ever, this sinister war sits side by side with peace.'

Later that month his company was transferred to Weymouth where they built fortifications on the shore against an expected German invasion.

> The beach is completely fortified. Everywhere there are endless wire enforcements, and on the roof of the big Marks and Spencer there are soldiers in steel helmets, with MGs and AA guns. The sirens have sounded four times since yesterday evening. The detectors report the time when the Nazis leave France – it's amazing!

He experienced several raids whilst at Weymouth, but otherwise found the work to be monotonous and suggested to the War Office that refugees from Nazi Germany might be better employed in propaganda work amongst the British, since they knew first-hand about the evils of Nazism. Nothing came of his suggestion and he found solace on leave in beautiful Chipstead.

> The house lies on a slope in the valley, and nearby cottages are hidden in their gardens. The wind rustles through the trees, just as it used to rustle in my childhood in the Taunus mountains. On the wild meadow which slopes down softly behind the house grow thousands and thousands of white daisies, intermingled with dark lilac-coloured clover and yellow buttercups. The cuckoo calls, and blackbirds, thrushes, finches and tomtits sing. It is inconceivably lovely, but even more inconceivable that there is a war on!
>
> Whenever we tune into the radio there are German voices and German military music. When will this persecuted, tormented mass of humanity be able to enjoy eternal peace and all this beauty – the most natural thing that life can give?

Meanwhile Beate was still struggling to deal with the authorities about compensation for their bombed London flat. Giving 'a complete list of the chattels lost or damaged with the price against each of them' and finding details of insurance was not simple and she shared her anxieties and confusion with Herbert:

> Yes, I am nervous. I don't want to make any mistake with the war damage things, and I rather imagine that people do not believe us. I don't think it's important to refer to the fact that we have lost everything. That doesn't interest them at all: it has happened to hundreds of refugees.

Other news added to their sadness. They heard from Ernst that Professor Salomons – the stepfather of Herbert's first wife – had died of a heart attack, which particularly upset Herbert's daughter, Dorothee, who was very sad about her grandfather dying. Then, in August 1942, Beate found out that her mother, Frau Scherk, had been deported from Berlin to Theresienstadt. It became difficult to continue to feel positive about the direction of the war. Herbert recorded in his diary that:

> For more than two years I have been stationed with my company all over the south of England. It has been hard work to build fortifications and defences, and at the same time it has been a strain always to be prepared for invasion.

Herbert took inspiration from the young men in the British forces, especially from the airmen, whom he admired as real heroes. In October 1942 he cut out – and kept until he died – a letter from the *Daily Telegraph*. Under the heading, 'Spirit of the Brave – An Airman's last letter home' it read:

> Sir, parents with sons in the RAF must frequently wonder how their sons really feel in their life of high adventure and great danger. May I proffer one letter in the hope that it may help and console other parents?
> My son, a pilot officer, has recently been reported "missing, believed killed" in the Middle East. A little before his final crash he wrote a letter to be posted only in the event of his not returning. This has just reached me. He says,
> "Please do not think that I have not enjoyed this life of suspense. I think it is great never to know from one day to the next where you will be – anywhere on earth or elsewhere.

'SOMEWHERE IN ENGLAND'

> "Believe it or not, I have enjoyed it all. And when that last action comes, I shall like that too. Well, don't worry about me, Dad. If there is one iota of a chance, I will be back, and if not...well, "I'll see you later"."

At the end of October 1942, Sulzbach's company moved to Hilsea, Portsmouth, where again he found his duties to be 'boring' – and his fitness rating remained at C, which upset him.

'From all our company am I to be the one non-combatant failure? Scrap metal! It is not only that I shall be scrap metal, but I won't be able to take part in the final battle and the final victory,' he fumed in a letter to Beate.

In February 1943, he and his company continued their move along the south coast, this time as far as Beaulieu, in the New Forest. Although his duties took him to Southampton, which had been heavily bombed, Sulzbach found the countryside unbelievably lovely. He told Beate:

> God, this Beaulieu is a charming, sleepy village – just like the Middle Ages. In the cloister gardens of the Abbey it is as though the world has stood still for seven hundred years. The silence in the nearby graveyard is incredible. I sat there in the sun and could not imagine that the world from before August 1914 had disappeared.

The following month, March 1943, Sulzbach was transferred to 251 Company at Thame and he enjoyed visiting nearby Oxford, where he took tea in the elegant Randolph Hotel. But, keeping up with the news, he took note of the tonnage that was being dropped in RAF bombing raids onto his beloved Frankfurt and Berlin – and felt uneasy.

He was curious about his feelings of being Jewish in this particular war. A few months earlier he had told Beate that he had enjoyed the Jewish Hanukkah festival, and he was concerned that his *Soldier's Service and Pay Book* had an incorrect entry for 'religion'. Beate tried to help:

> Can't you leave things as they are? If it says Jewish in your military papers, that's alright – let it stay as Protestant in your pass. Why does everything have to be tidy? Today you cannot withdraw from the Jewish community, even if you have never actually been of the Jewish faith.

Herbert only knew that: 'I feel neither Jewish nor Aryan, but inter-confessional (like inter-national).'

He was immensely cheered by the Allied victory in North Africa and attended a special Thanksgiving Service on 16 May 1943. Exactly thirty years earlier, just out of school, he had visited Tunis and his memories of that time mixed with this joyful wartime celebration.

> I thought of the soldiers and generals of the 8th Army, the 1st and USA Army, and the Free French regiments and their dead. It was "Onward Christian Soldiers", as in *Mrs Miniver* [from the 1940 novel and 1942 film], and in reality.

He was particularly moved by the words of the Czech foreign minister, Jan Masaryk, which echoed his feelings about the British soldier:

> I am moved with gratitude to the British soldiers, to those small humble citizens who are capable of being the greatest heroes. But they do not speak about it; they do not boast, and as soon as the war ends, they will modestly disappear into their little homes and cease to be glorious. That is their greatest glory of all.

During the summer of 1943, Sulzbach went to Bradford for an interview about his prospects in the army (hoping to be transferred to an Intelligence unit). There was no immediately positive outcome, so he continued with his company to Buxton, in Derbyshire. The weather was hot, duties remained boring, and the soldiers' main relaxation was playing cards.

In September 1943 Sulzbach was made a lance corporal and he was moved to the newly formed 506 company at Tidworth, in Hampshire. His fitness rating was improved to B1 and he became busier with various duties and attending courses.

But he also became aware of an escalation of events outside the camp.

> In the evening lorries whizz along the road, full of American soldiers on night exercises. The soldiers are wonderfully equipped and dressed, and wonderfully trained. High above, the bombers fly on to the continent and on Wednesday

'SOMEWHERE IN ENGLAND'

8 September we knew that something big had been signed, but we didn't know the details. Then on the nine o'clock news we heard of the armistice between Italy and the Allies. The report astonished everyone. Then the English national anthem was played, and I was quite overwhelmed. Good God, overwhelmed. In the Club, everything to eat and drink was free. "Nothing to pay today." "Why not?" "Ask Italy".

Tidworth housed a large contingent of American forces and in their Service Club at the beginning of October, on the Jewish New Year, 'was a poster saying, "Happy New Year to our Jewish forces", and then Jewish food was available in the canteen.' Sulzbach was moved by this unexpected display of freedom and democracy.

Meanwhile, Beate was taking her turn at fire-watching duties in Chipstead. She enjoyed working with her neighbours, but Herbert was concerned that she might be in danger and urged her to excuse herself. She was furious:

It would make a dreadful impression if I were the only person in Walpole Avenue to shirk my duties. As an alien and as a Jewess it is impossible. I won't do it and I will no doubt survive. Anyway, I am only a reserve and once a week doesn't make a big difference.

Towards the end of 1943 and the early part of 1944, Sulzbach heard of enormous air attacks on both Berlin and Frankfurt and couldn't fail to be aware of the build-up of troops around him in the south of England. Christmas at Tidworth was celebrated cheerfully in the American Red Cross Service Club, although as the Christmas tree twinkled, and his birthplace was pounded by bombs, Herbert thought back to those magical Christmases of his childhood.

In April 1944 he attended an interview in London where he was questioned about his knowledge of languages, and only a few weeks later he watched as aeroplanes massed overhead on D-Day.

Invasion has begun. Today I woke early in my tent, conscious that I had been hearing the powerful humming of planes while I was half asleep. Then our guards explained to me that masses of gliders and troop carriers had been overhead. Before midnight they had seen hundreds and hundreds of powerful bombers, all of them – until they reached the Channel – lit up with red and green lights so that they didn't ram each other as they flew through the night. I cycled over to the post to collect the papers and hear more details. There was no radio in the camp, so I went to a nearby house to ask the owner if we could listen to their radio.

I have just had a ten-minute break to go outside where I saw that hundreds of gliders had been hitched to motor planes which were full of troops. Once airborne they would land in France in forty or fifty minutes. The sky was black with aircraft and I found myself holding my breath, wishing the brave men up there "God bless". Then we heard over our landlady's radio, "Under cover of large naval forces and air support we have begun to disembark our troops in northern France."

Meanwhile, Beate was watching the skies over Chipstead.

We see the rocket-gun flying over our house every day. From the terrace we see it flying over the hills, taking a direct course for London. I take cover as soon as the gun comes near. The blast has caused a lot of damage.

In early July 1944 she wrote to Herbert that:

By day we count about eight or nine flying bombs. We are just now preparing our shelter. We have got wood for benches, but it will only take two beds. Saunders [in the house next door] has invited me to go to their shelter at night. They always sleep in the shelter and there is ample space. When the real battle comes, I will take up this offer.

She wrote just one day before a bomb fell in the garden of *The Plain House*, injuring Nellie Kaula and causing considerable damage to the house. Herbert was given compassionate leave for two weeks as Beate was in shock and Nellie was in hospital with an eye injury. He had a difficult train journey via London:

> There was an alert at Paddington, and everyone went into the Underground. At King's Cross it was "all change" because the line had been hit. In the tube hundreds of small children who were being evacuated were coming up the escalators and policemen received them with open arms – kindly, helpful, and selfless. Later I went by tube to London Bridge from where I took a train to Chipstead. Straight away the sirens were howling again but Londoners and everything carried on. I scanned the sky for flying bombs but saw nothing.

At Chipstead, he found Beate lying exhausted on a sofa in a doorway between the house and garden.

> Roof tiles were piled on the terrace and everywhere there were splinters of wood jutting into the open air. There were no windows anywhere; they were all boarded up. *The Plain House* is uninhabitable. Most of the roof has come off and the water drips through.

It was a noisy few days, as they were now under attack by the new V-1 bombers – the 'doodlebugs'.

> Hardly had I arrived when there was an alert and immediately afterwards, they got nearer – these beastly things, with their monotonous drone, which suddenly stops, and then the crash follows. Eight or nine came. People can get no peace: warnings and all clears alternate without pause. We made our beds in Mrs Saunders' shelter and the alerts continued until eleven o'clock, while the cats came and went during the night.
> During the day the roofers came, and so did a Home Guard Lieutenant – Mrs Bell. Between the alerts I tried to cook, eat, shave, and go to the toilet! Breakfast in the garden, amongst the dead roof tiles and the living garden flowers, was wonderful.

A JEW WHO DEFEATED NAZISM

On 14 July 1944 Sulzbach wrote to his commanding officer requesting an extension of his compassionate leave on the grounds that:

> Repair of *The Plain House* will start in the next few days with the entire roof, ceilings, pipes, etc. Somebody has to be present to attend to things and my wife's health after the incident is very bad. She suffers from shock and is unable to see to all that matters.

The request was granted for a further week and the Sulzbachs lived through:

> ...quiet days and quieter nights, which alternate with loud days and louder nights. Alerts are followed by flying bombs which either go over or drop down very nearby. Beate is in a dreadful state and worries about where she should go now.

Then on 21 July 1944 they 'heard on the evening news of an assassination attempt on Hitler, and then two days later of a German generals' revolt.' Shortly afterwards Herbert had to return to his company and Beate went to stay with her sister at her place of work near Guildford.

Sulzbach's company was then stationed at Market Lavington, near Devizes, and it was here that he had two slightly conflicting experiences. First, he heard of the death of a German, Lieutenant-General von Drabich-Wächter, in Normandy. He reflected on his feelings in his diary:

> Until now I have been pleased at the death of each German. I no longer had the feeling that he was a human being. For me, he was the murderer of the Poles, the Jews, the Belgians, the Serbs, the Dutch, the French. The Nazi and the German were one for me. But today when I read Alan Moorehead's report [in the *Daily Express*] from Normandy, I was thoughtful for the first time.

Drabich-Wächter had been the adjutant of an infantry regiment during the First World War, at the same time as Sulzbach had been an adjutant of his regiment's covering batteries.

'SOMEWHERE IN ENGLAND'

> Drabich and I were a good collaborative team. He was dashing, courageous and a good comrade and friend. He was certainly never a Nazi and never an anti-Semite. We chatted together a lot in our leisure time and when there was no shooting. It was during this same hot season of July and August, when we worked and fought together, and it is only 150 km from there that he has now, twenty-six years later, fallen.

Sulzbach's second significant experience at Devizes occurred at the end of July 1944 when he saw German prisoners working in the American barracks.

> My heart shook with hate, rage and revulsion when I saw the uniforms, the disgusting, stupid, brutal faces, the murderous swastika on the right breast. Never would I have thought that the sight of something like that would disturb me.

But generally, during August 1944, in the peaceful surroundings at Devizes, Sulzbach was optimistic about the eventual outcome of the war.

> There will soon come a time when we listen to the radio one evening and hear that the Germans are asking for an armistice. This moment is not far away. The European war will end soon. When Eisenhower and Monty take advantage of the situation, absolutely everything is possible.

He was disappointed that his application for work in the Intelligence Corps had been turned down because there were no vacancies, but was encouraged that his superiors were trying to find him more congenial work in the army – such as a job with Amgot, the Allied Military Government of Occupied Territories. Meanwhile, he enjoyed the facilities at his camp at Tidworth.

> Every evening I go to the American Red Cross Service Club where I can do some typing. It is only about five minutes away, in a palatial house in the woods [Tedworth House]. The rooms are huge and there is a dance hall, a concert hall, a cinema hall, bathrooms, and writing and reading rooms.

> There are thousands of magazines and weekly journals, and several newspapers, a library, games rooms, with comfortable armchairs in all the rooms, as well as a canteen which offers a wonderful selection of food and all possible hot and cold drinks.

Like so many others, Sulzbach avidly marked the progress of the Allied troops.

> The American army stands one mile from Aachen. On 27 August a week ended which had seen the liberation of Paris by the heroic Maquis and the French and American divisions. Paris, France – the symbol of all freedom, culture and love of life. Bordeaux, Marseille, Toulon, Grenoble and Avignon have been taken by the southern invading army. USA Panzer divisions are near the Swiss border.

As the end of the war came closer, Sulzbach brooded on the future – not only his personal future and that of his family, but also the future of Europe after such a cataclysmic war. He recognised the part played by everyone, and in a letter to his brother in Sweden he explained that:

> What is carried out here as civilian heroism, would never be quite understood by outsiders. But what has been undertaken recently by Beate, and in 1940 by Ruth – and what they have been through – is heroic. About my own future? I have no idea and no money.

In fact, despite his lack of money and prospects, his future would be good. As more and more German prisoners flooded into Britain, Herbert Sulzbach's ability with languages was an asset. He was assigned to an interpreter pool for prisoner of war camps. An administrative muddle meant that he was first sent to a camp near Aldershot with Russian prisoners, though he spoke no Russian.

> It took them two weeks to realise that I was in the wrong place, and then I was posted to Comrie in Scotland, at the beginning of January 1945, and there my new life started.

PART II

(1945 – 1951)
Turning Men's Lives Round

Chapter 5

Comrie. Confronting Nazism

Squashed into their train compartment, Herbert Sulzbach and other military personnel shared sandwiches and chocolate, but 'we were six, then seven, eight, nine, ten, eleven hours late. No cup of tea anywhere.' It was a slow journey, and wartime Britain made the journey especially difficult. The cold was intense, the frost and ice spectacular, and snowdrifts lay high along the tracks as they inched their way from London to the Scottish Highlands. But Sulzbach was relentlessly optimistic. He told Beate:

> A storm howled from the mountains, like the Hound of the Baskervilles. In the summer it must be a perfect dream.

It would be a few months of great change before summer arrived in the village of Comrie, not far from Perth, and even longer before Sulzbach would realise some of his own dreams. This was January 1945 and he was on his way to be an interpreter in a prisoner of war (PoW) camp. He guessed that it would be a tough assignment even with his formidable success as a German officer in the First World War, and his past four years in the British Army.

Sulzbach was extremely anxious about meeting German PoWs, all of whom he assumed were Nazis. He had had little choice about volunteering as an interpreter. As more and more Germans had been taken prisoner in 1944, anyone in the British Army who could speak German had been ordered to report to the authorities. While always quick to oppose Nazism vehemently, he was reluctant to have to confront anyone who had actually had a part in the destruction of his family, his business, and his privileged lifestyle in pre-war Germany.

His fears were not unjustified. 'Our camp is a black camp, where the fanatics are brought,' he later wrote to his wife.

It could hold 4,000 men, and the arrival of large numbers of German prisoners at the railway station, followed by their march to the camp –

'with defiant demeanour and proudly singing' – is still remembered by some villagers who watched them pass. Most of the prisoners were under 20 years old, and there were very few officers among them.

In the 'peculiar atmosphere' that Sulzbach noted when he arrived, the ardent Nazis amongst the prisoners controlled their compounds. Shortly before his arrival, and two days before Christmas 1944, a prisoner had been suspected of lack of fervour for Hitler's cause. Nazi leaders had searched his belongings overnight and discovered a diary in which he had recorded his doubts about Germany's ultimate victory. The prisoner, Wolfgang Rosterg, was thus considered a traitor, and was immediately tortured, brutally attacked, and hung up to die in the latrines. It was clear – as a journalist wrote later – that 'the atmosphere at Comrie camp was poisonous with hatred, bitterness, and frustration.'

Over the next few months Sulzbach became a much liked and respected member of the British staff at the camp. He was a slightly built man, and not particularly tall – and had astonishingly blue eyes. It was these eyes that people always noticed first, and which held their attention so strongly. Whether friendly, piercing, or twinkling, they were unfailingly direct. Capable, debonair, witty – and very hard-working – Sulzbach had arrived at Comrie as a staff sergeant.

He was forced to question some of his assumptions about Nazis on his very first evening in the British compound. As he told Beate:

> I saw my first prisoner, and thought that he helped there, and that he would later be taken back behind barbed wire. However, he was a barber and was cutting the hair of one of the sergeants. I urgently needed a hair-cut, so I had one too.

As he chatted to the barber, he was surprised to hear that not all the prisoners held Nazi views. Those anti-Nazis had been moved to separate quarters for their own safety and many of them were trusted to work with the British camp staff – including those in Sulzbach's office.

He also chatted to the Polish guards that evening and was taken aback by their hatred of Germans:

> Every single person has a story to tell about murder in cold blood. They dragged me into their recreation hut, where they listen to the 10 pm BBC German radio programme.

Sulzbach listened with the Poles to Hitler's latest speech, and noted that: 'He spoke nothing about victory – and nothing about how the Russians stood at the door.'

From the start, Sulzbach liked his British colleagues. The commandant of the camp, Colonel Archibald Wilson, was an ex-police chief constable who had been appointed shortly after the prisoner's murder. Wilson and Sulzbach were not only new at Comrie together, they also had similar personalities. Both of them could empathise with others, had confidence in their abilities, and a rich sense of humour. The Wilson-Sulzbach team would become a powerful force for good amongst the young men held in this 'black camp'.

The camp was divided into four compounds, each of which had their own internal discipline, with a 'camp leader' who reported to the commandant. Living quarters for the British staff and the guards, as well as the camp offices, were situated in a separate area of the camp outside these compounds.

The prisoners lived in Nissen huts – eighty men to a hut, with double-tier bunk beds. A coal stove in the centre gave some heat, although the Scottish winter and a depleted fuel supply meant that the men needed to be ingenious in stoking the fire. They had to go to separate huts for the washing areas and latrines, for the kitchen and dining facilities, and for recreational and cultural activities such as the theatre and library. Barbed wire surrounded the camp, with watch towers and armed guards at regular intervals.

In December 1944 the young German PoWs had become increasingly confident that the Ardennes Offensive would bring them victory. When this offensive stalled, their morale plummeted, and the bullying Nazi element reasserted itself. When Sulzbach heard that these Nazis had earlier been moved from a camp at Devizes, his blood ran cold. During his time working with the Pioneer Corps near Devizes, he had seen these same prisoners from a distance. Just by seeing the swastikas on their uniforms he had felt again all his fear, horror and revulsion of Nazi Germany.

It was brought home to him again a few months later by a statement from a witness at Rosterg's murder investigation who told the court that when he had spoken up against Rosterg's brutal treatment – dealt out to him just because Rosterg had held a certain point of view – he had been told by the murderers:

> You are as bad a criminal as he is. If you think like that you had better keep your mouth shut.

Sulzbach shared an office with his superior in the interpreter office, Captain Bauer, and ten PoW clerks. As he told Beate:

> Captain Bauer put me in charge of the mail to and from the prisoners. He spoke to me privately, saying that I should take another name, for use here in the German office, and I said immediately "Salbrook". Captain Bauer speaks excellent German with an accent, and he advised me to speak broken German sometimes at first.

As censor for the whole camp, Sulzbach read all the prisoners' outgoing mail and so began to understand more clearly how they viewed things.

> One letter said, "I will not allow myself to be misled from my belief in our great Germany, in our beloved Führer and our unique victory". Yet the Russians are eighty-two miles from Berlin, and the British-American army is on the Rhine! All such letters are allowed to go smoothly on their way; no one hinders them.

He was occasionally amused by certain aspects of his situation.

> All day long Nazis are coming in and out with queries about the post and other documents, and they click their heels and say, "Yes, Sir Herr Sergeant". That's me!

And once, when he escorted a group of prisoners on a walk:

> I found it funny when a Nazi asked me what a particular tree was called in English, another asked me where I had learnt such good German, and another said, "If the Herr Sergeant allows it", and then heels were clicked (in front of the refugee Jew).

In those first weeks at Comrie, he remained steadfast in his opinion, repeating to his wife that:

> Ninety percent out of the four thousand here are fanatics and I am right when I say that there are only ten percent anti-Nazis in Germany.

On 8 February 1945, the prisoners went on strike in response to an alleged shooting by a Polish guard. No fatigue parties of prisoners turned up to hump coal, shovel snow, or generally clear up. It was Sulzbach's birthday. In a letter to Beate he wondered:

> ...whether an English or Polish, French, Dutch or Norwegian prisoner would dare to strike in a German PoW camp. Immediately the firing squads would march out, and in accordance with war justice the PoW would promptly be shot dead.

The commandant went with some of his officers to the PoW compounds to demand which prisoners would work, and they were received in silence. As they turned to leave:

> The PoWs shouted with one voice "Sieg Heil" three times, so that the camp shook. When the Polish guards heard the roaring of the prisoners, they rushed from their barracks, with guns at the ready. Afterwards the commandant put the camp on seven days detention, with three days of only bread and water – and no coal.

Sulzbach was impressed by a Norwegian officer from the War Office who was part of the resulting Court of Enquiry. The German camp leader was brought in front of the assembled British officers and Allies and stood limply, without saluting. A British officer reprimanded him, so he lifted his arm in a Nazi salute. Writing to Beate, Sulzbach described what happened next:

> Then the Norwegian captain springs on top of the Nazi and roars at him in German. How dare he give the German salute

> to British officers? He forbids it, he roars at him again, then in Norwegian he orders him to about-turn. The Nazi stood straight as a candle and obeyed. I laughed heartily to myself.

Clearly, no known anti-Nazi prisoner was safe in the camp and sometimes a man could be transferred elsewhere.

> Captain Bauer allowed three anti-Nazis to transfer to another camp in Scotland, because of the current atmosphere. I saw them leave and spoke with two of them. They were extremely glad to be getting away from this camp. One was so terribly depressed, and you could see that he is a more honest man.

The whole event, including the non-compromising attitudes of the Norwegian officers from the War Office who attended the subsequent Court of Enquiry, only confirmed Sulzbach in his belief about Nazis.

> One can see what vicious danger they will present, when they are set free and released again into humanity. They will rule Germany with mob rule and lawlessness for years to come. This generation must be exterminated, like rats.

During those early months of 1945, the increasing number of PoWs who began to question Nazi ideology kept very quiet. If their doubts were suspected, they could expect death as traitors. Sergeant Schwänke, the chief clerk in Bauer and Sulzbach's office, just managed to escape this punishment. One night he was paraded in front of a kangaroo court of 300 PoWs for his 'crime' of 'treason', and the 'verdict' was pronounced by men hidden behind a curtain. They gave him one hour to leave the compound and forty-eight hours to leave the camp.

Once outside the 'courtroom' Schwänke appealed for help from the guards and was immediately taken into safe custody in a single cell in the detention barracks. But from then on, his life, and that of his family back in Germany, was in danger.

Sulzbach visited the PoWs in protection every day, taking them something to read or eat. His intuitively friendly, helpful and optimistic personality was a powerful influence on the disillusioned young men.

He still saw every German as a Nazi, but his reactions began to soften a little as he talked with the segregated prisoners. It was his conversations with those who could be receptive to other ideas that began the slow process of a change of attitude amongst the PoWs that would later become a basis for re-education.

In 1945 there were many people in Britain who felt that there must be something intrinsically evil in the German character that had led to the horrors of the previous years. Sulzbach also held that opinion but was gradually becoming aware of the contradictions that he saw every day. At the time of the camp strike in February he had noted in his diary how many of the prisoners shared his love of the outside world.

> Yes, they feed the birds, building around the food so that the new snow won't wash it away. And they stand for a long time in the morning watching the sunrise lighting up the tips of the snow-covered mountains and shining on vast areas of snow. They are enchanted as they look at this – and yet murder, murder, murder.

He had no expectation that things would improve in the immediate future, and told a friend, 'Those bad Nazis in our hands should not go home for a long time.'

Over the Easter weekend, another Court of Enquiry met at Comrie, this time to investigate the murder of Wolfgang Rosterg. A captain from the Secret Service attended with another from the military court in Edinburgh, and Sulzbach was the interpreter. The Crown Witness was PoW Bultmann, a friend of the murdered man, who had been immediately taken into protective custody on the day after the murder and transferred elsewhere. Sulzbach described what happened.

> I had the seventy or so men who had lived in one of the huts on the day of the murder paraded on the lawn in front of my office. Then Bultmann stepped forward to the three rows with the two officers and our adjutant. He went calmly and surely, without any commotion, along the front of them. All seventy of course knew what was going on, and who Bultmann was. For better or worse they had to repress their hate. I admired Bultmann's calm composure.

He picked out five men whom he thought were possible witnesses but there were still two men missing who must have been among them, and whom Bultmann had not picked out. So, we all went to the compound where the murder had taken place. I had earlier arranged for English sentries to be posted at the front and back of Hut 2. We went inside: three captains, two of our sergeants, myself, Bultmann and two Polish guards to protect Bultmann. It was a dramatic picture as we went past the seventy men lined up by their beds; fanatical Nazis, any one of whom expected to be identified by a "traitor". With the same calmness and without any fear, Bultmann went up and down the hut and picked out the two with deadly certainty. As we left, a cry rang out against Bultmann: "Traitor!" I allowed the guards to show their Stenguns.

The suspects were immediately taken to single cells in the detention barracks. I showed the captain from the Secret Service the statements that had been made for me a few weeks before by an anti-Nazi, who had in the meantime gone to an anti-Nazi camp. In this, three men were named who were heavily involved, whom Bultmann did not know. The captain asked to see them, so I went to the compound to collect them. There was a deadly hostile atmosphere as I and two Polish guards entered the huts; the fury of each of the one thousand men in the compound was enormous. So ended Easter Saturday.

On the evening of the final day of the enquiry, Sulzbach sat in the detention barracks with all those PoWs who had at any time asked to be taken into protective custody. One of the group was due to be repatriated the following day, but – instead of being pleased – he was terrified at the prospect. First, his family was in Russian-held territory, and secondly, he feared for his life as he travelled home, with his anti-Nazi views now well broadcast. Sulzbach tried to appreciate the man's predicament.

> These are his two fears: facing the enemy who is friendly towards him here and facing his comrades who are possibly his deadly enemy. That is Germany – Hitler's Third Reich.

The enquiry caused Sulzbach to reflect on the different values represented by the two world wars in which he had fought.

> In this murder, a paratrooper with the name of Joachim Goltz is involved and participates as one of the worst. He bears the same name as Joachim von der Goltz, the author of *Der Baum von Clery*, in which the soldier Karl says to his comrades in the middle of battle in 1915, "then I noticed that I loved this poor, downtrodden French earth." And here is this Goltz from 1940, who puts a rope around his comrade's neck, when he has already been beaten to death. The awful decay and decline of a country are demonstrated by these two bearers of the name Joachim Goltz.

The camp at Comrie received regular copies of *The Scotsman* and the *Glasgow Herald*. Most of the PoWs refused to read the papers, convinced that they were printed solely as propaganda. However, Sulzbach painstakingly translated cuttings from these papers and used an old duplicating machine to make copies that he distributed. He did not preach to the prisoners but allowed them to develop their own ideas and come to their own conclusions. The most worthwhile discussions were usually those that were held amongst the men in their barracks.

He was aware that – in spite of the evidence – most of these young men vehemently denied that Germany was losing the war. They held on to their belief that Hitler had a grand plan for victory and that German paratroopers would soon land, occupy England from the air, and set all PoWs free.

Even so, the news of Hitler's death on 30 April 1945 was not entirely unexpected by most of them. Many PoWs, though shocked, heard it with indifference. The news, a few days afterwards, of the unconditional surrender of the German armed forces was often received with apparent apathy by German PoWs, wherever they were held in camps across Britain, America or Canada. But at the same time, the prisoners felt desperate, fearful and utterly betrayed.

By then, postal links between Britain and Germany had completely broken down. This became a grim situation for the many PoWs who relied mainly on their families for any sort of personal support. One prisoner's letter, written just before Hitler's death, was passed by the censor – Herbert Sulzbach – but the postal service had become non-existent and so his letter could not be sent. He had agonised to his family:

> Where remains any civilisation? And where is the intelligence? We have exterminated the latter, stamped it into the soil, in order to allow stupid people to govern.

Sulzbach was able to encourage him and help him not only to come to terms with his questions but also to find some answers. They kept in touch after his repatriation, with Sulzbach writing to him that: 'With young men like you, Germany will certainly recover, and that is what you and we hope for Germany.'

For Sulzbach, British victory was a great and glorious event. By then, his wife had come to live in lodgings in the nearby village, 'five minutes by bike from the camp', and he had four days leave due on 7 May. Together they took the train from Scotland to join in the emotional celebrations in central London. He later described events to his brother:

> On 8 May I stood in Piccadilly Circus. It was hot and sunny, just as it had been on 3 September 1939 when war was declared. I squeezed through the streets and got stuck in the West End. The crowds were singing, dancing, cheering and were very high-spirited. Three young officers ran out of a restaurant towards the Eros fountain, which had been protected from bombing by wooden boards. After several attempts they got to the top, amid cheers from the crowd. Within half an hour even more people had joined them; officers from the commandos, artillery, air force, tank corps, two sailors from the royal navy, a few ATS girls, some elegant blue Wren girls, three Norwegian air force chaps, American soldiers, Poles, all shouting and singing and kissing each other.

That evening Sulzbach wrote to Mrs Booker – who, as Gertrude Stone, had been his childhood English governess. He was exultant:

> No words exist to express the atmosphere of these days. It is a mixture of joy, deep emotion, and highest pride.

He was delighted to receive a celebratory telegram from his brother, Ernst, in Sweden, and reminded him that: 'In 1918 you sent me a "Welcome back" telegram to Frankfurt. But this one is a Victory telegram!'

Returning to Comrie after the celebrations, Sulzbach was acutely aware of the changed mood there, and the altered circumstances of the PoWs. He noted that:

> They began little by little to see how much their so-called "Führer" had lied to them and cheated them, and at the same time they saw that what they had taken to be propaganda was the truth – and what they had taken to be the truth was lies and invention.

Sulzbach's own anxiety about a Nazi invasion of Britain had now become a thing of the past, his personal confidence had recovered, and his pride and delight in his work had been re-invigorated. He wrote to Basil Liddell Hart: 'My job is the most interesting I could imagine, and I love it and am as happy as a soldier can be.'

But it was still a terrible time for the young German prisoners at Comrie. Whatever their home backgrounds had been, their childhood and youth had been lived solely within the ideology of National Socialism. Most of them had little understanding of any other values and had fought valiantly for the ones that they had been taught. Many of them became deeply depressed, very confused, and completely discouraged.

A month after the end of the war, the first written educational materials from the re-education programme arrived. These were brochures containing photographs from the recently liberated concentration camp at Belsen. Sulzbach sent the brochures to every hut for the prisoners to see and added a few words of his own. He was typically forthright:

> Don't just glance through it! Belsen was not the only camp of horror. The crimes committed there were not the crimes of a few. Hitler himself gave the orders and Himmler initiated them. Millions of innocent men were imprisoned, died of hunger, were tortured to death. What was their "crime"? They had another political opinion – were of another race.

> Read it! Get into your mind what that regime really was. Try to understand why the entire world now hates Germany.
>
> It is up to you, when you go home, to rebuild Germany, to cleanse the soiled name of Germany. To rebuild a Germany in which liberty, justice and humanity regain their value.

Many of the prisoners found reading the booklet both harrowing and shaming. One wrote to Sulzbach:

> Many in this camp have no idea about politics and are educated only from one side. We were too young to think these things over or to talk about the times before 1933. We should very much like to occupy our minds with democracy as we see everything through the "brown spectacles". Please help us by giving us some books or other ways to learn.

Sulzbach found the books. Other prisoners requested 'writings and newspapers about the Nazi regime and about conditions in Germany', or 'an English grammar book', or 'a book about guidelines and objectives of democracy so that later when I go back to Germany I can help with the building of a democratic Germany'.

Despite the willingness of many to learn more about democracy and a different system of values, the PoWs had further horrors to face. They were required to sit through a film of the liberation of Belsen. It was a British government decision that this should be shown in PoW camps and all prisoners had no choice but to view it. Those at Comrie could not believe what they saw. 'Made in Hollywood' was the opinion of one confounded young man.

Immediately after the showing of the film, Sulzbach visited the huts to talk with the men and was encouraged by what they said to him.

> I told them again and again that Germany and the world would need such men as them, who realise that they have been cheated and betrayed for twelve years – in order to rebuild Germany and make a decent and free country out of a ruined and evil Germany.

Sulzbach received several letters from prisoners who expressed both their personal remorse and a desire to work in labour groups to make some sort of amends. One man wrote:

> We stand appalled before the documentary pictures of the German concentration camps. I have a great wish to work soon and to put my knowledge to the service of a free and democratic Europe.

Another said:

> I condemn National Socialism and its deeds which stand blindingly in front of our eyes. I ask that at the earliest opportunity I should go to a working camp in which one can think and feel freely.

Physical work offered not just a release from their pent-up emotions, but also a way of demonstrating their willingness to offer goodwill.

With the collapse of the Nazi regime, re-education of the prisoners became a practical possibility. Ever since his arrival at Comrie, Sulzbach had been talking individually to those PoWs who could be persuaded of a different point of view, and he had encouraged them to talk to other prisoners. Rather than imposing his own beliefs on others, he wanted them to find their own answers. Herbert Sulzbach was always extremely effective in one-to-one encounters. This underpinned his success at Comrie, had always been true of him, and would become the hallmark of his future work.

Although at the Potsdam Conference, in July 1945, the Allies agreed to 'de-nazify and democratise' the Germans, they did not produce an agreement on its practice or administration. In Britain, the commandants of PoW camps were given little guidance in their role in the re-education process until a leaflet was produced much later in December 1945 – and this was mainly to exhort their support.

As soon as the war ended, Herbert Sulzbach reverted back to using his own name, and was always proud of the fact that he remained true to his roots – a man from a respected banking family in Frankfurt, with racial roots in Judaism. Prisoners never experienced feelings of revenge from Sulzbach, and they were always deeply impressed by this. His humanity and respect for every individual – together with his persistence, his warm sense of humour, and his innate goodness – allowed him to enjoy good relations even with former enemies.

Many years later, a journalist said of Herbert Sulzbach that he, 'was a curious combination of angel and imp. His combination of courage, waspish humour, and sheer goodness broke down many barriers.'

At Comrie, Sulzbach came to realise that his earlier opinion about who was and who was not a Nazi needed to change. He was helped in this by memories of his experiences in pre-war Berlin.

> This is a warning for all who like to generalise, amongst whom I myself once numbered. In my biased way, I had believed that anyone with a swastika absolutely must be a Nazi. I had almost forgotten what had happened to us in Berlin in 1938, when I went back there from London to bring out my family. The honest police constable, Ott – who had already helped to falsify my wife's passport – celebrated our farewell with us in a pub, wearing a huge swastika in his buttonhole. How courageous he was, to spend our last evening in Berlin with us – an action which by Nazi law could have cost this brave man not only his job but also his life.
>
> You often hear, "Well, he was a member of the Party." Do not forget, you who generalise, that every postman, every railway worker, every policeman, had to belong to the Party, if he did not want to sacrifice himself or his family.

In order to try to determine which prisoners were Nazis and which were not, 'screening' was introduced. It had initially been used to select suitable labour for work outside the PoW camps and had then become useful in identifying and removing hard-core Nazis from camps where they caused trouble. Sulzbach was responsible for the screening at Comrie.

Prisoners had been screened – in a rudimentary fashion – when they first arrived at the camp, being graded as 'white', 'grey' or 'black' – with ardent Nazis graded as 'black'. During the second half of 1945 the process became more refined so that it could be used as a constructive tool in re-education. Before the authorities had initiated any particular system, Sulzbach had devised one of his own, which became much admired by the man in charge of the PoW re-education programme, Major Henry Faulk.

When Faulk visited Comrie in September 1945 he reported that:

> The results of re-education in this camp, and they are striking, are the direct work of the commandant and the interpreter. That the present inmates of the camp have not sunk back into despair is due to the tremendous influence of Lieutenant Colonel Wilson and Staff Sergeant Sulzbach. It is a triumph of personal influence.

Faulk described Sulzbach's screening system:

> Sulzbach interviewed his PoWs, had them watched by reliable men, put through a test period, interviewed again and finally graded. So reliable is Sulzbach's system that I have no doubt that the official screening figures will closely correlate with his own. The vast majority of all grades from "C redeemable" upwards are the result of Sulzbach's re-education. Staff Sergeant Sulzbach would be a treasure in any camp.

The new screening grades used a letter system, with 'A' grades given to evident anti-Nazis, and a 'D' given to confirmed Nazis who were not thought to be 'redeemable' – with pluses and minuses refining all grades. Unsurprisingly, screening remained controversial amongst all PoWs and many of the British staff.

On this visit to Comrie, Faulk also arranged a debate with the prisoners.

> With the consent of the commandant I organised the first political meeting, starting with a talk on the basis of democracy and the mechanics of the House of Commons and proceeding then to run a debate on Commons lines.

He explained to them that they needed to become accustomed to thinking independently, to tolerate other opinions, and to answer calmly.

The following day, Sulzbach noted that, 'The PoWs were deeply, very deeply, moved. Early this morning my clerks told me how they had talked about this experience late into the night in their huts.'

Sulzbach was intensely interested in all that he saw and heard about re-education for PoWs. He had long discussions with Faulk about the opportunities, challenges, and tools needed to achieve even greater success. His own work thus far had been mainly on a one-to-one basis with those individuals who had expressed a desire to learn about alternative values to Nazism. He had helped them to create cells of like-minded PoWs around them and had seen prisoners change as a result. He was now absolutely passionate about what needed to be done. As he reported to the Political Intelligence Department:

> We have the chance of our lives to re-educate all PoWs.
> We CAN make out of the German people a peace-loving country, but we must jump to the task.

Generally, re-education of German prisoners in Britain began to gain momentum towards the end of 1945, but there was one particular camp where Faulk especially wanted it to succeed. This was a camp for German PoW officers. In October 1945 Faulk requested the War Office that Herbert Sulzbach should be transferred as interpreter there. But the bureaucracy of finding a replacement for him meant that Sulzbach was still at Comrie a month later when the first Remembrance Day after the Second World War was celebrated on 11 November 1945.

At the first armistice in November 1918, Herbert Sulzbach had been much the same age as many of the prisoners now in his care. Like them, he had experienced the despair and humiliation of unexpected defeat. Remembrance Day in 1945 now had added significance for Sulzbach and he wanted to use the event constructively for the prisoners. He copied out the poem *In Flanders Fields* by John McCrae and distributed it amongst the PoWs, together with his own explanation that 11 November in Britain was not a day of triumphalism but one of memories and reflection, and of mourning the dead.

He suggested that they, too, could follow the observance of their 'host-country' in commemorating the fifty million dead of both world wars. Sulzbach proposed that all PoWs should parade for the two-minute silence at eleven o'clock – with the condition that each prisoner should only participate if he could take a vow, which would be:

> Never again shall such murder take place. It is the last time that we will allow ourselves to be deceived and betrayed. It is not true that we Germans are a superior race: we have no right to believe that we are better than others. We are all equal before God, whatever our race or religion. Endless misery has come to us, and we have realised where arrogance leads.
>
> At this moment we swear to return to Germany as good Europeans, and to take part as long as we live in the reconciliation of all people and the maintenance of peace.

All but a very few of the 4,000 PoWs at Comrie joined the parade on 11 November 1945. Herbert Sulzbach kept his own worn, folded, and frequently repaired copy of *In Flanders Fields* in his wallet until the day he died.

A few days before this ceremony, Sulzbach had heard that he had been given a commission in the British Army. His wife was delighted for him.

> For the day's celebrations, I have taken up my best writing paper, and I congratulate you with all my heart. It is such a satisfaction to know that real competence, reliability and love of one's job finds acknowledgement in this world. It is wonderful, Herbert – I am so very happy!

The prisoners at Comrie were sad when Sulzbach left the camp, and many wrote appreciatively to him. One letter was signed by over a hundred men.

> You gave us new belief. Most cruelly deprived of your own German nationality, you rescued each German man who showed goodwill for our new Germany. We came to this country as humiliated and desperate men. You gave us perception, faith and confidence.

As an interpreter not only of words but of culture and values, Herbert Sulzbach had helped these young prisoners to begin to view the world through something other than 'the brown spectacles'. He left the PoW camp at Comrie on 11 December 1945 to go on leave to his family in London. Within a few weeks he would need to travel north again. In Northumberland was a PoW camp with 4,000 German officers who desperately needed to turn their humiliation, defeat and shattered dreams into something better for themselves and their country. Neither they nor Herbert Sulzbach could know what an astonishing journey lay ahead.

Chapter 6

Featherstone Park. Trust, Confidence and Humanity

It embarrassed Herbert Sulzbach on his first evening in Northumberland to hear that the camp commandant, Colonel Vickers, had announced at the weekly staff meeting of fourteen officers that Sulzbach had been 'especially selected as the best man on the job' by Colonel Faulk. 'And Faulk', as Vickers reminded everyone, 'knows what he is talking about.'

Now a captain in the British Army, Sulzbach had arrived at PoW Camp 18 at Featherstone Park, Northumberland, as the interpreter officer. He was delighted with everything that he saw. It was 25 January 1946 and he was to remain working at the camp for two and a half years. He would always consider it to be 'the most satisfying years of my life', 'my life's work.'

Vickers' supreme confidence in Sulzbach's abilities, and the teamwork that his own character encouraged, were some of the significant factors in the widely recognised success of the work done at Camp 18. In his first letter home, Sulzbach described Vickers:

> He is jovial, about 55 years old. Jolly-speaking, full of wit, never acts like a colonel around us. Big, kind, and genial, enormously energetic and loves life. Anyway, he sat down yesterday after supper with three officers and played cards. His manner in today's conference was uncommonly impressive: flying down all the points with an interpreter. He is exceptionally matter-of-fact and kind, of course, with the German officers.

Sulzbach and Vickers were of a similar age, and both had fought in the First World War. During that time, Colonel Vickers had been taken prisoner by the Germans, and this influenced his empathy and attitude towards the prisoners at Featherstone. He never failed to refer to his experiences during his welcoming speech to new prisoners. One newly arrived PoW, Hermann Ziock, noted in his diary what happened on his first evening at the camp:

> When we sat down to our first meal, the camp commandant came along. He asked us where and how we had been taken into captivity and inquired after our health. And – so that we knew that he was not stamped with hatred of Germans – Colonel Vickers gave a welcome speech, which was also very sincere. He himself had been taken prisoner by the Germans and had always been treated as a gentleman. For him, that was unforgettable. In any case, he would do all that he possibly could to make our captivity easier.

Ziock had been shipped to Canada when first taken prisoner in 1943. Once hostilities had ceased, he and other prisoners in Canada had been brought back across the Atlantic, many of them believing that they were on their way home. It was a shock for them to dock at Liverpool and be taken to further imprisonment in England.

There was at least one occasion when Sulzbach was called to the local railway station at Haltwhistle to placate a trainload of these angry German prisoners. After a tense march from the station, with few guards to keep order, the long column of sullen prisoners would come over the hill towards Featherstone. On one such day, with the beautiful River South Tyne on their right, the stunning bluebell woods of Burnfoot on their left, and Featherstone Castle beckoning ahead, the soldiers suddenly braced their shoulders, burst into song, and marched purposefully towards Camp 18.

Colonel Vickers was an extremely successful commandant. He brought order, optimism and good governance to a community of about 4,000 extremely dispirited men. He was also willing to share his administration and his vision with his staff. Officers working under him liked him, and appreciated his concerns for their families, his willingness to sit down with them and enjoy a game of cards – and his back-slapping cheerfulness when one of them was successful at, for example, winning at the races at nearby Carlisle. Colonel Vickers was great fun, and his officers (and the prisoners) welcomed his open, friendly and apparently informal administration, where everyone worked to the common purpose.

Soon after Sulzbach's arrival, Vickers decided to take down the barbed wire surrounding the camp and demolish the watch towers. He left the barbed wire at shoulder-level, telling the prisoners that this was not to keep them in, but rather to keep the cows out. At this time, commandants had not been given official orders to remove security fencing, but Vickers merely required a promise from the prisoners that they would not try to escape.

Right from the start, Sulzbach's work at Featherstone needed a large support team. In his interpreter's office were three British staff sergeants to help him, and in an adjoining room were twelve PoW clerks. His workload was enormous and carried a huge responsibility. Camp 18 housed the cream of the German Wehrmacht, mostly colonels, and almost all the captured general staff-officers.

When Sulzbach first arrived, many of these men were still in a severe state of distress. Some had been in captivity for many months, even years. Sulzbach held consulting hours in his office, when prisoners could talk to him individually, and he reckoned to see about thirty or forty prisoners a day. In these one-to-one encounters he recognised the prisoners' need to talk through their depression, fear and humiliation.

Vickers gave Sulzbach a free hand to act on his own initiative, and usually trusted his judgement absolutely. Sulzbach worked extremely hard. It took much time, tact and patience to build up the necessary confidence and trust between himself and a prisoner.

Sulzbach also encouraged (morally and materially) a wide range of leisure and cultural pursuits within the camp. He instigated and sustained the academic and training programmes that took place, and spent hours writing to influential people to gather support for re-education and to promote Anglo-German reconciliation.

As the re-education programme gained momentum in early 1946, lecturers were invited from far and wide. Sometimes it was difficult for Sulzbach to find people who combined the necessary subject knowledge, language skills and required attitude towards the prisoners. Some speakers were sent from the London section of the Foreign Office, and Sulzbach also used his considerable network of contacts to invite people to give talks at the camp.

TRUST, CONFIDENCE AND HUMANITY

The object of the lectures was 'neither reproach nor conversion but enlightenment that will help the prisoners to form their own opinions,' and this required lecturers with a command of German. As Major Faulk later explained:

> The mass of PoWs expected an official British pronouncement on policy. To them at the beginning, any speaker was an official representative of the government. With their background it surpassed belief that any government should send speakers to them who had not been politically vetted and briefed. Lectures in English failed. They were unable to clear the language barrier, especially for discussion.

But Sulzbach found that obtaining the necessary resources was perhaps the most difficult part of the whole job. Every single PoW struggled to acquire paper, ink, pens, pencils, or slide rules. Without the assistance of the Young Men's Christian Association (YMCA) and the International Red Cross, he knew that he would not have been able to achieve even what he did.

It was also part of Sulzbach's job to gather together what was needed to enable the rest of the cultural programme to run smoothly. Hermann Ziock was astonished by the extent of this programme and described in his diary how:

> Featherstone Park has developed into such a study-camp that there is no other comparison. Theatre, newspapers, academic studies, radio, agricultural work, archaeological excavation at the Roman wall, and many other forms of mental or physical work illustrate the variety of activities. Where is there anywhere today that supports more than one stage? In Featherstone Park there are four.

He did not mention the four orchestras and the camp radio.

This enormous camp was located in the parkland adjacent to Featherstone Castle. From the earliest days of the war, the castle had housed a school for young boys, and the parkland had been requisitioned for a PoW camp – initially for Italian PoWs. After May 1945 the camp had been used solely for German officer prisoners. There was not a great deal of contact between the prisoners and the castle in the immediate post-war period, although one ex-pupil remembered that he had been taught music by one of the PoWs – and was told that this man had been the organist of Leipzig Cathedral.

There was one occasion when one of the PoW theatre groups used the dramatic castle courtyard as the setting for a powerful production of Hugo von Hofmannsthal's *Jedermann* (*Everyman*). Following the example of late medieval mystery plays, the drama traced the finite nature of man's life and the nothingness of earthly possessions. The performance at the castle was remembered vividly more than sixty years later by both an ex-pupil of the school and an ex-PoW of the camp.

As far as possible, the prisoners themselves invented ways of creating what was needed for their shows. Hours were spent ingeniously making – almost from nothing – costumes for theatre productions, puppets for the marionette theatre, and sometimes even instruments for the orchestras.

Herbert Sulzbach had one particular great strength in his work: he was able to understand the mindset of a German soldier in a way that no Englishman could. The prisoners' country had once been his country too, and he had fought heroically for it. He was still proud of the Germany that he had known, and of its past cultural life. He had been educated in the same system as many of the older PoWs and cherished many of the values that they had once held. There had been a time when both he and some of the prisoners had all been part of the same vibrant social life of either Frankfurt or Berlin.

Although he had since been forced to flee the country, this pre-Nazi Germany remained dear to Sulzbach, and he conveyed this passionately to the PoWs. His birthplace – Frankfurt – had been Goethe's too, and he was fond of quoting Goethe to the prisoners. Some of the poet's verses were pinned up in his office. He was especially inspired by the opening lines to *Das Göttliche* (*On the Divine*):

Edel sei der Mensch, Hilfreich und gut!

(Let man be noble, generous and good!)

Many of the prisoners shared this cultural link to the Enlightenment. Writing an article entitled *Despair or Responsibility?* in the camp newspaper in June 1946, PoW Ziock noted that:

TRUST, CONFIDENCE AND HUMANITY

It is up to us to avoid old mistakes and learn a lesson from our past. By the spirit of democracy, we mean that freedom and respect for individuality which the most intellectual of Germans saw as the highest value of mankind; poets and philosophers with a world-wide reputation like Goethe or Schiller, Herder or Kant.

One of Sulzbach's clerks was a young Marine officer, Herbert Schmitt, who had surrendered his U-boat in May 1945 and who remained a prisoner at Featherstone for two further years. Thirty years afterwards, he still remembered very clearly his first talks with Sulzbach in the summer of 1946:

> At that time, I had practically given up any hope of ever coming home. I eventually came round to believing (and feeling guilty and ashamed of) the horrid tales of Auschwitz and Bergen-Belsen. At that time, I also felt the world would never forgive the Germans and that our personal future was extremely bleak. I told Sulzbach about my feelings and found him to be a sympathetic listener. Eventually I found him comforting me and what he said was:
> "You shouldn't lose hope in the future. Germany didn't only produce concentration camps, it also produced great composers, philosophers, poets, artists who gave so much to the world." And then he reminded me of the inscription on the Frankfurt Opera House: *"Dem Wahren, Schönen, Guten"* ("To the true, the beautiful, and the good"). This, he said, should be my motto. I've tried ever since to live by it and whenever I pass the Opera House ruin (which happens quite frequently), I think of Herbert Sulzbach, the man who made me an Anglophile.

The Opera House in Frankfurt had been a familiar place for Sulzbach. His grandfather had lived in a magnificent house overlooking the square in front of it, and as a child Herbert Sulzbach had watched the celebrations for the Kaiser's birthday from his house. His vivid memories from forty years earlier were able to help to inspire more than this one struggling young Marine officer.

Herbert Sulzbach's own personal qualities were clearly a huge factor in the success of the re-education of the prisoners. His humanity was remarked upon by thousands of PoWs who remained in touch with him, and with each other, for many years after the end of their captivity. More than thirty years later, Engelbert Hoppe – an ex-PoW who had arrived at Featherstone Park in mid-1945 – recalled the atmosphere at the camp:

> I met Herbert Sulzbach in 1946. I was twenty years young, desperate and humiliated, as were many of my comrades, by what had caused the German nation's downfall. Herbert Sulzbach and Colonel Vickers had been sent by Colonel Faulk to Featherstone Park to take command. We prisoners of war regarded it as a routine substitution. But then something happened, almost like a miracle. Despair stiffened with defiance made way for winning our self-respect and finding a positive sense of the future. Herbert's impartial belief in humanity set an example. He convinced us that he would not and could not forget about Nazi Germany, but at the same time was willing to strive with us for a better Germany, a better relationship with Britain, and the peoples of the world. He made us understand what a German general had said after the war, "If we had won this war, we would have lost ourselves".

Sulzbach's influence was also recognised by those in authority. When all the prisoners eventually went home, in 1948, an inspector from the Red Cross wrote to Sulzbach:

> When Colonel Vickers took over Camp 18 it began to be a model camp in every respect, but there is no doubt that it was largely your close, personal contact with the PoWs which (though strictly within the regulations) brought this about. I think your methods are one of the best arguments I know for the humanitarian ideals embodied in the Geneva Convention!

TRUST, CONFIDENCE AND HUMANITY

Just before the camp closed, one of the prisoners wrote a letter to the *Manchester Guardian*, explaining simply that: 'Captain Sulzbach, by his conduct towards us, gave us a perfect example of a humanitarian.'

Certainly, those prisoners who worked closely with him were particularly affected. The German camp spokesman, General Heim, wrote to tell Sulzbach that: 'All my life it will be a pleasure and satisfaction that I should name you as my friend.'

General Lieutenant Ferdinand Heim was the third member of the influential leading team at Featherstone Park. Vickers and Sulzbach had been keen to find a spokesman for the PoWs whose outlook and vision reflected their own, so on 7 May 1946 Sulzbach travelled to the PoW camp at Bridgend in Wales to visit Heim. Quite quickly, the two men agreed to call each other by their names instead of their formal rank. Sulzbach liked this lean, serious man who was of a similar age to him, who had worn the uniform of the Imperial Army in the First World War, and who had later (in the second) contradicted Hitler's orders at the siege of Stalingrad. Heim became the much-respected leader and spokesman for all the prisoners at Featherstone.

When Sulzbach first arrived at Featherstone much of his job involved interviewing and screening the prisoners – who viewed the whole process with suspicion, contempt, and some fear. Twelve months previously, with the large influx of prisoners towards the end of the war, screeners had become overwhelmed by the amount of work and one ex-PoW remembered his fury and resentment when he was screened in May 1945. Apart from his turmoil of emotions at that time, he had been a boy of 8 when Hitler had come to power.

But the same man also remembered that screening changed when Sulzbach arrived. 'He very quickly found out if people wanted to flatter him, or something like that.'

Sometimes Herbert Sulzbach found himself interviewing men he had known years before. One day a Colonel Stock – who seemed vaguely familiar – sat in front of him. When questioned, the colonel gave his pre-war profession as a legal officer in Frankfurt and Sulzbach was astonished to find that he recognised a man from his childhood who was now a 'wanted war criminal'.

The screening process required subsequent interviews, and several months later Sulzbach was amazed to discover that he and Stock had both attended the same school. Stock could only remember his interviewer from one occasion during their school days. As Sulzbach recounted with amused delight in a letter to his wife:

> He had once been in a performance of *Der Nachtwächter* [*The Night Watchman*] by Körner, in which I had also played a part. I had only said one sentence. "You are really like boozy swine". Isn't that odd, that a PoW tells me this after about forty years?

Over and over again, Sulzbach's previous life in Germany caught up with him. In March 1947, PoW Major Schulz introduced himself. He had been transferred eight weeks previously from another camp and had immediately recognised Sulzbach's name. Not wishing to give the impression that he hoped for preferential treatment, he had hesitated in coming forward, but had eventually asked a clerk if the interpreter had once directed a fancy paper factory in Neubabelsberg. Sulzbach was delighted to meet the husband of his former secretary, Martha von Cardinal, and especially to see letters that described how she had – with much courage, and at great risk – helped Jews in Breslau, where she and Schulz had married.

On 1 June 1946 a new camp newspaper came out. It was called *Die Zeit am Tyne* [*The Times on the Tyne*]. *The voice of the German prisoner*. Both Colonel Vickers and Herbert Sulzbach encouraged and supported the appearance of the newspaper and wished it well. There was one particularly important aspect to this piece of journalism. The PoWs were amazed and impressed by Sulzbach's refusal to censor any article, which was an entirely new experience after the reign of the censor in Nazi Germany.

Most PoW camps had a newspaper, and the one at Featherstone Park was one of the most successful in the country. It was written and produced (in German) by the prisoners and printed on the presses of the local Northumberland paper, the *Hexham Courant*. Membership of the editorial team changed as prisoners were repatriated, and some of them became influential in the new German media when they returned home.

Hermann Ziock wrote the first editorial, entitled *What we want*. In it he explained that: 'We do not want propaganda and illusion. We want truth and outspokenness, not prejudice and hate, but objectivity and real teamwork.'

TRUST, CONFIDENCE AND HUMANITY

Die Zeit am Tyne carried not only political articles, but also general information about the camp and the wider world, sketches, illustrations, as well as reviews of theatrical and musical events. Production reached 2,500 copies, and these were sold to the officers in the camp, and also sent to other camps in Britain, as well as abroad. The paper was popular amongst the prisoners, and its contents were debated in their huts and canteens. Several prisoners took back to Germany an entire collection of the editions of the newspaper that were produced during their stay at Featherstone Park.

The final edition came out in May 1948 and in it Sulzbach wrote his *Farewell*:

> During the years of my stay here I have said "*Lebewohl*" ["Farewell"] to thousands of you. Go home, please, without bitterness and take something of the freedom of spirit you enjoyed here. Take home the "Featherstone Park Spirit", as you named it yourselves. Remember the tolerance you witnessed here and remain as stable-minded as you became here. Take home positive values such as consideration, reflection, enlightenment, a widening of your outlook on the world. Make use of this involuntary School of Life in Camp 18. Germany is geographically the heart of Europe. Let her become not only – with God's help – the heart of a united Europe, but also the true heart which radiates goodness, humility, truth and humanity.

As soon as the war in Europe had ended in May 1945 – and certainly by the time Sulzbach arrived at Featherstone Park at the beginning of 1946 – the main concern of the prisoners had been when they were going home – and why not as fast as possible? There were many British people who increasingly asked the same thing and in July 1946 Richard Stokes MP chaired a public meeting in London of churches, parliamentarians and welfare organisations to address these questions. They passed a resolution demanding PoW repatriation, permission for fraternisation with British people, a decent pay for prisoners, and a chance for them to send parcels home.

By August, the press was in full support. The Bishop of Chichester, George Bell, wrote a letter to *The Times* that autumn, recognising not only the severe personal strain on individual prisoners, but also the serious long-term negative effect that could be expected on relations between Germany and Britain.

Herbert Sulzbach, glad of this support, wrote to the bishop expressing his thanks and asking Bell to come to the camp to talk to the PoW officers. 'I feel that you would help to keep up morale until they can all go home,' he wrote. Alas, the bishop was too busy.

At Featherstone, although repatriation was still not a possibility in July 1946, there was a substantial transfer of PoWs to other camps (which made them feel as though they might be nearer going home), and also the one year anniversary of the day when Colonel Vickers had arrived at Camp 18.

A special operetta performance was produced for the men who would be leaving the next day, and afterwards the commandant spoke kindly and warmly to the departing prisoners. His final sentence was simply, '*Auf wiedersehen, au revoir*, so long!'

The British Army depot at Catterick had sent an escort for the prisoners who were transferring, and these soldiers joined in the festivities. Finally, the band played *Lili Marlene*. The British soldiers sung in English and the PoWs in German before the 'magnificent' event came to an emotional end.

Such occasions always brought home to Sulzbach how torn he felt between his allegiance to Britain and to the Germany he had once loved. That night he wrote in his diary:

> When the band played *In der Heimat, in der Heimat, da gibt ein Wiedersehen* [*In the homeland, in the homeland, we shall meet again*], a picture of my two lives rose up in front of me for the thousandth time. How often had I sung this song as a young soldier and German officer thirty years ago in the 1914/18 war!

As some of the prisoners departed on that fine day in July 1946, when the sun shone, the sky was blue, and the Northumberland landscape compellingly beautiful, the commandant and his wife, the British officers, and hundreds and hundreds of PoWs all stood around in cheerful mood. To Sulzbach, it reflected the atmosphere of the camp, 'the total humanity which the commandant has built up, and the rare interdependent trust that he has brought into being.' He had come to believe passionately that, 'if only in all camps such men on both sides could develop this understanding, and if that understanding could be taken to Germany and Europe, then we would have the guarantee that "it could never happen again"!'

Shortly afterwards, Colonel Vickers encouraged Sulzbach to invite his wife to visit from London. She stayed in a spare accommodation hut near to Herbert. It was an idyllic time for them both, and afterwards he missed her hugely – especially as he felt that she now had a greater understanding of his work, shared his love of Featherstone, and appreciated his care and concern for the German PoWs.

Sulzbach was extremely sorry when Colonel Vickers was posted to another PoW camp in September 1946. He had valued their working partnership immensely and wrote appreciatively to him:

> We are losing more than one can express in words. The Germans lose the commandant who gave them freedom, who gave them back confidence, hope, and the spirit needed for the new life that they will have to start in Germany. And we officers lose this permanent happiness, gaiety, this happy laughter of yours, which has made everyone else happy too.

Vickers was much missed, and when he paid an impromptu visit to Featherstone a few months later everybody again relished his sense of fun – and hearing his terrific stories. 'The mess rocked with his vitality,' Sulzbach remembered.

Towards the end of September 1946, all PoWs were eventually told the plans for general repatriation. They were also told their screening gradings, which had been kept secret from them until then, and they were given the right of appeal against those gradings. Their hopes were raised for an imminent return home, but they were to be bitterly disappointed. Three months later, morale had dropped again as repatriation remained very slow.

The PoWs were, of course, interested in events at the Nuremberg trials, which took place towards the end of 1946, but the attitude of some of the Marine captains at Featherstone disappointed Sulzbach. Having seen that re-education was gradually becoming successful, Sulzbach was sorry to discover that some of the Marine captains wanted to send a petition to the king for mercy for Doenitz and Raeder. Almost all the young Marines had been carried away by the captains and put their signature to the petition – and it wasn't easy for Sulzbach to find 'his pupils' apparently back-sliding.

Twelve months after Herbert Sulzbach's significant experience of Remembrance Day at Comrie, he was pleased to commemorate Remembrance Day 1946 at Featherstone Park, although it was a less dramatic celebration.

At 10.58 am he gave a sign to the trumpeter to start playing. Wherever a PoW was, or wherever he worked, he stood to attention and took his cap in his hand, until 11 am when the trumpeter ceased. For Sulzbach, 'it was simple and wonderful. We honoured the dead in every country.'

A few days earlier, he had been curious to discover that Otto John was at the camp seeing every colonel who was being released for repatriation. He described John as 'a young-looking man of about 35.' When the British officers talked with him and asked him when he had left Germany, he said '20 July 1944'. Sulzbach fetched his book *Officers against Hitler*, and John showed him the reference to 'Otto and Hans John'. Otto John had been in the anti-Hitler clique since 1936, and after the assassination attempt on Hitler on 20 July 1944, he had escaped by plane. His brother was tortured for six months and then hanged.

The strength and work of those who had stood against Hitler became increasingly important to Herbert Sulzbach. It encouraged and comforted him to learn more about those Germans in positions of authority who had rebelled against the Nazi regime.

The free, relaxed and confident atmosphere at Camp 18 had changed when Vickers left Featherstone Park. His successor, Colonel Hubert McBain, felt that he had inherited a situation that was too relaxed. Sulzbach welcomed the more refined, gentlemanly commandant, but differences between the attitudes and styles of the two men gradually became more apparent over the following months.

Colonel McBain made two very welcome changes at Featherstone Park within a few weeks of his arrival. He completed the removal of the boundary wire at the camp, and also encouraged many more of the officers to volunteer to help bring in the harvest on local farms. This farm work culminated in a magnificent Harvest Thanksgiving at nearby Hexham Abbey, when a thousand PoWs joined the service. The local papers were full of praise and gratitude.

'The "enemy" in our midst. But he has beaten his sword into a ploughshare,' wrote a journalist in the *Hexham Courant*. It was indeed a very moving occasion.

McBain was a committed Christian soldier. Soon after his arrival, PoW Siegfried Böhner, an architect, was asked by Colonel McBain to carry out his plan for a cultural/religious centre for the camp in the form of a chapel for all denominations. A Nissen hut in the British part of the camp was made available for conversion. The architect's design envisaged a reshaping of the hut along the lines of a small timber church in the Bavarian style.

Sulzbach was delighted with this enchanting church and enjoyed the celebrations of the consecration of the chapel in April 1947, when the Bishop of Newcastle and various local clergy were invited, with lunch and tea for the visitors. But – even as the chapel was being planned – in October 1946, German PoWs in Britain were, in general, having doubts about religion of any sort.

Prisoners at Featherstone Park wrote in their camp newspaper that:

> Innumerable decent Germans broke down when their Fatherland collapsed. They felt utterly empty. They want nothing to do with the Christian Church. In their opinion it has failed. It does not mean that these men reject the Christian ethic as such; but they doubt very much whether it can be realised.

The initial concern that Colonel McBain had with Sulzbach's work appeared to be Sulzbach's involvement in the screening process for PoWs. McBain was not alone in his concerns that a Jew of German origin was authorised to make decisions that affected the repatriation of a German prisoner. Amongst the British population, too, there was a widespread assumption that Jews could not be expected to react normally to Germans and that therefore their employment, particularly on the issue of re-education, was compromised. Questions were even asked in the House.

As a result, Sulzbach's screening procedure was double-checked. When his gradings were found to be perfectly in line with government guidance, Sulzbach was invited to widen his screening programme to outlying camps. Colonel McBain was very generous, both publicly and privately, to Sulzbach, who was extremely grateful for the acknowledgement and praise from his commandant. But he never quite felt the personal warmth and fellow feeling, nor the sharing of professional ideals, that he had felt with Vickers.

Restrictions on fraternisation between the British population and PoWs were officially relaxed at Christmas 1946, by which time public and parliamentary pressure had made the process both redundant and inevitable.

So, from the end of 1946 the prisoners at Featherstone Park began to take their concerts, plays and puppet shows all around the locality. On 1 May 1947 there was a concert of sacred music at Haltwhistle parish church, with musicians from the PoW camp. A few months earlier, the Methodist church in Haltwhistle had held a joint service of passion-tide music. The programme, for 'the Evangelical Congregation of Featherstone Park Camp and the congregation of Westgate Methodist church', was written in both German and English. Events such as these – and there were very many – helped to form those personal Anglo-German friendships that Herbert Sulzbach so earnestly wished to promote.

Once fraternisation was allowed, contacts with local people and visits to local places of government also gave PoWs the opportunity to widen their understanding of the democratic process. Groups of prisoners visited Newcastle Council to see how democracy worked in practice, to visit the assizes, and to see local government in action. In May 1947 Sulzbach organised a twelve-seater bus to take himself and eleven PoWs, including General Heim and Baumgarten (one of his clerks) to Newcastle. On arrival, they had two hours to explore the town, so Sulzbach, Heim and Baumgarten ambled through the busy streets, sat in a 'nice café', and relaxed in the sunshine on a bench in the town square.

At one o'clock, all twelve men met again at the YMCA and then went to the Town Hall, where they attended a council meeting. The town clerk explained the procedures. They would debate, 'which interested the PoW lawyers very much. Then we went back to the YMCA, where high tea was laid on, before returning to the camp for 7.30.' For Sulzbach – and possibly the PoWs – it was an intriguing and pleasant experience to wander around the streets of Newcastle 'with nobody taking any notice.'

These contacts with friendly and welcoming local people were healing experiences for many of the prisoners. One PoW, Kurt Schwedersky, much later remembered that:

> It must have been in springtime of 1947 that I was walking alone outside the camp. When I came to a small village,

I sat down on a wall facing the street, enjoying the warmth of the sun. I was about to eat a slice of dry bread I had taken with me, but at that moment I was addressed by an old man standing behind me in a garden. He said that I should wait a moment because his wife was just going to make a cup of coffee for me. A short time later he returned and passed me a cup of good hot coffee. This friendly gesture of humanity will stand in my memory until the last day of my life.

The first friends I used to meet regularly were some road workers. They were elderly men who had fought during the First World War in France. From them I got time and again a piece of cake, an egg or something else. When I thanked them, they used to say, "Don't mention it. In this country we say the poor help the poor."

Some of the prisoners at Featherstone, especially the younger ones, worked towards academic qualifications whilst at the camp. Many of them had missed out on the last years of their education as they were called up into the army. Arrangements between German and British universities enabled German PoWs to study and gain qualifications whilst in Britain. For Engelbert Hoppe, this meant that once he was repatriated, he had already completed the first year's study towards his teaching qualifications.

People like Herbert Sulzbach hoped that the re-education programme at Featherstone Park would not only inform and convince the prisoners of the positive aspects of a democratic political framework, but also equip them to play a major part in the rebuilding of their country. It was, he had noted within his first week at Featherstone, 'a hard, very hard, job – but it can be done.'

Many years later Colonel Faulk explained that although his job meant that he was responsible for the re-education of the PoW, it was impossible actively to do so in a didactic manner. He saw re-education as giving people the opportunity and tools to come to their own point of view, on their own. Faulk knew that for this to be successful, he needed to employ people whom the prisoners would trust.

When the PoWs at Featherstone learnt of Sulzbach's Jewish background, they were deeply impressed. Engelbert Hoppe, even as an elderly man, became very emotional as he remembered how 'Herbert often made excuses on behalf of the Germans, which moves me so much, you know.'

The success of Sulzbach's approach came to be called 'The Featherstone Park Spirit' and Camp 18 became known as the 'camp of confidence'. A visiting journalist from a national English newspaper reported in May 1947 that:

> The atmosphere of the camp was exceptionally happy. Relations between British and Germans were more than cordial; this in itself is not unusual. What was unusual were the remarkably liberal and anti-Nazi sentiments of every prisoner with whom one spoke. Everyone seemed to be looking forward to the future, and not backwards to past injustices and failures. This renunciation of Nazi ideals by two thousand officers appears to be sincere, and one forms the opinion that if they are deceiving the British most of them are also deceiving themselves.

In August 1947, a new commandant took charge at Featherstone Park. Like Vickers and McBain, Colonel Bartlett brought his own personality to his work. As Sulzbach wrote to Beate:

> On Saturday evening he was here with his family; everyone went to the concert, and then there was poker for us seven, Colonel Bartlett included.

Throughout 1947 Sulzbach began to wonder (and worry) about his own future, once his service with the British Army was over. He really had no idea what to do next – or where. He considered trying to pick up the threads of his pre-war business life, but it would be no easy matter to reconnect with his previous customers from pre-war Copenhagen, Amsterdam and Paris. He had not kept himself informed about the industry for some years, and suspected that demand for a luxury market such as fancy paper was very limited.

Repatriated PoWs kept him informed about conditions in Germany, and in November 1947 he heard that the Berlin flat that he and Beate had shared at Prinzregentenstrasse 80 was nothing but a heap of rubble.

TRUST, CONFIDENCE AND HUMANITY

Sulzbach became increasingly torn between what he knew that his wife wanted in this post-war world, and what he hoped might be possible for himself. He recognised that he wanted an occupation that would be more closely linked to his current work, and he began to realise that he would like to continue to work towards reconciliation – by working within Germany.

He hoped to persuade his wife that a job in post-war Germany (for maybe no longer than a year or two) would allow him to develop his work – but he wanted her to accompany him. 'It gives me such an ache in my heart to be separated from you for only a few days.'

He knew with absolute certainty that his wife would find being in Germany extremely difficult, if not impossible. When the war had ended, Herbert and Beate Sulzbach, like most Jewish refugees from Germany, had gradually been able to piece together news about their family and friends. Several members of both of their families, and many of their friends, had been murdered, or had died as a result of persecution, by Hitler's regime.

There was a great deal of sadness for both of them, but Sulzbach had had the opportunity at Featherstone not only to come to terms with his own feelings, but also to empathise with the feelings of other Germans. He had not only helped German prisoners to regain their trust and confidence in themselves and their country, but the prisoners had helped him to regain his trust in the Germany that he had once loved so much.

He was frequently asked about his feelings of hate and revenge. 'Thank God, I never had those feelings. Hatred leads to self-destruction.' 'Hate and revenge are revolting and are unworthy of peaceful men', were some of his comments.

In March 1948, Herbert Sulzbach learnt officially that the camp at Featherstone Park would close on 15 May, with a working party remaining until the end of June to clear up. There was already an atmosphere of departure, and Sulzbach felt very keenly that an important section of his life was once again coming to an end.

When it came, it was an impressive departure for the last PoW. Herbert Sulzbach broadcast his short farewell speech on the camp radio at 10.30 pm. Then Heim's successor, Colonel Merkel, spoke before the *Leonore* symphony from Beethoven was played on the gramophone. For Sulzbach, it was a dignified farewell celebration.

A JEW WHO DEFEATED NAZISM

When Hermann Ziock had left Featherstone Park over a year earlier, he had realised that he would never be able to leave the PoW camp completely behind. In his farewell speech, he had told other PoWs that:

> One of the things that we must all take with us is the searching and hopeful spirit that always inspires us, when with seriousness and deliberation we reconsider what we should say about the events of these times.

Many other PoWs recognised that their time at Featherstone had been of value. As one wrote to Sulzbach, 'It has been not a bad, but rather a more beautiful, dream. The involuntary seclusion developed so many insights.'

Herbert Sulzbach might have said the same for himself. As Engelbert Hoppe said thirty years after his repatriation:

> At the end of our PoW days in Britain, we left with what we called the Featherstone Park Spirit. Born out of this spirit is the most noble and touching confession of Herbert Sulzbach finding his way back to Germany through his prisoners of war.

When the gates closed on Featherstone Park in May 1948, Herbert Sulzbach's service with the British Army still had six months to run. Events in Europe dictated his next posting. When he left Camp 18, he did in fact return for a few months to Germany, to his beloved Berlin. He returned now to a city under siege, but at Comrie and Featherstone Park he had forged strong and unbreakable ties with those soldiers who had once represented the ideology that had originally driven him away.

The Featherstone Park Spirit did not die. Many years later, Yehudi Menuhin spoke of how:

> Featherstone Park camp healed and encouraged the human heart and spirit. Instead of wounding and destroying life, instead of awakening hate and intolerance, it furthered and generated the only basic principle of mankind's survival – that is, mutual respect and mutual trust.

Returning to Germany would test the strength of this spirit even in Herbert Sulzbach.

Chapter 7

Berlin. City of Ghosts

Beate and Herbert Sulzbach celebrated their twenty-fifth wedding anniversary on 19 June 1948. They had been married in Berlin in 1923 – in a year of continuing social upheaval during the revolutionary days of the Weimar Republic. Less than a week after their anniversary in 1948, Berlin was under siege again – this time as a result of increasing post-war political tension between the Allied occupiers of the city.

The Soviet members of the military occupation wanted complete control of all Berlin – as well as of the surrounding countryside that was in their zone – and moved towards excluding the other Allied armies from their sectors of the city. Just before midnight on the night of 23 June 1948, without warning, they turned off the electricity supply to the Western Sectors of the city. A few hours later they closed the only rail network into the city and shut down the only motorway by which the Western Powers transported personnel, goods, and equipment to their garrisons. The Soviets also stopped all barge and waterborne traffic.

It had been clear for some time that there were serious differences between the four Allies' post-war approach to Germany, with special tensions over the control of the capital. One result of this was that throughout May 1948, Herbert Sulzbach had received a series of memoranda (that were each as quickly cancelled as they were re-issued) from the British War Office concerning his next assignment, as the Soviets adopted increasingly threatening behaviour towards their former allies. It seemed that no compromise could be reached between the Allies over Soviet war reparations, German unification, or ideology – and the Soviets wanted the Western Powers to leave Berlin.

Many observers agreed with the diplomat Harold Nicolson who wrote from Germany that, 'the prizes are so enormous, the losses so terrible. The Barbarians are at the gate.'

Sulzbach's posting was at last confirmed, and on the evening of 28 June 1948 he reported at Liverpool Street Station in London. Amongst his papers he had a rail warrant to Harwich and authorisation to proceed to Berlin for employment with the Royal Pioneer Corps in the British Army of the Rhine's (BAOR) part in the Berlin airlift.

He did not enjoy the ferry journey from Harwich 'on a troop ship with every discomfort' but – with his experiences at Featherstone Park fresh in his memory – he was intrigued by a remark made to him about luggage handling. When he asked an officer how he would get his bag off the ship, he was asked whether he had given it to a German PoW. When he said that he had, the officer replied, 'Then you need not worry – they are reliable.' He arrived at the Hook of Holland the following day, exchanged his money, and waited to board the next BAOR train. He remembered his first image of Germany as that of a railway carriage, 'an old German express train carriage, gone to rack and ruin, its livery faded, and in complete disrepair.'

Chatting to a fellow officer on the train, Sulzbach mentioned that he knew people in Amsterdam. He was advised that if he wanted to see them, he should leave the train quietly at Utrecht, take the Dutch train to Amsterdam, and repeat the journey in reverse the following day. Although he knew that it was against orders to leave a BAOR train, Sulzbach nevertheless decided to take the risk and later that afternoon was amongst his old friends, the Bergenthals, in Amsterdam. In the evening, they invited a friend to supper at their beautiful flat and they all talked together about Sulzbach's recent work amongst the German PoWs.

He was overjoyed to be back in Amsterdam, which he had first visited in 1904 as a 10-year-old boy. In a letter to his wife he enthused about it:

> I love it. The canals are the same as ever, and so are the wonderful streets. The shops are full of beautiful things. Everything is rationed, even cigarettes, but it is the same for everyone. Amsterdam breathes like the continent: the cafés are full; the tables and chairs are out on the streets just like in Berlin or Paris. Everything is so different from England – everything.

The next day's return to a train at Utrecht passed off without incident and although Sulzbach marvelled at the countryside, the dilapidated German

Above: 1905. The Sulzbach villa at Friedrichstrasse 57, Frankfurt am Main.

Below: 1908 autumn. The Sulzbach family (Herbert in the front) motoring in the Spessart mountains.

1908. Herbert's father, Emil Sulzbach, in front of their house at Friedrichstrasse 57, Frankfurt am Main.

1911 14 September. Lili and Ernst Sulzbach on the balcony at home.

Above: 1911 April. (l to r) Hans, Hedwig, Hertha, Karl and Herbert Sulzbach on a cycle ride.

Right: 1911. Herbert's mother, Julie Sulzbach, on the balcony at Friedrichstrasse 57.

Left: 1914–1915 Herbert Sulzbach.

Below: 1914–1918. Herbert Sulzbach third from left.

Above: 1916. Evricourt field kitchen.

Right: 1919 19 April. Herbert Sulzbach and Margot on their engagement.

1923 May. Herbert Sulzbach's staff outside the factory at Neubabelsberg.

1928 24 March. Herbert Sulzbach and Beate in front of their hotel at Cannes.

Right: 1936. Neubabelsberg factory (photo taken 2010).

Below: 1938 18 May. Leaving Germany. A last view of Prinzregentenstrasse.

Above left: 1938 20 May. Beate and her sister, Ruth, on board the 'New York' to Southampton.

Above right: 1943 November. Herbert Sulzbach working as a private in the Pioneer Corps at Tidworth.

Left: 1939 16 August. Herbert Sulzbach.

1944 24 July. Herbert Sulzbach in the garden of 'The Plain House' in Chipstead after the bombing.

1945 July. Herbert Sulzbach and Beate in the garden of 'Earnside' in Comrie.

Sonntag 18.11., 19³⁰

MUSIK-VORTRAG

aus Oper und Operette

MITWIRKENDE: STRELAND-QUARTETT / K. WENNINGER BARITON / ANSAGER: F. BEYER

I. TEIL:

Grosse Fantasie aus der Oper „Margarete" (Faust)	Gounod
Violinsolo aus „La Traviata"	Verdi
Arie d. „Falstaff" aus „Die Lustigen Weiber von Windsor"	Nicolai

~ PAUSE ~

II. TEIL:

Walzer aus „Walzertraum"	Osk. Strauss
Potpourri „Ein Abend bei Paul Lincke"	Lincke
„Ich bin verliebt" aus „Clivia"	Dostal
„Deine Lippen sie küssen so heiss" aus „Guiditta"	Lehar
„Isolabella"	Lincke
Grosses Potpourri aus „Maske in Blau"	Raymond

1945 November. Concert programme at Cultybraggan PoW camp, near Comrie.

Above: 1945. Cultybraggan PoW camp near Comrie amongst the Scottish mountains (photo taken 2010).

Below: 1946. Drawings of Featherstone Park camp by a PoW.

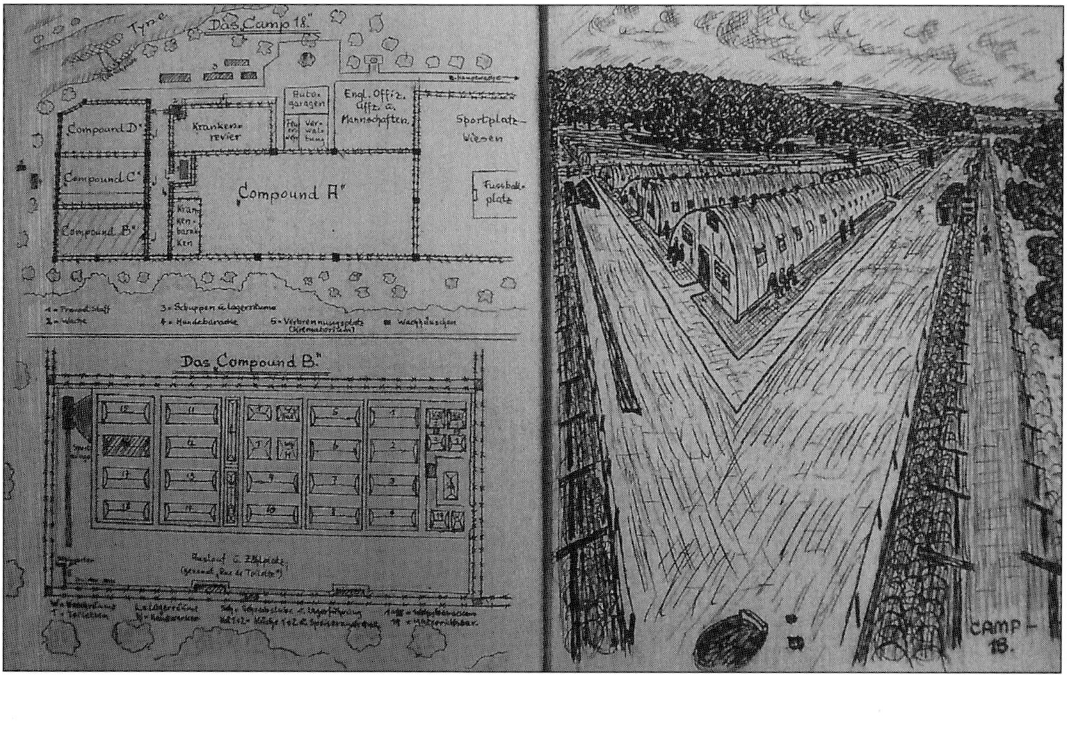

Above: 1946. Herbert Sulzbach (4th from left, rear) and other British staff with their families at Featherstone Park.

Below: 1946. Herbert Sulzbach in his hut at Featherstone PoW camp.

1946. Herbert Sulzbach.

1949 31 January. Herbert Sulzbach at Emil Sulzbach Strasse in Frankfurt.

Left: 1971 8 February. Herbert Sulzbach receives the Grand Cross of Merit from Ambassador Karl Guenther von Hase.

Below: 1973 2 July. Herbert Sulzbach (3rd from left) at his book launch at the German Embassy with Ambassador von Hase and military attache.

Above: 1978 December. Herbert Sulzbach in his office at the German Embassy.

Below: 1982 The plaque on the gatepost to the site of the Featherstone Park PoW camp.

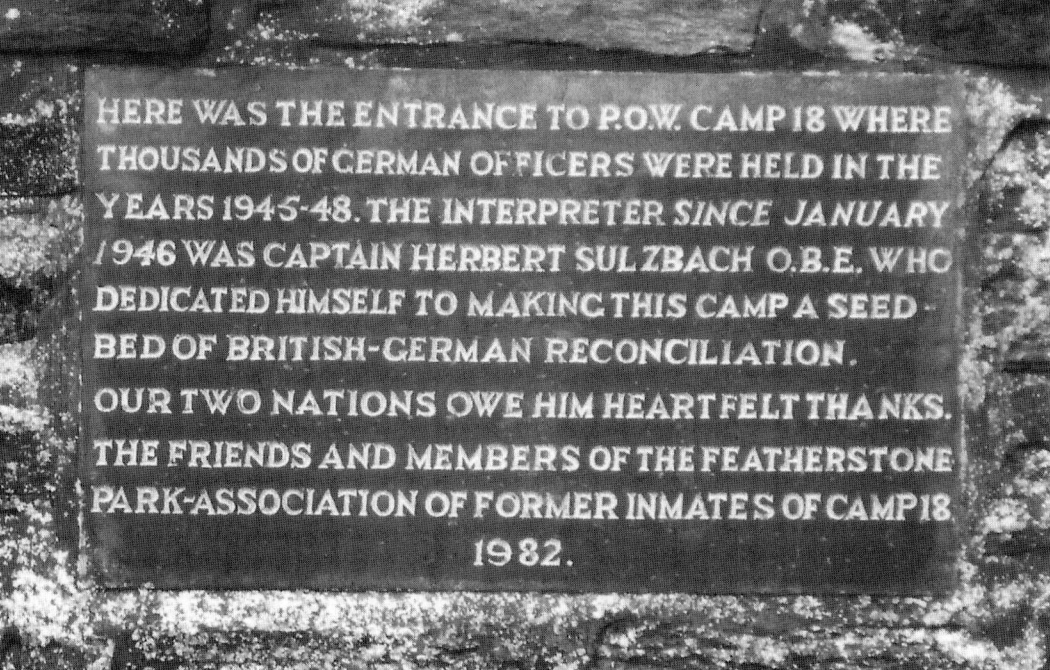

Above: 1982. Henry Faulk, Kurt Schwedersky, and Herbert Sulzbach at the Wallace Arms after the opening of the plaque at Featherstone Park.

Left: 1984 26 August. Herbert Sulzbach and Chum James Clegg at the last parade of the Old Contemptibles in Ipswich.

fortifications that he saw on his journey through Holland reminded him of sights that he had seen after the First World War in Flanders.

When his train passed through Bentheim, which had once been a German customs frontier post, he was momentarily seized with fear. The last time he had been there had been in May 1938, when he and his wife had fled Germany. He had strong memories of being abused then by 'a disgusting official from Customs Investigation'.

Also at Bentheim, he saw a sign in English: 'Do not throw food to the begging German children! They risk their lives if they are attracted on to the railway lines', and he was disgusted that Hitler had brought the German people to this situation.

At Osnabrück he remembered the many times that he had read of RAF raids on the town, and saw for himself the result – 'debris and piles of rubble, an almost dead town' – and yet as he travelled through Germany he recognised a sense of home-coming. He was, in many ways, glad to be back.

> It is strange. When you look out of the window, and when the air snaps, it smells continental: sad, sweet and beautiful. The huge lime trees are in bloom. Only in Germany can they smell so wonderful. The blackbirds and finches sing in the evenings with continental warmth and melancholy, as they don't in England!

Sulzbach arrived at BAOR headquarters in the ancient spa town of Bad Oeynhausen in the evening of 30 June 1948. He had known it thirty years previously and now found the inner town to be a complete garrison. Every hotel and every villa had been used to accommodate British staff and administration, and the spa park – although still beautiful – had become overgrown.

He was booked into a pleasant room in a former hotel that had been turned into a visitors' mess. The food was good, and the beer and French cognac were extremely cheap. The waiters and other service staff were mostly local Germans who tended to live in the outer areas of the city.

All around him were the elegant and luxurious hotels, where he had once stayed as a young man. He found the famous 21 Club to be 'quite feudal'. The ground floor rooms had been set up as a luxury steamship, and there were side rooms with 'bars, reading/writing/bath rooms, gaming rooms, shops selling wonderful things, a dance hall' – and all at the service of British officers and their wives. The hotels in Westerland, where he had stayed after his wedding twenty-five years earlier, were now being used as leave centres for British forces personnel.

'If only Hitler could see this!' Sulzbach commented.

The Allies' administration was struggling to keep up with the rapidly changing demands of the airlift emergency and Sulzbach found that although his arrival had been expected, he had not been allocated to any particular work. So he found himself sitting around indoors without a job – just waiting – with no congenial companions as he didn't know anyone there. And during the following three days there was continual torrential rain.

He cheered himself up by visiting an ex-PoW from Featherstone Park, Major Heimann, who lived not far away. He was pleased to find Heimann doing well and working in his father-in-law's factory. The two hours that they spent talking together were the 'best part of the few hideous' days that Sulzbach spent in Bad Oeynhausen.

Then, on 3 July 1948, there was an appeal for more officers at the aerodrome at Wunstorf, a huge former German airfield near Hanover. Sulzbach was sent there immediately, and was given accommodation in the 'pretty, clean, undamaged town' of nearby Neustadt.

Wunstorf had become the main RAF airfield for the airlift. In those early days the RAF poured all their available aircraft into the emergency, but this rapid build-up meant that several Dakota squadrons arrived with their necessary servicing personnel and crews before there was adequate accommodation. Also, the three days of heavy rain that had so depressed Sulzbach at Bad Oeynhausen had caused havoc to an airfield that as yet had no hardstanding for aircraft.

Sulzbach was fortunate to have his good accommodation. Many pilots remembered arriving to find all available beds taken and having to sleep in armchairs – or on the billiard table. These RAF pilots were also professional transport pilots and many of them had served in Bomber Command during the war. Sulzbach was very impressed by them, and by the atmosphere at the airfield. The RAF mess had at one time been the German Luftwaffe mess and resembled a large hotel. Sulzbach reckoned that there were probably about 200 RAF officers there, 'all old fighter pilots and navigators – many with the Distinguished Flying Cross or Distinguished Flying Medal.' The atmosphere was reminiscent, he thought, of 1940 – hazardous and stressful, but with airmen showing much courage, laughter, and a certain gaiety.

A few days after his arrival, he described the operation in a letter to his wife:

> An aircraft takes off fully loaded towards Berlin every six minutes. The enormous airport is seething and there is an atmosphere of emergency. Everybody has been working day and night since last Monday when it began: 2.5 million Berliners in our zone of Berlin must be fed by air. There are now colonels, captains, majors, and hundreds of our boys loading, unloading, and loading and unloading.
>
> It amounts to a war campaign in peacetime: that really is the atmosphere here. Everyone works without a break, backwards and forwards, asking nothing. A tent city has sprung up round the whole place where the soldiers sleep when they are replaced. There are canteens in the huge tents, also kitchens. Cars rush around with commands and everyone is slightly bullish.

Aircraft were expected to fly around the clock, so aircrew and ground crews worked in rotas throughout the twenty-four hours. Within a short time, civilian airlines were also chartered to assist the RAF, and these were generally manned by former Bomber Command crew.

Flying conditions during the airlift were new for all the pilots. They were required to fly in very narrow corridors over distances of a hundred miles or more, following along behind one another while maintaining a safe distance and the same speeds. From Wunstorf, the RAF flew into Gatow airfield in Berlin. Gatow lay on the south-west edge of the city and was surrounded on three sides by fields – all of which were in the Soviet zone.

These 20-mile-wide air corridors (there were three of them) providing access to the city had been agreed in a post-war agreement between the Allies on 30 November 1945. When the Soviets blockaded Berlin, 1,534 tons of food were needed daily to keep the people alive.

Political tensions amongst the Allies impacted on the people of war-damaged Berlin in several ways. One very noticeable difficulty was the variation in currency. Once the western Allies had lost any expectation of being able to work with the Soviets, they had moved independently towards a plan of economic reconstruction for Europe. This included a sound banking system, a currency to replace the barter economy, and the eventual establishment of an independent and sovereign German government.

In March 1948 a central bank had been established in the western zones and on 20 June 1948 the United States and Britain introduced currency reform in their zones and sectors. As well as a Deutsche Mark for the western zones, the Allies also introduced a Berlin Mark that was only valid in Berlin. The Soviets then quickly introduced a Berlin Mark of their own – so Berliners then had two currencies.

Visiting Berlin from Dresden on 1 July 1948, during the time that Sulzbach was at Bad Oeynhausen, the writer and academic Victor Klemperer noted in his diary that:

> The vexation of the triple currencies: West Mark, new East Mark, old East Mark, everywhere a different reckoning-up and a different attitude on the part of the shopkeepers – one doesn't accept this money, the other not that, goods are being held back, prices fluctuate.

So, from 24 June 1948 there were two currencies in circulation in Berlin – and the black market flourished. On the day that Sulzbach arrived at Wunstorf, the Soviet military governor in Berlin had told his British counterpart that the blockade would continue until the West abandoned its efforts to set up a German government.

The hectic activity of the early days of the airlift was exhausting. Right from the start, Sulzbach found the work physically tiring, with strenuous duties from seven in the morning until nine at night, or twelve-hour night shifts. During his time off work, he was fortunate to be able to get away from the airfield to his accommodation in a peaceful house in Neustadt that belonged to one of the colonels from Control Commission. He and a Major Dempsey had each been allocated a room there, and Sulzbach's pretty and light room was 'on the first floor, looking over the garden, with birch trees and weeping willow, and with a view over a small sports field to the edge of Neustadt – a typical small German town.' It was a quiet and rural retreat. A Frau Walter also lived in the house and cooked their breakfast, as well as other meals when they were not eating in the RAF mess.

BERLIN. CITY OF GHOSTS

As the political situation in Berlin grew increasingly tense Sulzbach became more and more apprehensive, knowing that the western Allies were impossibly outnumbered by Soviet troops. Along with his colleagues, he felt that he was 'sitting in a mouse trap' and was very worried about the worsening international situation – being aware that 'it could kick off any day'. He sought advice from his elder brother, Ernst, for the best steps that he should take to protect his family in case of further war. Meanwhile, there was little that he could do except get on with his job.

His department was made up of German labour. About 600 Germans took part, working day and night shifts. Freight trains (coming mostly from Bremen) drove into a siding at the airfield, and the German workers unloaded the goods there. Sulzbach and his superior, Major Dempsey, were responsible for the supervision and organisation of this, and the whole enterprise was under the control of the Royal Army Service Corps.

Once a train had been unloaded, the next was already moving in. Trains carried, for example, powdered milk, canned foods, butter, potatoes, flour, and coal. Some of the goods went directly into the aircraft and some went into two huge hangars – which had once been German aeroplane hangars. Loading of the Dakotas and Yorks was done by British troops, while the Germans unloaded the goods trains and filled the hangars. A loaded aircraft took off every six minutes and would be unloaded in Gatow one hour later. The planes flew in an unbroken stream, day and night.

Even before the war, Germany had imported much of its food. Until the last few months of the war, Germans at home had been fed by food taken from those countries that they had subjected. Now hunger was growing in Berlin, where the official daily ration was still only three-quarters of the daily minimum recommended by the Red Cross. It was not only food that was required: in a growing but still frail economy, Berlin's industry remained dependent upon raw materials and components being imported into the city.

After working feverishly for three weeks at Wunstorf airfield, Herbert Sulzbach decided that he had to go and see Berlin for himself. On Sunday afternoon, 25 July 1948, he took off.

He went in a four-engine York that was loaded with ten generators, and he marvelled that it ever became airborne with this load on board. The four-man crew consisted of experienced fighter pilots who since the end of the war had been operating on the civilian England-Singapore-Nairobi route. On the outward journey, Sulzbach sat in the front next to the pilot and listened to the constant radio contact between Wunstorf and Gatow. Before long, they were flying over 'enemy territory'. On the whole route of 200 kilometres he saw 'only two cars, a lot of cattle, and one cyclist. Where the people lived, seemed to us to be a mystery.' The flight captain told him that it was always as quiet as this; he found it eerie.

Sulzbach was very familiar with the area on the ground that he saw below him. He had lived there throughout the 1920s and early 1930s, during which time he had directed his small factory on the outskirts of Berlin not far from Potsdam. He looked out of the window with keen interest and recorded in his diary how:

> Potsdam came in sight, and the Havelsee, and I confess that my heart pounded. We left Neubabelsberg to the right, and I thought of the years 1920 to 1936, and of my little factory out in the country. At that moment we went downwards, the second pilot let out the undercarriage, and the landing at Gatow began. We rolled down the airfield and I was in Berlin.

Sulzbach thanked the pilots and walked towards some nearby cars, hoping to hitch a lift into Berlin. As he talked to a driver, he was approached by a German, who greeted him with, 'Captain Sulzbach, may I, in the name of Camp 18, welcome you to Berlin?'

He was completely speechless. The first German he saw in Berlin was a Lieutenant Schenk, who had been discharged from Featherstone Park in May and now worked as a clerk at Gatow aerodrome. Although Sulzbach didn't at first recognise him, he was really touched, taken aback and pleased.

He managed to hitch his lift, and a short while later got out of the car at the home of Irene von Reitzenstein, a young woman who had visited England (and Featherstone Park camp) the previous year as part of an Anglo-German education project. She accompanied him to his British officers' hotel, the Savoy in the Fasanenstrasse, and then acted as his guide through Berlin.

Irene von Reitzenstein had been educated in Switzerland but had returned to Berlin in 1944 so that her mother would not be alone during the bombing raids. She had been injured in one of the raids and had subsequently had her leg amputated. In the immediate post-war period, she had been active in working towards a new democracy in Germany. Sulzbach admired her not just for herself, her intelligence, and her beauty but also the way that she represented what he saw as the best in German young people.

She had recently written to him, saying, 'We love your aircraft, which come to us in an endless chain from the free world, and we pray to God that you will stand firm.' Sulzbach viewed Irene as a shining example of a young European with a sense of justice and great clarity of thought. The two of them began their journey through the city in the early evening of 25 July 1948 and Sulzbach could not believe what he saw.

First, in the twilight he saw the remains of the Kaiser Wilhelm Memorial Church, and the first empty burnt-out houses on the Kurfürstendamm. When they much later stopped for a meal, they lost track of time as they talked – only realising too late that it was past midnight and so impossible to summon a military taxi. They had no choice but to carry on walking, which was tiring for Sulzbach's companion. They began a trek through the ghost city, which Sulzbach vowed he would never forget as long as he lived.

There was nobody on the street. From time to time a private car of an American or British officer flitted past, but they were all full so there was no possibility of a lift. At last a car stopped for them, took Irene back to her home, and Sulzbach eventually arrived back at his hotel – at four o'clock in the morning, and with very sore feet.

Early the next morning he called at the house of his nephew – his sister Lili's son. They had a great deal to talk about together, and then his hosts took Sulzbach on a tour of the western part of the city. As he returned to Wunstorf later that day, Sulzbach sat alone at the back of the aeroplane. Looking out of the window, he tried to put his thoughts in order. He hoped that the ruins of Berlin were not, as Irene von Reitzenstein thought, a symbol of the end of Europe, but rather a reminder to the world of the outcome of war. More than anything else, he yearned for people to work to understand themselves and to believe in good – 'to do good, and to be good.'

Herbert Sulzbach was stunned, horrified and completely overwhelmed by what he had seen in Berlin. It surpassed even what he had felt when he had first seen Hanover a few days after his arrival in Germany. Then, he had been unable to understand where people lived in 'this heap of rubble' – never mind comprehend their attitude towards their victors.

When he had first hitched his lift from Gatow airfield, the driver had taken him through neighbourhoods that were familiar to him from his years spent living in Berlin. They had gone past the Havel, from where his brother had frequently launched his canoe, and had driven along the roads that he had once known well. The last time that Sulzbach had seen Berlin had been in 1938, when it had been a flourishing city. Now he was faced with a level of destruction that he had never thought possible, despite all that he had read and seen throughout the years of the war. In Pichelsberg, the large iron bridge hung on its side, and the beautiful villas in the Heerstrasse were almost all burnt-out, with their gardens gone wild. He no longer recognised streets that had once been so familiar to him because the houses no longer existed.

He realised that since he was seeing Berlin after the city had been blockaded for four weeks, it was perhaps 'characterised by an even greater bleakness, emptiness and ghost-like quiet than otherwise.' But he remained horrified by what he saw. Even though he had been familiar with press reports from May 1945 onwards, with thousands of photographs in newspapers and magazines, he was shattered by the reality of bombed-out Berlin. In his diary and letters, he tried to describe everything with appropriate expressions, but he simply couldn't find them. 'There would not be sufficient superlatives in the world to describe the horrors.'

At one point on his tour of the city, he had left Irene von Reitzenstein resting on a pile of stones and gone on alone to Prinzregentenstrasse, where he had lived with his wife between 1923 and 1938. He stood in front of number 80, which was 'not so much a ruin as a totally collapsed house.' He stood there for a few minutes and 'didn't really know what I was thinking.' He felt that, surely, at some time the moment would come when the rubble would stop. 'But no, it is never-ending!'

It was not unusual for visitors to Berlin in the immediate post-war years to be stunned by the scale of destruction, and to liken the ruins to those of Pompeii and Herculaneum. Herbert Sulzbach had been similarly affected as he looked about him during his walk around the city. At seven o'clock in the evening, a pale light had shone on what had once been Berlin. As he stood on Wittenbergplatz, as far as the eye could see up to the Nollendorfplatz was a string of ruins. Houses were not so much burnt-out but rather between where he stood and the Nollendorfplatz stood only isolated walls. The whole district seemed like Messina after the earthquake of 1908, which he had seen in ruins in 1913. He was left speechless. 'It took my breath away.'

During their walk, Sulzbach and Irene had eaten at 'Venetia', a small restaurant in Joachimsthaler Strasse, where only two or three tables were occupied, and a pianist and a violinist played to the few guests. It could have been a romantic setting – but Sulzbach found it 'spooky'. The mood was candle-lit – but only because there was no electricity except during certain hours. Time and again he had the impression that he had wandered into 'a totally dead city.'

Berlin had not been self-sufficient in energy for many years. Before the blockade, electricity – and the coal to power the electric power plants – had come from the surrounding areas to the east of Berlin. When the Soviets cut off electricity supplies from the power plants that they controlled, and also cut off the delivery of coal to the few small and obsolete power stations located within the western sectors of Berlin, there were serious consequences.

The city's water pumps and sewage systems relied on electricity, as did the public transport system of trams and underground trains. Without electricity, Berlin's industry would collapse. The generators carried by the aeroplane that Sulzbach had taken to Berlin were part of an urgent attempt by the airlift to supply electricity to the city.

The Allies planned to rebuild a major power plant, but until this could be done not only did existing plant have to be fed by airlifted coal, but the supply of electricity to users needed to be severely restricted. It was a dire situation, with households reduced to just a few hours of electricity each day – and on a rota system so those hours would sometimes be at night. The trams and underground trains only ran between 6 am and 6 pm and there was no electricity for radio broadcasts. Berliners who experienced the blockade had strong memories of the darkness.

At three o'clock in the morning of 26 July, as Sulzbach and Irene sat and rested on their trek through the city, they watched the moon rise and shine with a ghostly light into the rubble of the Kaiserallee. Suddenly, just like a ghost, an elderly woman scurried past carrying a basket in each hand. They saw neither from where she came, nor where she went. Then they trudged on, and each and every house for miles on end was a ruin and a heap of rubble. From time to time they saw a light come on in a ruined building, and they realised that there lived a family that was cooking the next day's dinner, 'because Wilmersdorf only had power between two and four o'clock at night.'

Sulzbach was intrigued by these 'ghosts of the city', but in his diary noted how:

> There is not, thank God, any ghost! It is astonishing, remarkable and wonderful how the Berliners are alive; they have their old native wit, they work, they have faith. They are strong, despite all the present hardship, despite the siege, despite the nights of bombing raids that came in almost unbroken succession from 1943 until May 1945.

Not everyone was as optimistic about the future of Berlin as Sulzbach. There were serious doubts amongst the Allies, partly because the airlift seemed technically impossible, and partly because they assumed that when their efforts inevitably failed the Berliners would choose communism – with subsequent civil unrest and riots against the Allies for staying in the city, rather than against the Soviets for imposing the blockade in the first place.

However, although the Berliners shared the Allies' doubts about the technical feasibility of the airlift, their main fear and expectation was that the Allies would stop trying. It seemed unlikely that they would be willing to go to such trouble and expense for their former enemies and risk a war with the Soviets. Sulzbach's personal view was that the city had an immense strength. He was inspired by Eden's proclamation that 'We can't let these people down' – but not everyone shared this view.

On one occasion, as Sulzbach made his way around the ghost-like ruins of Berlin during the daylight, there was some sudden activity. A loudspeaker van came through the city, stopping on every corner so that the announcer could report that in two minutes the latest news would be transmitted. Without electricity, there could be no radio, so this was how the population of besieged Berlin could keep up to date. During the blockade, news was vital to the Berliners. The most popular station was Radio in the American Sector (RIAS), which broadcast twenty-four hours a day. The station sent out trucks with loudspeakers – such as the one that Sulzbach had witnessed – to cruise the city's streets and announce the news.

There was also an acute shortage of petrol. None was available for private vehicles, and even petrol for official vehicles was strictly rationed as buses and ambulances had priority. Consequently, there was hardly

BERLIN. CITY OF GHOSTS

any road traffic; only one or two electric trams, no taxis for civilians, and hardly any pedestrians. Sulzbach watched as every half hour a tram went past (in which the conductor still wore the same green uniform) – but the tram carriages had become scruffy and colourless, just like the railway carriages, which he could barely recognise and which he saw as 'a symbol of today's Germany.'

The people of Berlin had become almost completely dependent on limited public transport, bicycles, or their own two feet. Open trams clanked along ringing their bells to warn the horse-drawn carts and bicycles to move out of the way. Bicycle tyres wore out and could not be replaced – giving the memorable sound of rimless bicycle wheels on the cobbles of blockaded Berlin.

For Herbert Sulzbach, so much in the city had changed beyond all recognition. During the 1920s and 1930s, when he and his wife had lived a charmed life there, Berlin had been an exciting place with its artistic experimentation, elegance, wealth and hedonistic lifestyle. There had been amusement parks, a zoo, and glorious countryside that had been easily accessible by the modern transport system. Not far away had been large areas of forests and lakes that were frequently visited by people like themselves with the wealth and leisure to enjoy it all.

Berlin's café culture had been famous. Throughout the 1920s, the Café Josty on Potsdamer Platz had been a regular haunt for Beate Sulzbach and her friends. It had been a large and popular place for well-off society men and women, artists and intellectuals, who frequented its pavement tables in large numbers, and enjoyed its patés and confectionery. How sad Herbert Sulzbach was to find every trace of this way of life completely extinguished. As he recorded in his diary, 'you could see the sky through each and every house. I looked for, but could not find, the building on the corner where Josty's café had been. House after house was yawningly empty, burnt-out, disused.' It was very difficult for him to come to terms with what he was seeing. The Germany that he had left in 1937 had been such a different place from these experiences as a British captain in 1948.

Sulzbach's period of duty with the Berlin airlift had opened up once again the differences that had developed between his own and his wife's attitudes towards Germany and the Germans. Beate could not share his belief in the possibilities of post-war Anglo-German friendship and reconciliation, nor identify with his experiences.

But Herbert Sulzbach was very much affected by his experiences in post-war Berlin. He was, above all, confused. In some respects, he felt that he had never left Berlin, and yet he had become deeply attached to Britain. As he wrote to Beate:

> Have all those years in-between been just a dream? Has Berlin been destroyed overnight by an earthquake? Or am I living a second life? Thirty years ago, I was a German soldier and officer, and I loved this country. Now it is as a British captain that I see Berlin. I love England and its people, but I still keep that feeling of friendship for my first love, and I still revere this old friend.

When he had eaten at a restaurant, and listened to an organ grinder playing – in the ruins and rubble of the courtyard – the same tunes that he had once heard as a child in Frankfurt, he had felt 'nothing but wistfulness and melancholy' because in those childhood days in Frankfurt his wealthy father had frequently invited an Italian organ grinder into their luxurious garden to play for his children, and had made sure that the man had been well rewarded.

Sulzbach had also been with Irene von Reitzenstein to the Grunewald – a large area of woods on the edge of the city – and had found it difficult to take in the apparent normality of what he saw. On a perfect cloudless day, children and adults bathed in the lake, just as he had once done. Everything there seemed unchanged – the lake, the sky, and the wonderful pine trees – and it smelt unchanged. 'It smells as it always smells in the Grunewald. A strange peace reigns here and it is rather surprising that nobody comments on a man sitting here in an English uniform, talking in German.' Meanwhile, above them American aircraft circled constantly, bringing foodstuffs from Frankfurt to Tempelhof, and flying boats landed on the Havelsee.

Writing to Beate and searching for words to describe the depth of his feelings, Sulzbach drew on a Hebrew description of the earth before the creation of light:

> Berlin – the city of ghosts and the city of the dead. I can no longer recognise it. It is a whirlpool of impressions, a *Tohu wa bohu* – chaos – in me. It is incomprehensible.

A week after his first visit, Sulzbach returned again to Berlin. His horror at the results of the Allied bombing of the city, for which he felt partly responsible, had – if anything – intensified. He recoiled at the thought that 'thousands of anti-Nazis had been killed with our bombs'. He agonised over the comparisons: three years previously he had maintained that 'the Germans who were given orders to shoot Jews should have refused' and in the same way he now wondered whether 'our RAF boys should have refused to destroy towns which only held civilians?'

His wife did not support this position. She was very 'disappointed' in what she termed his 'weakness'. This upset Sulzbach very much, and he responded to her letter: 'What you say is inhumane – that even one house left standing in Berlin is one too many. We are worlds apart!'

In many respects, he wanted to remain in Germany, expressing a desire to 'help the Germans to become Europeans instead of Germans'. He was certain that it should be possible to re-educate the German people. 'We could do it!' he wrote enthusiastically to Beate.

However, he was also desperate for peace and stability at home, although he recognised that his life could never again return to what he had known before the war. 'I long for you, for a home life, for quiet, for an ordered life. I am so mentally tired, so deeply sad, as never before,' he wrote in anguish to his wife. Neither he nor Beate could find any answers to their situation and she tried to be generous to him, telling him that she would support him working in Germany if that would give him happiness. She also sympathised with his feelings about his current work. 'That you feel so miserable and that the duties are so strenuous, distresses me deeply,' she told him.

Sulzbach's desire to find effective work in Germany stemmed almost entirely from what he saw around him. Many observers had expressed concern about the moral attitudes of the young people whom they met in post-war Berlin. Victor Gollancz had written about it on his earlier visits to Germany, and in 1948 Victor Klemperer noted how people were worried about: 'Adolescents going to the bad in bombed Berlin; stealing, black marketeering amidst the ruins.'

Young people who had been raised in the Third Reich had grown up with the indoctrination of Nazi schools and the Hitler Youth. Many of them had experienced dislocation and violence during the war, and lost homes and family members. It was not unusual for their fathers to be dead, missing, or in PoW camps.

Herbert Sulzbach had, since his arrival in Germany, been struck by the differences in outlook between the young people he met there and the young PoWs he had known in his camps. On 9 August he held a meeting with some of the young Germans who were working at Wunstorf airfield. He had asked his superiors if he could meet with a few of the German civilian workforce for a voluntary debate. Instead of an expected ten to fifteen attending, thirty-six young people came. Sulzbach sat them round him in a circle and began talking. He stressed what had struck him when he had arrived in Germany: 'the big difference between the Germans who had been in captivity in England, and those here'. He explained what he saw as the reasons, that few of the Germans had learnt to think outside their experience, and that they didn't know what tolerance or freedom were. He gave examples from his work at Comrie and Camp 18, talked about what he had learnt between 1945 and 1948, and gave a brief history of his own experiences.

Afterwards there were many questions and an animated discussion. Sulzbach asked if they would be interested if he had individual consulting hours, where they could bring their worries, and to this came an enthusiastic and unanimous 'Yes'. He was reminded of a comment made to him by a young Nazi at Comrie – 'We have never seen or learnt anything else; show us a new way.' Sulzbach very much wanted to find a way to help these young Germans.

The PoWs Sulzbach had known at Comrie and Featherstone Park were never far from his thoughts and he took every opportunity to visit those who lived near Wunstorf. On one visit to Hanover he stopped on the way to visit Dr Neumann, who had been the doctor at the Featherstone Park camp hospital, and he was delighted to be received extremely enthusiastically by his ex-PoW friend.

But he was deeply distressed at some shocking news of ex-PoW Mohn, who had been one of his clerks – and a strong supporter – at Featherstone Park. In October 1948 Mohn died after being involved in a tram collision in foggy weather. Sulzbach grieved for 'the splendid Mohn'.

On 20 August 1948 Sulzbach travelled to Hamburg for a meeting with several of his ex-PoWs. Fifteen attended, along with two journalists from the BBC and two from the local radio station. They had 'a grand meeting'.

By the end of July 1948, and only a few weeks into the airlift, the RAF was already meeting its cargo target of flying 3,000 tons a day into Berlin – and the anticipated riots in the city had not materialised. Indeed, morale had increased and respect for the western Allies had surged. Berliners had recognised that the West really was trying to sustain them.

Even as the airlift held firm, the political situation remained tense. Trains arriving in Berlin were frequently met by eastern sector police who blocked all exits from the station and relieved passengers of any food or worthwhile goods that they had brought from elsewhere. On 9 September, the mayor of Berlin, Ernst Reuter, spoke to a crowd of over 300,000 people at a mass demonstration in front of the Reichstag and near the Brandenburg Gate. He was formidable in urging the West to hold:

> We cannot be bartered, we cannot be negotiated, we cannot be sold. Whoever would surrender this city, whoever would surrender the people of Berlin, would surrender himself.

The airlift continued, expanded, and gradually became more structured. The administration became smoother, although the work remained demanding, and Sulzbach began to enjoy his work more once the intense shock of his first visit to Berlin had begun to recede.

Then the Wunstorf airfield experienced its first tragedy when, on 19 September 1948, after almost 22,000 flights without a crash, a York took off and after a few minutes two out of the four motors cut out. At a height of only 50 metres there was nothing they could do – the plane struck the ground, exploded and all five men were burnt. The horror touched everyone deeply because they had been together for months.

By the end of October, the airlift was becoming a much more regimented operation, but by then Sulzbach had heard that he was to be demobbed. On 31 October 1948 he arrived back in London. He had very mixed emotions. In one sense he had 'come home' – but he also remembered similar feelings that he'd had on 12 December 1918, when he had arrived back in Frankfurt at the end of an earlier war. 'What a strange feeling,' he had written then, 'to be back home and not have to go away anymore.' As he travelled by train from Waterloo Station to Aldershot barracks for demobilisation, he felt glad to be back in 'this old world-dominating city' and relieved to have left behind 'the dull, grey, and aloof world' of the previous four months.

After lunch and administrative formalities at Aldershot, Sulzbach was given civilian clothes ('a good suit, shirt, shoes, socks, hat, and a raincoat') and returned to meet Beate at Waterloo Station. His eight years as a British soldier had come to an end. In a few months' time, Herbert Sulzbach would be 55 years old, and the whole world had changed since he had fled Germany eleven years previously. The lifestyle that he had known before the Second World War had completely disappeared, along with all its ease of wealth and position. But Sulzbach realised that he too had changed, and so had some of his values.

While he had no idea what he could do to earn a living, he knew that if at all possible he wanted to build on his work of Anglo-German friendship and reconciliation that he had begun at Comrie and Featherstone Park. His few months in Germany had shown him both the realities and the opportunities that existed in the country of his birth, and he recognised that he had the skills to make his own contribution to the new Germany – if he could find a way, while still providing financially for his family.

But after so long away, he also had to try to rebuild the emotional bonds of home. In particular, his attitude towards Germany and the Germans was not well received by other members of his family, nor by some of his friends in the local Jewish community. Sulzbach's cheerful and normally optimistic nature was severely challenged by the enormity of the task ahead. With no money, few plans, and no promise of employment he was going to need all his customary charm, determination and hard work to make a success of the next few years.

Chapter 8

'Somewhere in Europe'

Within two months of his return from the Berlin airlift, Herbert Sulzbach had exhausted all his ideas of ways of working among young Germans in Allied-occupied Germany. So, he turned again towards trying to make use of his business contacts in Europe.

At the beginning of January 1949, he travelled abroad for the first time as a British civilian. Taking the ferry from Dover, he went by train through France to Barcelona, to discuss business possibilities in the cork industry with Walter Scherk, a rich and generous cousin of Beate. He was shocked by what he encountered as he travelled through post-war France. His cup of black coffee (with sugar but no milk), three slices of toast without any margarine or butter and just a dab of jam cost the equivalent of two shillings – and he was made aware that 'in England we still live in a paradise when you see France.'

He stopped overnight at a hotel in the centre of Paris – in Rue de la Paix, famous for its jewellers and fashionable shops – and met with some of his business associates from the 1920s and 30s, Fritz Heymann, Monsieur Der and Alfred Muller. He had first visited Muller and Sons – in their 'wonderfully solid and elegant warehouses and offices' in Rue de Flandre – twenty-five years previously to do business with Alfred's father. Since then, various members of the Muller family had perished in Auschwitz, or worked in the French Resistance, and Alfred was the only one of four sons who was still alive to run the business.

The next day he travelled on to Barcelona and considered himself fortunate to be only one hour late arriving, compared with the customary five- or six-hour delay. Walter Scherk and his son Kurt welcomed him warmly at the station and then Kurt drove them all in his father's huge American car ('which cost £2,000') to the Majestic Hotel in the centre of Barcelona. Although he reckoned the hotel to be 'good and certainly first class', with hot and cold water, he was surprised to discover the electricity was only on from five in the evening until the morning, so he had to shave by candlelight.

After so many years of experiencing wartime restrictions and continuing rationing in Britain, Herbert was startled by the luxury that he found in Barcelona. He was surprised to find a second car, 'just a Chevrolet', standing outside the Scherks' house the following morning and wondered aloud if they really needed two cars for four people to travel to the factory.

Herbert met with Walter Scherk's business contacts to learn about the mechanics of the cork industry in Spain, where it had become particularly profitable since Germany's post-war collapse in the market. He talked with the head of the Brazilian department of the Corporacion Internacional de Comercio, which was a large export and import organisation, and also met their agents for the USA and Spain – all of whom were Germans with experience of the industry. Their proposal was that Herbert should become the corporation's representative in Germany, using his many contacts there to build up business.

Herbert spent a week trying hard to learn the complexities of the cork industry (with which he was completely unfamiliar) and also making arrangements for a visit to Germany to begin negotiating with potential customers and clients. Meanwhile, he was taken aback by the splendid hospitality of the Scherks and by the warmth and beauty of his surroundings. One day he went for a drive with Walter's wife, Alice.

Within ten minutes they were in the mountains, with a wonderful view of the sea, and Barcelona lying white and hazy beneath them in the hot sun. Back in the city, Alice invited him for Cinzano and oysters on a piazza that reminded him of the Reichskanzlerplatz in Berlin. They sat outside at a pavement table, surrounded by elegant and happy people, and a barrel organ played nearby. Sulzbach was enchanted by the warmth, colour and luxury, writing to Beate:

> My God, our life in the UK is so dull! We must live in this sort of country, where there is still vitality. Why are we poor in England when there is a paradise here with palms and sun throughout the year?

'SOMEWHERE IN EUROPE'

The Scherks lived in a large, white villa – Moorish in style. The interior was modern, with floors laid with stone slabs against the heat, and a 'Moorish-Arabic' courtyard inside, with a glass roof. Sulzbach went for a walk on his own down to the sea. The water lapped in small waves on to the sandy beach, and on the path between the street and the sea he found hundreds and hundreds of lizards – all of them slim, nimble and graceful. For him, it was almost impossible to imagine that there could be such beauty – such peace and serenity. 'How poor we are in England, that we cannot enjoy such things.'

It was all so very different from anything that he had experienced in the eleven years since he had left Germany. It was also an acute and painful reminder of the luxury that he had himself enjoyed during his childhood and youth.

Sulzbach left Barcelona on the afternoon of 22 January 1949 for his trip to Germany and spent the next twenty-nine hours travelling by train to Basel. He immediately went into negotiations there, on Walter Scherk's behalf, with the banker Hans Seligmann, who was also a personal friend of the Sulzbach family. He felt at home in Basel, where he had lived, worked and campaigned during the immediate pre-war period. For several years he had been friends with many of the journalists and editors from the Swiss newspapers and took this opportunity to visit Peter Dürrenmatt, chief editor of the *Basler Nachrichten*. As a political columnist for the paper, Dürrenmatt had written glowingly of Sulzbach's work with German PoWs after he had visited Featherstone Park in 1947.

That evening he also met with many of his old Frankfurt friends now in Basel – the Franks, the Seligmanns, and Professor Otto Reise – and was brought up to date with others, such as the Goldschmit and Rothschild families. Herbert found many similarities between Basel and the pre-1914 Frankfurt he had known. There was the same wealth and comfort, the same kind of restaurants and cafés, the same good, solid food, 'as well as the same fine *petty-bourgeoisie*. Even the trams make the same noise!'

When he set off for Frankfurt the following day, he was exhausted and rather depressed. As he wrote to Beate:

> I am tired from nine years of soldiering, from being 55, and going back into business without any break. I don't

understand ninety percent of what Walter says and I sink
into bed at nine o'clock feeling simply ill with tiredness.

He was apprehensive about this first post-war visit to his home town and hoped that it would not be as disturbing as his first visit to Berlin – and also hoped that it would make a difference that he was returning as a civilian rather than as a member of the occupying forces.

He arrived in Frankfurt on the evening of 27 January 1949, and in the darkness his first impression was that the area around the railway station was unchanged. He could see that the Carlton Hotel was still standing, as was the Schumann Theatre. It was only on the following morning that he realised that all the buildings were roofless, and most had their windows blown out. He was appalled by the traffic – 'American trucks, German juggernauts, huge luxurious American cars, clapped out German cars, and military jeeps tearing about in an almost unbroken succession. From the central station at night, Frankfurt seems more like an American colony than a German city,' he wrote in his diary.

He found that all the Allied hotels were full and it took two hours of searching before he could find one night's accommodation in the English/American press hotel, the Park Hotel, but the next day he found a room in a German guesthouse in the Hansa Allee.

For the next fortnight he was frantically busy not only chasing contacts and opportunities for the cork business but also trying to straighten his family's financial affairs – as well as meeting with some of the ex-PoWs from Featherstone Park.

But first he needed to make a pilgrimage around his home city. On 28 January 1949, he recorded it in his diary:

> It is cold and foggy, and everything is covered in a hoar frost. I have discovered that my first love, Mieze Kindervatter, was killed in an air raid and my other young love, Maxi Siebert (later Frau von Körper) died of a heart attack when she heard of the death of her son. The beautiful Jella Ettlinger perished in Auschwitz with her entire family – her parents, husband and children.

To complicate his memories, the house at 7 Oberlindau, where the Ettlinger family had once lived, had since been divided into flats and in one of these he found an ex-PoW whom he knew. Herr Horlitz had been the mess caterer at Featherstone Park and was now working as a confectioner in Frankfurt. When Sulzbach called on him, he was received with great pleasure – and Horlitz was still wearing his chocolate-coloured PoW shirt as his house jacket.

The vast I.G. Farben building, which Sulzbach had often visited during the 1920s and early 1930s in connection with his fancy paper factory, had remained intact and now housed the Supreme Allied Command. To Sulzbach, when he visited, it seemed as though he was 'in the middle of America'. Amongst the many American authorities was the Joint Export Import Agency, which especially interested Sulzbach as it controlled the entire German import and export.

He also went to the premises of Kirchholtes Bank, which had once been his family's bank, Gebrüder Sulzbach, and was disappointed to discover that he now knew only one of the employees there. He spent the evening with the bank's owner, Heinrich Kirchholtes, and his wife, Gertrud (who was Herbert Sulzbach's cousin). Sulzbach's guesthouse was very close to the Heinestrasse where his childhood tutor, Dr Löffler, lived so he paid him a visit. It was a sad occasion as an old and changed man opened the door to Sulzbach.

At the Opernplatz, where his grandfather's house had once stood, he found nothing but a heap of rubble, with the beautiful park running wild. It was the same at the Oppenheimer's palace next to his grandfather's house. At the burnt-out Opera House, only the façade remained. Near its top, apparently newly carved, were the words *Dem Wahren, Schönen, Guten* (to the true, the beautiful, the good) 'as though it were necessary that these words should be newly engraved – and even more necessary that they should be etched onto the hearts of all Germans and all peoples.'

The whole town was devastated. None of the beautiful half-timbered houses any longer existed. Every once-familiar building was missing. On every corner throughout the town people had set up shacks for selling – fruit, food, shoes, clothes, and household things. The whole of Frankfurt seemed like a permanent Christmas market and in the alleyways there were signs indicating where a shop had been re-established.

It was a very melancholy journey for Herbert Sulzbach. 'I never meet a soul I know, and nobody knows us anymore,' he lamented.

Later, he met with his lawyer, Dr Heertz, and was relieved and pleased to find that he could expect to receive at least some compensation for his family's wartime losses. Having commented that he was no longer recognised on the streets of Frankfurt, he was gladdened by an unexpected encounter.

In a side street off the Eschenheimer Landstrasse, he saw a taxi that had stopped at a petrol station. He found the elderly driver in the garage waiting room and asked for a lift. The driver told him that he was an American taxi so Sulzbach agreed to pay in dollars. Looking more closely at Sulzbach under the streetlight, the driver exclaimed 'But I know you!'. When Sulzbach gave his name, the taxi driver was delighted.

> Oh, the son of the banker Emil Sulzbach in the Friedrichstrasse! I was often at your place with your chauffeur, Herr Blank. Those were the days! What good things we had to eat there, but those times have passed now,' he said.

Sulzbach's subsequent meeting with a small number of ex-PoWs in a local restaurant was a success, although he had learnt too late of others who could have attended. Amongst those who were there were some of the senior PoWs from Featherstone Park. Sulzbach was pleased to find that 'the spirit of Camp 18 is still sky-high. All of them said that they would not have wanted to have missed their time there.'

His negotiations for the business in the cork industry were proving to be much slower and far more complicated than either he or Walter Scherk had expected. He wrote to Beate to explain that he would need to stay longer before making his way home via Hamburg, Bremen and Amsterdam.

He had little time for relaxation, but one afternoon went to an Allied cinema where he was bemused at the playing of *God save the King* at the beginning of the film. Everyone in the audience, including German girls with their American soldiers, stood for the anthem. As usual, there was a supporting film and, on this occasion, it was a film from London about the high courts of justice. When Sulzbach saw footage of Lincolns Inn, the Temple 'and all the other magnificent buildings', and heard a judge speaking about old London and its sense of tradition, he felt homesick. 'For the first time in my life I had a yearning for my second home – for England, for London. I felt that what I saw in the film was my real home, and in Germany I am a foreigner,' he later wrote in his diary.

'SOMEWHERE IN EUROPE'

By mid-February Sulzbach was on his way back to England. He stopped first in Hamburg and was surprised to see a hotel with a placard advertising *Operation Plainfare* – the new name for the airlift to Berlin. He went inside and the first crews that he saw were his friends from Wunstorf. He was overjoyed to see them, and very touched when they invited him to fly to Berlin that night. 'But I was so tired, and I had so much to do the next day.'

He travelled on to Bremen for further negotiations about cork (and also to meet with some ex-PoWs) and then went back to London via Amsterdam.

Throughout the next twelve months, Herbert Sulzbach went backwards and forwards between London, Barcelona and Germany but finally – in February 1950 – he had to admit defeat in his negotiations. It had been impossible for him or anyone in Spain to receive permission to establish a branch in Frankfurt as foreign investments were still not allowed there.

Many of his experiences during 1949 had moved him profoundly. He had eventually been able to make contact with his great friend from 1917 – Hans Ado von Seebach – who had served alongside him during the First World War and stayed in close touch as a good friend until the end of the 1930s. In 1950 they met once again in Bonn. They stood together on the Rhine bridge – von Seebach having been a colonel in the German Army during the recent war, whilst Sulzbach had been serving with British forces and fighting him. Nearly thirty-two years before, they had marched together over that very bridge, both as lieutenants in the defeated Imperial German Army.

But Sulzbach's most haunting memory had been standing before his childhood home in January 1949, almost thirty years – and a cataclysmic time – since he had last lived there. As usual, he recorded it in his diary:

> I walked along the Friedrichstrasse, which is relatively unscathed, past some burnt-out houses, to the Freiherr-vom-Steinstrasse. The synagogue on the corner stands curiously complete, and I went past number 29 where the Liebmanns lived.
>
> Then I was in front of Friedrichstrasse 57. I could hardly remain standing. The house that had enfolded our childhood and youth stands undamaged. I looked briefly into our

former garden, where there is now a villa, but I did not want to linger and reflect. Opposite, the Siebert's house still stands, except that – like a symbol – Maxi's room is burnt-out. Number 61, the Riesser's house, now accommodates an American War Crimes Investigation Unit.

It was a strange homecoming. Frankfurt had been the place where he had lived and loved during an idyllic and privileged time in what was now a distant time and a foreign land. That was all in the past and he still had no idea how to move into the future.

PART III

(1951 – 1985)
Friendship and Reconciliation

Chapter 9

German Embassy, London. Building Bridges

Many years after this unsuccessful job-hunting in Europe, a German ambassador was known to tell his members of staff, '*Nie verzagen, Sulzbach fragen*' ('Never despair, consult Sulzbach'), but it was Sulzbach himself who was close to despair by the time that he finally went to work at the new German Consulate in London in April 1951, after over a year of looking for employment in Germany and failing to establish anything connected either with his early business ventures or with his work among PoWs.

'If you should ever join with me, never give up your British nationality!' These were the words that Sulzbach remembered after his first meetings with Dr Schlange-Schöningen, leader of the post-war consulate in London. After much discussion and soul-searching Sulzbach did join him. At last, his long search for a job had come to an end and everyone who knew him was pleased.

Sulzbach's friend Hans Ado von Seebach had known Dr Hans Schlange-Schöningen in Germany when the latter had been Minister for Food and Agriculture in the British zone during the late 1940s. As soon as von Seebach heard of Dr Schlange-Schöningen's appointment to London, he spoke with him about Sulzbach's successful work amongst German PoWs at Featherstone Park and also urged Herbert to consider working with the consulate.

The German Consulate opened in London on 16 June 1950, although the new Federal Republic of Germany had not yet become a sovereign state. When sovereignty was approved in June 1951 the consulate was accorded diplomatic status and became an embassy four years later. Herbert Sulzbach joined its staff in April 1951. Within the next few years, he had his German nationality returned to him – but, as advised, he always kept his British nationality.

GERMAN EMBASSY, LONDON. BUILDING BRIDGES

His friend, Dorothy Buxton, understood how important his appointment was to Sulzbach – and to the new Germany. She sent her congratulations to him, noting that, 'your position there will create one more little bridge of rapprochement and understanding between people of German and of Jewish race.' She also wrote to Dr Schlange-Schöningen:

> I doubt whether anyone else in this country is on terms of personal friendship with so many Germans as Mr Sulzbach – and I fear that there are many Jews who let him know their resentment.

It wasn't only Jews who were wary of attempts at Anglo-German friendship. Initially, the consulate operated out of two three-storeyed blocks of flats with tiny rooms at 4 and 6 Rutland Gate. There was a staff of twenty and they were frequently subjected to verbal and physical abuse.

Herbert Sulzbach had only just arrived in his new job when a British national paper published a double-page feature of two articles speculating on what might be going on at Rutland Gate. One journalist was clear about his difficulty in accepting the idea that Germans would be doing anything other than furthering their own ends on this mission and hoped that their activities were being closely scrutinised. Another asked a direct question as to what was really happening at the German Legation. A member of the consulate gave the answer:

> We are operating here on a shoestring. Our main task is restoring confidence and promoting trade between two peoples.

Sulzbach wrote 'Idiot' in the margin of his paper against the articles and fired off a letter to the editor:

> How much better would a warning against activities in a consulate or embassy have been between 1933 and 1939 when so many people in this country flirted with Ribbentrop? I came in close contact with the new German officials in July 1950 and came to the conclusion that Bonn

can be congratulated on sending Dr Schlange-Schöningen to this country with a staff of enthusiastic Europeans.

When he was asked, many years later, about his early work at the German Embassy, he told the interviewer that he had started in the social welfare department, became a specialist assistant, and then moved to the press service. During the last twenty-two years of his employment, he worked in the cultural department, where he had various responsibilities that were quite similar to what he had been doing in the Featherstone Park PoW camp.

Thirty years after the consulate was opened, Dr Jacob Gewirtz, a senior member of the London Jewish community commented that:

> ...the rehabilitation of Germany after the Second World War, and its re-entry into the family of nations, were not so much the result of reparations agreements or of Nuremberg Trials but of the single-minded dedication and unshakable faith of those like Herbert Sulzbach who believed – and even more important taught others to believe – that kindness and decency transcend race and nation.

Sulzbach's employment was extraordinary for its time. As Rainer Dobbelstein, a friend and diplomat at the embassy acknowledged, 'Herbert was an absolute gift to the embassy. He, a Jew, had volunteered to work in the new embassy, thus giving much valued validity to the new post-war Germany. He was a bridge between Britain and the new Germany at a very difficult time.'

When Herbert Sulzbach joined the Consulate General he was 57 years old and had developed countless friendships and contacts with people from different races, countries and walks of life. This gave him a unique position at the embassy. He was delighted not only with his new job but also with the way that it reinforced his contacts with the PoWs he had known. He used his many connections both from his pre-war life in Germany, and from his life and work in Britain, to develop friendships and encourage reconciliation. A journalist working for the *News Chronicle* wrote gratefully to Dr Schlange-Schöningen, in September 1951:

> On no previous occasion since I began visiting Germany as a journalist have I had anything like the number of

interesting and useful introductions that I have today. Thanks to Sulzbach's work among prisoners of war, he has been able to put me in touch with a quite extraordinary variety of people, who are playing some part in the rebuilding of Germany.

Terence Prittie, a British journalist working in Germany, recalled how he was sceptical as he watched events unfold in post-war Germany. When Herbert contacted him and talked about the long task that lay ahead, Prittie was impressed by his honesty and optimism – and began to look for the positives in post-war German life. 'There had to be real grounds for hope, if people like Herbert could be so very hopeful.'

Although Sulzbach worked in the press and then cultural departments at the consulate, he tended to 'operate as a one-man band', as a former colleague noted. There were initially only four people in his department, and he was not in a senior position.

Some years later, another colleague described him as 'the special embodiment of two cultures and his Jewishness. He was charismatic, funny and charming, in the way that aristocracy were. He told a good story. He was a good man. When he spoke to you, you felt that he really cared about you as an individual – and he was like that with everybody.'

Since the end of the war, Sulzbach had been keen to make his own personal reconnections with Germany and in July 1951 the consulate issued him with a six-month travel permit. His childhood summer holidays, which he always remembered with great affection, had been spent at Zandvoort and other nearby resorts. He wanted to return to the many places that still held special memories from the past. As soon as he had his travel pass, he and his family left from the Hook of Holland to holiday at Herrenalb, a health resort in the Black Forest. The following year he received a twelve-month travel permit.

His niece remembers how she was taken on holiday by her uncle to introduce her to his childhood. Hours and hours were spent planning these holidays. 'We went on the Rheingold Express. I can still smell the cups on the Express. They were dark green cups – white inside, with a gold rim and green outside. We went to Holland, often to Germany, and on to Italy.'

Throughout his early years working at the consulate, Sulzbach remained concerned about the unconfirmed nature of his position. He had been taken on as a local employee by Dr Schlange-Schöningen without, it would appear, final agreement from the authorities in Bonn. 'If Bonn says "No" it will be over!' he wrote to Dorothy Buxton before he had even been there a month.

He was depressed by a third refusal to have his position confirmed a year later, as well as by his low wages ('the same salary as a girl typist'), and the fact that his pay became further reduced because he had to pay income tax in both Britain and Germany.

He asked Hans Ado von Seebach if he could use some influence.

He wrote to von Seebach:

> I don't complain. I love the work, I love the atmosphere, and the whole embassy is a great team of happily working people, all of whom are worthy to represent the new Germany. I see the successes and am pleased – but now and then something comes over me when I see that the youngest legation counsellor earns more and is entitled to more pension. It has already been said in the *Express* that the average pay of an English employee is £24 a week – and mine is £22! I must be able to put aside a few thousand Deutschmark each year, don't you think?

Sulzbach's concerns about pay and position would remain a source of disappointment until he retired, although in the meantime he eventually received some restitution money (and also a monthly old age pension) from Germany, which eased some of his financial hardship. But his inability to recoup anything like the financial security that he had once enjoyed occasionally made him feel slightly bitter.

The Second World War had left a legacy of hate and Sulzbach's first few years at the embassy were marked by intense anti-German feeling amongst some sections of the British population. But things gradually changed, even in the immediate post-war period. Sulzbach was particularly moved by the occasion in November 1952 when the German president, Theodor Heuss, laid a memorial stone at Bergen-Belsen concentration camp, declaring that, 'No one can take this shame from us.'

Responding to those people who wanted all Germans to be made responsible for such crimes, Heuss also said, 'I reject collective guilt but accept for all of us collective shame,' which corresponded exactly with Sulzbach's own views.

GERMAN EMBASSY, LONDON. BUILDING BRIDGES

As a politically conservative person, a monarchist and a British patriot, Herbert was delighted with the coronation of Queen Elizabeth II in June 1953. He watched the celebrations on television, enjoyed the 'tradition, grandeur and dignity' and felt 'proud to be a British subject.'

The year 1957 was a busy year for the new German Embassy. Harold Macmillan visited Bonn as prime minister, and this visit was reciprocated by Chancellor Konrad Adenauer the following year. A few months later there was a state visit to England by Theodor Heuss. These official visits kept the employees of the press and cultural departments very busy, and there were many events and receptions at the embassy in London.

Herbert's personal engagement diary for 1957 shows that apart from his daily work at the embassy, he went to meetings and social events of the Anglo-German Circle. He and his family went to a nearby Jewish restaurant at 20 Abbey Road – or to Cosmo's – about once a month. Visitors to his home, and visits to friends, were frequent, involving about forty different local families. He enjoyed going to the local cinema, as well as walking on Highbury Hill and Primrose Hill with his family. A monthly game of poker with friends was a regular feature in his diary – and he kept a close eye on the horse racing.

One young student from Germany – the daughter of Kurt Schwedersky, an ex-PoW officer in Featherstone Park – remembers her visit to London in the early 1970s, during which time the Sulzbachs held a reception at their home:

> It was packed with people, many of them well-known, and the modest room was transformed in the candlelight. Beate was beautiful. She would be sitting in a dream, smoking with an elegant holder. And Herbert worshipped her.

Sulzbach regularly scrutinised the newspapers for anything written about Anglo-German relations and was always quick to respond to journalists. In a sharp letter in 1959 he complained about the press frequently writing about 'unpleasant events' in Germany – which he agreed should be done – but never mentioning the positive ones. He noted how he had not read such anti-Hitler articles before the war, as he now observed anti-Adenauer ones.

He was critical of – and frustrated by – the seemingly incessant negative British media coverage of Germany. He wanted the views and actions of students in Germany to be more widely known and appreciated.

A JEW WHO DEFEATED NAZISM

In 1959 there was little acknowledgement of young Germans' interest in Anne Frank, and the annual pilgrimage of students to her grave. (The Frank family had been friends of the Sulzbachs in pre-war Frankfurt.)

German newspapers gave publicity to the trials of Nazis, and Sulzbach felt that this was under-reported in the British press, and that important personalities such as Willy Brandt were little known in Britain. It frustrated him that the press failed, as he saw it, to portray the positive changes in post-war Germany and he wished that it could be recognised that Germany was beginning to face its past. He was concerned about the way that negative media attention fuelled anti-German sentiments. His letter to the *Daily Telegraph* in January 1960 was published:

> A recent BBC television interview showed that the man in the street still regards all Germans as Nazis and does not know much about the great changes in the Federal Republic since 1949. I fear that sections of the press which never mention positive development have had a bad influence.

By the end of the 1950s, Sulzbach was responsible for much of the administration of the cultural department – periodicals, books, films and gramophone records. He dealt with the post, and with enquiries about anything to do with Germany – on his own and without a secretary. He frequently received and advised German, English and Commonwealth visitors, as well as British teachers. He was 65 years old and reckoned that he usually worked a ten-hour day.

He was also involved with the setting up of various Anglo-German Circles and helped provide speakers for their meetings, as well as supporting the youth group of the Anglo-German Association. Increasingly, youth groups visited the embassy and Sulzbach showed them around and explained its work.

In the summer of 1960 Sulzbach stayed at a health spa in Germany and was heartened to see for himself how the country was dealing with its past. From Bad Nenndorf in Lower Saxony he wrote to his wife:

> On the radio, every morning, two Hebrew songs are sung in the original text. The presenter, a Dr Fischer, speaks of the greatness of the Israeli people and against 'disgusting Teutonic boasting'. He talks about 'our evil past' and about hiding things. This happens every morning between five and seven o'clock.

GERMAN EMBASSY, LONDON. BUILDING BRIDGES

Anglo-German friendship was given a significant boost through initiatives such as town twinnings. This was a conscious effort to develop links between local authorities and communities in Great Britain and Germany to heal the wounds of war. It required understanding, enthusiasm and commitment (which initially often came from only a few people) for the hope and vision of a more peaceful and united Europe to be realised.

Engelbert Hoppe, who had been repatriated from Featherstone Park to become a teacher and had been greatly influenced by what he had experienced in the PoW camp, became passionate about creating and continuing links between Germany and England. He was involved with twinnings from 1952 when many people thought it was too early for such things. As he always acknowledged, 'I owe so much to Herbert Sulzbach and Colonel Vickers. Herbert was my great fatherly friend and England made me.'

People who had served in the war – in both the German and the Allied armies – were often those who best recognised the value of these links. Sulzbach himself was involved in the early stages of the formation of the Tunbridge Wells/Wiesbaden partnership during the 1960s. At first this was contact between ex-servicemen from both towns but grew into a partner agreement between the two towns, which was signed in 1961. Those who struggled to set up the partnership found that it was a difficult time as memories of the war were still fresh and many people were reluctant to make friends with yesterday's enemies.

Their Twinning Charter was eventually signed almost thirty years later, on 22 April 1989, in the Town Hall at Tunbridge Wells, and in April 2006 the City Council and the mayor of Wiesbaden were granted the Freedom of the Borough of Tunbridge Wells. Town-twinning arrangements were also begun in Bishop's Stortford. A local newspaper editor, Kenneth Cook, who was involved with his town twinning, told Herbert:

> I was fascinated by your great work for Anglo-German friendship, which has proved an inspiration to me ever since. It spurred me on through all the efforts that had to be made to build up an efficient organisation.

In 1945 Kenneth had been billeted in the Spandau Jail in Berlin as a member of the occupying forces. A developing friendship with a local German family convinced him that a lasting peace could best be achieved by individuals and families getting to know each other. By the early 1960s he was editor of the *Herts and Essex Observer* and was approached to see if he would support the twinning of Bishop's Stortford with Friedberg and Viller-sur-Marne. It was then that he met Herbert Sulzbach. The two men shared similar ideas and attitudes, and even after the embassy had bowed out of the twinning arrangements, and Kenneth had moved on from his editorship of the local paper, he kept up his links with town twinning. His friendship with Herbert continued until Herbert's death. Their friendship was not unusual. The people with whom Herbert was in contact for work often became his personal friends.

A curious episode in Sulzbach's work at the embassy in the 1960s was his involvement with Graham Sutherland's painting of a portrait of Konrad Adenauer. Negotiations had begun in the late 1950s, Adenauer had given his approval in spring 1959, and Herbert became an intermediary (on behalf of the embassy) in the early 1960s. Strict secrecy and confidentiality were required, at the insistence of both painter and sitter.

Sulzbach became increasingly frustrated and impatient with the lack of progress, as matters moved into their sixth year. However, in May 1965 Adenauer was eventually shown the portrait, expressed deep satisfaction with it, and accepted one of the pencil sketches as a personal gift from Sutherland. Sulzbach also received a small print as a gift from the painter, in gratitude for his part in the drama.

Sulzbach's work of reconciliation included trying to act as a bridge between the Jewish and other communities. Kurt Schwedersky was an investigating judge who, after repatriation from Featherstone Park, had used his legal skills to investigate war criminals from the Nazi period. His work took him to many countries to interview witnesses, many of whom were Jewish. When he was in London, the German Embassy gave him strong support. On one such occasion in 1965, Sulzbach wrote to Schwedersky, asking him to 'mix business with pleasure' and accept an invitation to a reception at his flat to bid farewell to the departing ambassador, Dr Hasso von Etzdorf. Apart from Schwedersky, the guest list included members of parliament, peers, military historians, journalists, and the director of the Wiener Library – as well as 'some English friends'.

GERMAN EMBASSY, LONDON. BUILDING BRIDGES

Schwedersky's visits, and his work, were often reported in both the national and the Jewish press, and Sulzbach and Schwedersky were very good friends.

The new German Ambassador to London in 1965, Herbert Blankenhorn, arrived at a momentous time. To many observers, the queen's state visit to the Federal Republic in May of that year was a turning point in Anglo-German relations. The queen and Prince Philip were cheered by thousands as they drove through the streets of Berlin at the end of their eleven-day visit. Sulzbach was delighted that Kurt Schwedersky, as chairman of the newly created Featherstone Park Association, had been invited with his wife to one of the receptions given for the queen.

And after this state visit it was noticeable that there was less negativity towards Germany in some sections of the British press. When Konrad Adenauer died in April 1967, Sulzbach (who was a great admirer of Adenauer) was pleased with the news reporting, commenting to Schwedersky that:

> The British press was wonderful about Adenauer's greatness, as a man, a statesman and a European. There was television coverage for hours, almost as much as for Churchill's funeral, with a commentary full of admiration for him and for the new Germany.

The 1960s were years of increasing awareness amongst young people in Germany of the need for Germans to confront and deal with their recent past. This younger generation, which had not been implicated in the Third Reich, took a critical look at the Second World War and asked questions of their parents. As a German president, Joachim Gauck – who had been part of this generation – was to say half a century later:

> My generation was confronted with the pitch-black hole of German history. The great achievement of the 1968 generation was and still is the hard-won blessing of being able to remember differently and more profoundly.

Nineteen sixty-eight was also the year in which the German Institute in London hosted a reception for Fabian von Schlabrendorff, a man who had opposed and resisted Hitler. Herbert Sulzbach prepared an explanatory handout for guests, in which he noted that:

> Little, if anything, was known about the German Resistance before the end of the war. In 1945 a few facts became public about the so-called Officers' Plot of 20 July 1944. Schlabrendorff was the man who planted a bomb in Hitler's plane in 1943 – a bomb which did not go off. The men of the German Resistance stood alone. Perhaps this day, and the presence of Fabian von Schlabrendorff, will contribute to a greater understanding between our two countries.

Since his time at Featherstone Park when he had first met Otto John, Sulzbach had become very interested and involved with the circle of resisters. When he had read von Schlabrendorff's *Offiziere gegen Hitler* (*Officers against Hitler*) when it had first been published in 1959, he had been intensely glad and relieved to realise that 'the other Germany' that he loved had never completely disappeared. He was proud to count himself as a friend of Schlabrendorff until the latter's death in September 1980.

But this prevailing attitude of honesty, retrospection and rebellion amongst the younger generation brought unexpected conflict to Herbert's own family. After staying with a German family as an au pair, his 20-year-old granddaughter returned to England with pro-Nazi opinions that horrified him, and seemed to be shared by Herbert's daughter, her mother. He was shocked and deeply hurt, and he and his granddaughter had a difficult meeting at the embassy. Herbert explained how he felt to another (non-Jewish) family member:

> There is a difference between contrariness, and not caring about the murder of one's own relatives! I want nothing more to do with her or her mother, because they both deny as Jews their grandfather and father respectively.

They remained estranged for many years.

At the end of this turbulent decade, a notable occasion took place in German-Jewish relations. In December 1970 Willy Brandt was the first German federal chancellor to visit Poland, where he unexpectedly and apparently spontaneously sank to his knees, visibly moved, after laying a wreath at the memorial to the Warsaw Ghetto Uprising. This remarkable demonstration of atonement was widely seen as a very special and great gesture. Sulzbach wrote personally afterwards to Brandt and was very glad to receive a reply.

During the 1970s the embassy and its work continued to expand and Sulzbach enjoyed working with the younger people there. Many of them remembered him with affection and gratitude. A young, and very apprehensive, Italian had joined the staff as the butler for embassy receptions (and was still working there forty years later). Only 18 years old when he started working there, Ezio le Donne was immediately welcomed by Sulzbach, who enabled him to fit into what at first seemed to be quite an alien environment. The young man remained forever impressed by Sulzbach's care of young people. As he recognised, 'Mr Sulzbach invested his time in young people because he said, "Young people are our future."' One young woman who worked at the embassy in the 1970s remembered him as 'like a grandfather' – concerned that she could find her way around London and was making friends. Like many others, she remembers that he rarely talked about the past.

Regine Schwedersky came to know Herbert Sulzbach through her father, Kurt. She also remembered that he never talked about the past – and since she was brought up not to ask questions that might be painful, she asked none of Herbert. 'Turning the page, repressing it, blanking it out,' she commented, 'Herbert had to do this – behave as if it didn't exist – just to keep going. He could only deal with the whole situation because he turned the page and didn't look back.'

On 8 February 1971, his seventy-seventh birthday, Sulzbach was awarded the German Grand Cross of Merit. He was extremely proud and pleased and wrote cheerfully to Kurt Schwedersky to thank him for his part in recommending him for the award. Amongst the many congratulations which he was pleased to receive was a letter from the German Embassy in Tel-Aviv (together with a newspaper cutting in Hebrew 'which no one can read').

A few months before his eightieth birthday, Sulzbach had particular cause to look back. In 1973 his First World War diaries were published in English (with a different title from the original), and there was a book launch on 2 July at the embassy. It was a very proud day for him, particularly as the German foreign minister, Walter Scheel, attended – and took away a signed copy to present to Britain's Sir Alec Douglas-Home as a seventieth birthday present. Heinz Bitker, the German Army attaché (and a former PoW at Featherstone Park) was also there in uniform.

There were 250 guests at the book launch and the ambassador said in his speech:

> I think the publication of this book, *With the German Guns*, after so many years is an acknowledgement of the fact that it was and perhaps is, even today, difficult to fully digest these two world wars. It is a story of loyalty to the true fatherland and a story of loyalty to an ideal: service for one's country, loyalty, comradeship until death, friendship among human beings and respect for the life of others.

Sulzbach was especially pleased that Hans Ado von Seebach was present for the occasion, and ended his own emotional speech by quoting from the book, 'Today my heart beats for Europe – and that is how it is.'

As a friend, Eva Reichmann, noted in the newsletter of the Association of Jewish Refugees, 'Herbert Sulzbach is a living example of the absurdity of our times.'

Publication of the book brought an increase in mail for Sulzbach. One letter came from a professor at York University, explaining that he had first started to read the book in its original 1935 German publication. He wrote:

> In March 1945 I was a *Jungzugführer* [student leader] of the Hitler Youth in Munich. I and others of similar rank were issued with copies of the book, *Zwei lebende Mauern*, which at our weekly gatherings we were to read to our platoons. I must have got about halfway through it when on Monday 30 April 1945 at the ripe old age of eleven and a half years I became a PoW of the Americans. My assault pack was searched, which contained this book. An American lieutenant thumbed through it and then threw it into the River Isar. Thus, thirty-six years later I have had at long last the opportunity to complete reading a book begun in 1945.

Correspondence also arrived from men who realised that they or their fathers had fought from opposite trenches to Sulzbach and were amazed that they were all still alive. Ian Angus consulted his father's war record and found that he and Sulzbach had fought in one particular battle – in opposing armies and both of them in the artillery, so probably shooting at each other. Still bemused about his discoveries thirty years later, Angus reminisced about how he tried to meet Sulzbach. His initial letter brought a swift reply and an invitation to the embassy. When the two men met, Angus remembered how he felt that he had known him all his life, 'and to think that he and Father might have killed one another had they come face to face, and here we were talking as old friends.'

Sulzbach immediately invited Angus to a forthcoming party at the embassy, and he described watching Sulzbach there:

> He would appear out of the crowd and say, "Ian, this is X, X this is Ian Angus. He's interested in this, and he's interested in the other", and then he'd dash off and be doing it with someone else. He had a remarkable memory for names and backgrounds. Herbert was active all the time, whisking people from one group to another; you never quite knew the nationality of the person to whom you were talking until well into the conversation.

The filmmaker, Bridget Winter – who also attended receptions at the embassy – noted how:

> Weaving in and out of groups that he has brought together (and never forgetting a name) it is fascinating to watch him in operation. He acts as a seed-planter, occasionally standing back to watch results with a smile. Indeed, his enormous sense of fun often tempts him to experiment with cross-fertilisations that more orthodox souls would never ever contemplate!

Herbert was indeed well-known for his impish sense of fun, and his telling of a good story.

Sulzbach was often contacted by schoolteachers who wanted help or information from the embassy. When he first started working at the consulate his old army boss, Henry Faulk (by then a language teacher in Glasgow) wrote looking for a way to take schoolchildren to visit

Germany – in 1951. The children were from poor homes and it was essential to keep costs to the absolute minimum. 'No hotels, or any such nonsense,' demanded Faulk. Both men were committed to finding ways to enable children and young people to connect with others in post-war Germany.

Official contact very often turned into personal friendship – with both Sulzbach and with people in Germany. Eric Henderson, a headteacher from a middle school near Newcastle, explained how in 1974 he decided at his school to do something on modern history, so 'I wrote to the German Embassy and Herbert picked it up.' They began to correspond, and through Sulzbach Eric Henderson developed other friendships, one of the strongest being with Kurt Schwedersky. Over the next few years, Henderson visited the Schwedersky family on several occasions, and the Schwederskys visited Northumberland, staying in the village where Henderson was working and becoming involved with the schoolchildren there.

Schwedersky and Sulzbach both sent tape messages at Christmastime, which Henderson played to the children and their parents. The children, aged 9 to 13 years, wrote their own letters in reply.

Sulzbach also had other contacts with students that were less encouraging. As he told Jack de Manio in a radio interview, almost daily he received letters from schoolchildren, sixth formers, and students asking for pictures and the life history of Hitler. In response, Sulzbach had eventually written a standard reply:

> The German Embassy should like to inform you that it does neither possess such material nor would wish to distribute it because it does not want to be party to the possible glorification of Hitler.

As Sulzbach emphasized, 'my fight is to try to convince the British people that the new Germany is there to stay.'

The press office at the embassy was busy during the 1970s correcting many such distortions and stereotypes of Germans that were still present in the British media, and Sulzbach was a good contact person for journalists and filmmakers. Never slow to express his opinion, he was interviewed on British and German radio and television, and frequently appeared in letters and articles in both countries. As he wrote to the producer of the *Dick Emery Show* in September 1976:

GERMAN EMBASSY, LONDON. BUILDING BRIDGES

> Why – in 1976 – ridicule everything German? These films or scripts are out of date and create the old animosity. We have to work for friendship and not for the contrary.

He was as ready to comment on the 'impartial documentaries' as he was on the comedies. The day after viewing a Panorama programme, *Blind Eye to Murder* in December 1978, he wrote to the producer:

> The documentary certainly was good, impressive and at the same time terrible – because every decent German would agree with most of what you said and showed. Yet, of course, damaging to my own cause – my work of reconciliation between our two countries – as the primitive viewer will generalise: Germans are bad, will ever be bad, and do NOT regret or want to see their past.

A significant television programme that was aired in the late 1970s was *Holocaust*. After the abusive reactions to the embassy from the earlier Panorama programme, Sulzbach was keen to set the film in context, and suggested to the journalist and broadcaster Ludovic Kennedy that he manage a 'post-viewing debate' as a balance. Some years later, Kennedy spoke about Herbert's relationship with the media:

> Hardly a month went by in all of the fifteen years [that I knew him] without him writing or telephoning or sending a sheaf of press cuttings to jog my elbow about a possible interview or film or article or introduction that would help forward his lifetime's task of bringing the British and German people closer together. His enthusiasm and good nature and, indeed, love meant that one inevitably found oneself doing – or rather trying to do, because Herbert never fully understood the exigencies of journalism – what he wanted.

In the same month that *Holocaust* was screened, Herbert Sulzbach was awarded the European Cross of Peace, on 6 October 1978. On Remembrance Day in the same year, sixty years after the end of the First World War, the *Daily Telegraph* published an article by Sulzbach under the heading, *Looking back without anger*. This long article was on the leader page of the paper in a prominent position, and the ambassador sent a memo about it to Bonn, in which he noted that:

> It is hitherto unparalleled that an important British newspaper should publish an article by a German on this particular day.

Having so many lasting contacts, in particular with circles aloof from the embassy, Sulzbach was an extremely useful contact for all his colleagues in the media and cultural departments of the embassy. Rainer Dobbelstein remembered that when he arrived in the cultural department of the embassy, he 'turned time and again to Sulzbach because he had lots of contacts. His role [at that particular time] was really in bridge-building and having all these contacts.'

Herbert Sulzbach retired on 30 April 1981, aged 87, after thirty years work at the German Embassy in London. Tributes were paid to him by many of his friends, colleagues, and work contacts and these were printed and presented to him bound into book form. *The Times* reported his retirement under the heading *The Healer*, which many of his colleagues found particularly fitting. They had learned not only to appreciate the skill with which Sulzbach had healed so many of the emotional wounds of war, and enabled people from two countries to engage in meaningful discussions with each other, but also the sensitivity and urbanity that he had brought to this role.

Many friends and colleagues agreed with the journalist who wrote of Sulzbach:

> You remember when countries were on opposite sides and you know that what really matters is friendship and real understanding which is what you have in plenty. So, it's absurd to imagine you actually retiring, because you will never retire from understanding people and countries.

A reception was held at the embassy for his retirement farewell. Amongst the guests were four ex-PoWs, all of whom had become firm friends with Sulzbach. In his speech, one of them – Engelbert Hoppe – described, movingly and with passion, the immense impact that Herbert had had on his life:

GERMAN EMBASSY, LONDON. BUILDING BRIDGES

My thoughts go back – as they have done so often – to Featherstone Park, where, as one of the youngest prisoners of war, I met Herbert Sulzbach in 1946. I was twenty years young, desperate and humiliated, as were many of my comrades, by what had caused the German nation's downfall, and connected with it the unbelievable and terrible things that proved to be true. The steady change of heart at Camp 18, with more than 4,000 German officers, became the great task of Herbert Sulzbach.

He convinced us that he would not and could not forget about Nazi Germany, but at the same time was willing to strive with us for a better Germany, a better relationship with Britain and the peoples of the world.

On behalf of thousands of ex-prisoners of war whose hearts and minds you touched, some of my fellow prisoners and myself have come to say a mere "Thank you, Captain. Sir, thank you so much".

Herbert Sulzbach was awarded the Order of the British Empire (OBE) on 31 December 1981. Remembering the German Grand Cross of Merit that he had received ten years earlier, the British Ambassador to Germany wrote to him:

It is very fitting that you should now wear both German and British honours on your breast. I hope that it may be some reward to you to know that the Anglo-German reconciliation is as near complete as these things can be in our imperfect world.

Sulzbach attended the investiture at Buckingham Palace in March with his niece. Beate was by then seriously ill with dementia and unable to accompany him. He was very impressed with the ceremony – 'the DIGNITY, tradition and ceremony; just unbeatable' – but he was almost overwhelmed by Beate's illness, and that year was an exceptionally sad time for him.

On 6 May Beate was taken into hospital and Herbert visited her daily, 'for 198 days', until she died on 25 November 1982. He was pleased that she continued to recognise him, smiled at him, and often said 'Wonderful!' But he was desolated by her death, telling Ian Angus that

'I cannot grasp it and there is no consolation after sixty years of marriage and sixty years of love.' He continued to attend receptions and events at the embassy, where he felt 'only a little bit distracted from sadness and grief.' Beate was buried in Hampstead Cemetery in north London and Herbert ordered a white Carrara marble headstone for her grave, 'to the dear memory of my unforgettable and beloved wife.'

Even when he had retired from the embassy, Sulzbach maintained links with his friends who were promoting Anglo-German friendship. For Christmas 1982, Sulzbach's message to the children at Eric Henderson's school ended with the words:

> Try to work for peace amongst mankind, think and work for others and it will give a purpose to life. God bless you and my good friend Eric Henderson.

As well as maintaining his links with schools and young people, Sulzbach continued to be involved with radio and television programmes. His objective remained to promote the message of Anglo-German friendship and reconciliation, and he did so tirelessly. Often this corresponded with the media producers' objectives, but when his aspirations were not met Sulzbach was bitterly disappointed.

For example, he had spent considerable time, effort and emotional energy working with a team on a two-part documentary called *Jailed by the British*, which was aired in February 1983. The first part focussed on the internment of 'enemy aliens' in the 1940s, and the second on German PoWs of the Second World War. The producers intended:

> ...to show the fierce prejudices and misconceptions which existed at the time and the way in which far greater understanding was achieved often in spite of governments and the military machine.

Sulzbach felt positive about the first instalment, but when the second documentary was shown he was furious. He felt insulted by the portrayal of his work with PoWs, and let the producers know his feelings in angry letters littered with capital letters and underscoring.

Many of his friends, and several influential people, responded to his call for support:

GERMAN EMBASSY, LONDON. BUILDING BRIDGES

'My greatest criticism is the failure of the film to show that reconciliation is alive and well,' wrote Eric Henderson.

'If I had known what would be the outcome of all the filming I would never have been prepared to help you,' said Kurt Schwedersky.

'Surely the main point of the whole operation was that it was one of the seed-beds of future democracy in Germany, which has proved so strong,' was the response of the historian and author Matthew Sullivan.

A collaboration with happier results was a radio programme that was aired for Remembrance Day 1983. *The Black and the Grey* told the story of PoWs at Comrie. It included a recording of Sulzbach reading *In Flanders Field* – the poem that he had shared with the prisoners almost forty years earlier at Comrie. A reviewer in *The Guardian* commented that the programme made him 'think about our changing attitudes. Sulzbach and his colleagues had a difficult and painful task, and his faith in the possibilities and the importance of re-education gave him and his colleagues a steadfast moral purpose.'

But one of the most joyful occasions for Sulzbach in the last years of his life was his inclusion in the final Old Contemptibles' Parade at a church in Ipswich in August 1984. He was invited as the special guest of these British veterans of the First World War in an act of reconciliation. The church organisers hoped to make this final event 'a more impressive occasion altogether' than previous occasions. 'We will sing the hymn *Glorious Things of Thee are Spoken* to the German National Anthem in honour of your presence with us,' wrote the vicar. 'After the hymn, we plan to have an "act of friendship and reconciliation". What we hope you will agree to is to come forward with Chum Clegg for the shaking of hands and exchange of gifts.'

Sulzbach asked Eric Henderson whether he should wear his Iron Cross or his OBE. 'Both', suggested Henderson, but in the event Sulzbach wore all his medals and glowed with pride and happiness.

> It was an occasion which went far beyond all my expectations. It was all incredibly moving, and I was proud to be there. How could I have imagined seventy years ago, as I fought against the British, that one day I would be welcomed as a friend?

Only a few months after this enjoyable occasion, Sulzbach became unwell and in April 1985 he was admitted to the King Edward Ward of the Royal Free Hospital in London. At the end of June, he wrote a note to Eric Henderson, 'Thanks dear Eric for postcard from Scotland. I don't feel well. Love, H.'

He died from lung cancer a few days later, on 5 July 1985. Condolences poured in from around the world.

Sulzbach had wanted 'a simple funeral' and to be buried alongside his wife. This took place at Hampstead Cemetery in London on 15 July 1985 and was attended by his niece and a few close friends, including Eric Henderson, Ludovic Kennedy and Kurt Schwedersky. A few months later, a memorial commemoration was held on Tuesday 5 November 1985 at the German Embassy. Ambassador Baron Rüdiger von Wechmar welcomed the many guests, and addresses were given by Sir Bernard Braine, Ludovic Kennedy and Bernard Levin. At the close, Yaltah Menuhin Ryce played Felix Mendelssohn-Bartholdy's *Variations sérieuses* on the piano.

The ambassador spoke of how:

> Herbert Sulzbach, an officer of the Kaiser and a king in two world wars, became an officer of peace. Neither Herbert Sulzbach nor his cause will ever be forgotten by this embassy. *Herbert Sulzbach hat sich um sein Vaterland verdient gemacht* [Herbert Sulzbach has rendered outstanding services to his homeland].

Herbert Sulzbach had indeed profoundly affected many people and lives. As one ex-PoW mourned, 'Herbert, who saved us from despair, and gave us back belief in fellow humans and human dignity, is gone for ever. But I'll never forget him.' The colleague who had arrived at the embassy as a young butler treasured the memory that 'Mr Sulzbach was a grand person to know. You didn't work with him; you lived with him. He had this kind of richness inside himself.'

There were also many who felt that 'the Sulzbach spirit' could not die with him. Thinking of their joint involvement with the schoolchildren in Northumberland, Kurt Schwedersky was comforted to recognise that 'I myself could visit a school in Northumberland and speak to the pupils about the Sulzbach spirit. It is so consoling to know that Herbert Sulzbach has set in action something which will be continued beyond his death.'

GERMAN EMBASSY, LONDON. BUILDING BRIDGES

Kurt Schwedersky, Engelbert Hoppe and Eric Henderson – with others – all wanted 'the Sulzbach spirit' to continue into future generations. Apart from bringing up their families and future schoolchildren to engage in friendship and reconciliation anywhere in the world, they had already – before Herbert Sulzbach died – moved to perpetuate the ideals that he held.

On the gatepost of the former prisoner of war camp at Featherstone Castle they fixed a plaque recording Herbert Sulzbach and his work there. It was done in the name of the Featherstone Park Association – which had itself been the inspiration of Herbert Sulzbach. Without the association, and the plaque, this journey through Herbert Sulzbach's life might never have been written.

Chapter 10

Düsseldorf, Germany. Staying Friends

Formation of the Featherstone Park Association

Herbert Sulzbach's success in his work with PoWs had convinced him that Germans who had been held prisoner by the British were in a unique position to further post-war friendship and reconciliation. Even as the gates at Featherstone Park finally closed in May 1948, he had maintained that 'there are no better envoys for peace and understanding than the German PoWs who have been in this country.'

For the prisoners themselves, their captivity remained forever an intensely significant part of their lives. They wrote in their thousands to Herbert Sulzbach after their repatriation to try to explain, all echoing the same feelings that this ex-PoW expressed:

> The years of captivity were years of a great experience, which I should not like to have missed. You showed us the way to contemplation, tolerance and world-wide thinking, and I would be very glad if I could keep in contact with you even after the closing of the camp.

Herbert Sulzbach added the names of his correspondents to his formidable list of contacts and during his period of duty on the Berlin airlift he used every opportunity to renew contact with ex-PoWs nearby. As early as August 1948 he arranged a meeting at the Rabs-Keller in Hamburg with fifteen ex-PoWs, including Herbert Schmitt, who had been one of his many clerks at Featherstone Park and who now worked as a journalist in Frankfurt. This time he invited two radio journalists from the BBC and the local German radio station. He told his wife that 'it was a grand meeting.'

It had not been easy for most ex-PoWs after their repatriation. Not only had they faced the need to restructure family life, but also their

DÜSSELDORF, GERMANY. STAYING FRIENDS

destroyed country was under occupation and they had not been able to be part of the immediate post-war rebuilding since they had been in captivity. But their experience at Featherstone Park helped them to remain hopeful. A prisoner, who had worked as one of Sulzbach's clerks at Featherstone Park, had written from Germany to a British national paper shortly before the camp had closed in 1948 saying that 'Captain Sulzbach, by his conduct towards us, gave us a perfect example of a humanitarian. The seed sown in Camp 18 will bear its fruit, of that there is no doubt.'

Throughout the busy, lonely and depressing year of 1949, during which Sulzbach travelled around Europe looking for employment, he also worked towards his goal of creating a confederation of ex-PoWs. He was most active in Germany, but he also wanted to involve people in America. His ideal was a worldwide organisation that would build friendship and reconciliation out of people's traumatic wartime experiences.

Throughout that year he met with as many ex-PoWs (whom he now considered 'friends' or 'guests') as possible. At the beginning of that year he had met with a small number of them in Frankfurt. The meeting had been a great success, with Sulzbach noting that, 'all of them had said that they would not have wanted to miss their time in Camp 18, and that many people wrote to them saying, "Oh, if only I had been a PoW"!'

He learnt that there were many more ex-PoWs living in the vicinity, including 'the charming oldest, 67-year-old Colonel von Lindeiner-Wildau.' Sulzbach called him and was touched by the colonel's pleasure and emotion. The two men arranged to meet at Sulzbach's guesthouse.

Later in the year, when Sulzbach needed to go to Bremen as part of his business negotiations, he – as usual – wanted to organise a meeting with local ex-PoWs and asked Helmut Hohnholz, another of the men who had worked as a clerk for him at Featherstone Park, to make the arrangements.

It was clear to both Sulzbach and many of the ex-PoWs that these networks could be enlarged to create something far more enduring and significant. Sulzbach had been pleased when an article in the *Basler Nachrichten* in 1947 had stated that, 'at Featherstone Park they have made a cell of reconstruction'. He had always hoped that this cell would expand, and its members play an influential part in the reconstruction of the new Germany. Whilst it was not unusual for groups of ex-soldiers to get together to reminisce, sing marching songs and swill beer, Sulzbach's group would have a very different purpose.

Back in London, he made his plans, and in July 1950 he invited about fifty ex-PoWs to a meeting in Falkenstein in Taunus, Germany. He advertised it through newspapers in Britain and Germany and also had an open letter published in *Picture Post*, receiving several calls and letters from interested people.

The meeting was scheduled for 3 September 1950, and it was probably no coincidence that this date marked eleven years since the outbreak of war. Herbert Sulzbach left London a week beforehand and toured the biggest newspapers and radio stations in Germany giving interviews about his project. The political editors of several German and American newspapers attended the meeting and reported favourably about it the following day. Sulzbach wrote his own account, and sent a copy to his wife:

> Ex-PoWs came from all parts of Germany. A First Lieutenant drove from Wiesbaden and bellowed into the hall, "I can't wait any longer to see our captain again!" An elderly couple came from Lower Taunus and the man told me that he had only come to shake my hand and to thank me for what I had done for his PoW son who had chosen to remain in England.

He received letters from all over Germany and a number of ex-PoWs who were unable to attend sent greetings and best wishes. One wrote that as a teacher he used Sulzbach's teachings about three or four times a week when he talked with his pupils.

Reginald Sorensen MP, whom Sulzbach had known since 1947, gave the main speech and the English and French visitors were 'deeply impressed with the spirit of the meeting'.

As Herbert told Beate, 'the English and French who were present were deeply impressed with the spirit of my friends. The elderly Colonel von Lindeiner-Wildau, who had once been commandant of Stalag Luft III – a PoW camp for RAF officers – before becoming a prisoner at Featherstone, gave a speech on behalf of the ex-PoWs. And one participant at the meeting was a young RAF flight lieutenant who had been shot down over Berlin in 1943 and been a PoW under von Lindeiner-Wildau.'

DÜSSELDORF, GERMANY. STAYING FRIENDS

A German writer wrote to Sulzbach, commenting on his suggestion for international meetings of PoWs, saying that 'with this good idea you show a new way for a peaceful direction in a politically restless time, and the promotion of a European exchange of ideas.'

In his diary, after the meeting, Sulzbach remembered that when Camp 18 had closed, he had written to General Heim saying, '*es hat sich gelohnt*' ['it has been worthwhile']. After the success of this reunion he felt able to reaffirm: 'It has!'

On his return to England he wrote to the *Manchester Guardian* giving details of the meeting, pointing out that it had been held 'within the first congress of the World Club, an organisation aiming at promoting friendship between people of all nations.'

Repeating his belief that former prisoners would be the best envoys for peace and understanding, he claimed justification in the numbers who attended 'from all parts of Germany' who – with visitors from Britain and France – were 'eager to help to work for the great cause of friendship.'

He announced his intention of organising 'a bigger international prisoner-of-war meeting next year and I should like to appeal now for greater support by anyone and any organisation agreeing with my ideas. Surely, we ought to encourage democratic-minded Germans, of whom there really are far more than is generally assumed.'

Over the following few years such meetings were repeated, and during this time many of the ex-PoWs moved into senior and influential positions in Germany – in administration, in the Foreign Office, in the economy and in industry. Sulzbach himself was given his position at the new German Consulate in London and used his many ex-PoW contacts in Germany to good effect.

Sulzbach was made acutely aware of the special atmosphere amongst these men when he attended a reunion of ex-PoWs from Featherstone Park in October 1957. It had been organised in Düsseldorf by one of the group, Peter Hehn, and Sulzbach recollected that about fifty men attended – amongst whom he 'saw so much loyalty, friendship, camaraderie, and gratitude. The men did not talk about the usual war memories but instead were full of admiration for the country that they had wanted to defeat.'

Several ex-PoWs remained enthusiastic that an association should be formed to continue to promote the ideals that they had inherited from Camp 18. In June 1960 they met in the Malkasten restaurant in Düsseldorf to discuss the founding of the new association. Two years later, the organisation and legal work were completed and on 14 November 1962 the *Arbeitskreis Featherstone Park* (Featherstone Park Association) was entered in the legal register at Düsseldorf. The executive committee was named as Peter Hehn (marketing director, Düsseldorf), Kurt Schwedersky (county judge, Düsseldorf), and Wolf-Dietrich Heimann (buyer, Frankfurt am Main). Herbert Sulzbach was to be the association's honorary president.

Sulzbach had worked indefatigably to gather influential support for the new association and as a result its list of patrons included Sir Ivone Kirkpatrick, Captain Sir Basil Liddell Hart, Reginald Sorensen MP, John Burns Hynd MP, Fred Bellenger MP, Sir Harold Nicolson, Yehudi Menuhin, Benjamin Britten, Victor Gollancz, Professor Norman Bentwich OBE, and Lord Longford (formerly Lord Pakenham).

Membership of the association was open to former PoWs of Featherstone Park and its aim was the nurturing and improvement of the relationship between Germany and Britain through personal contact, mutual instruction, and the promotion of reciprocal understanding. The association was to be based in Düsseldorf.

Sulzbach used his charisma and his contacts to gain support and positive reporting from both British and German journalists – in Britain and in Germany. Terence Prittie, at the time West German correspondent for the *Manchester Guardian*, remembered becoming involved in the early days:

> Herbert took me to one of his annual meetings of the *Featherstone Park Kreis* [Featherstone Park Circle]. I was struck by three features; there was an instinctive "camaraderie" among the participants, they discussed their problems with sober objectivity, and there was an underlying but palpable friendliness towards Britain. Some of the German ex-prisoners brought their children along; so, this was an association with a real future.

He sent his report to the *Manchester Guardian*, in which he noted that nearly a hundred former German prisoners of war from Camp 18 at Featherstone Park in Northumberland had attended the meeting in Düsseldorf to discuss whether Germany was today 'facing its past' and to

DÜSSELDORF, GERMANY. STAYING FRIENDS

examine the possibilities of contributing towards a better understanding between Germany and Britain. He wrote:

> Here was a normal cross-section of views, which contrasted strongly with the former Nazi indoctrination. The German community was progressing towards an understanding of past mistakes and crimes, and towards an essential self-awareness. Members of the association have already been active in developing personal contact at all levels, in writing newspaper articles and letters to the press, and in putting forward proposals for bettering Anglo-German relations. It is an interesting thought that these men look back to their time at Featherstone Park with pride, even with gratitude.

The very first meeting of the newly formed association was held on Saturday 29 October 1960. It was anticipated in the English press, where one newspaper noted the organisation's 'unique testimony to British decency and tolerance'. Reporters recognised that the setting-up of the association was centred on Herbert Sulzbach, whose life seemed to encapsulate the contradictions and confusions that Germany evoked throughout the world at that time. Reporting on the election of Sulzbach as the group's honorary president, one journalist drew attention to the remarkable honour that German officers had bestowed on a man who was both a Jew and a Briton – an honour that reflected their respect for someone who had helped them through a very dark time of captivity.

Many of the ex-PoWs were now attending the meeting as influential participants in the 'new Germany' – as members of the West German parliament, eminent judges, and businessmen. With their liberty and prosperity restored, these former prisoners reviewed their time in Featherstone Park with deep appreciation. By making their experiences there as widely known as possible, they hoped to foster Anglo-German understanding: this was the main aim of the new organisation.

The theme of the speeches in Düsseldorf was 'Surmounting the past to achieve Anglo-German Friendship'. Two hundred ex-PoWs had been located and contacted by the date of the meeting, and 130 managed to attend. Henry Faulk and Herbert Sulzbach were greeted with stormy applause and shouts of approval, and ex-prisoners shook their hands continuously.

Sulzbach was absolutely delighted with the event and eventually got to bed at 2 am. On the following day, he and the main speakers met for lunch.

Press reports after the event were favourable. The *Birmingham Post* reported Peter Hehn's welcome to Herbert Sulzbach and Henry Faulk as 'the ones who helped us regain our balance after the war by the noble way they treated us, not as Nazis but as humans'.

An article in the *Manchester Guardian* commented that, 'it is true that ex-servicemen of different nations have met before to talk of reconciliation. But in this case, it looks as if the forward-looking experiment of Camp 18 has had more lasting and positive results.'

The format for the first meeting was one that served the association well for several years. Speakers were invited and on this first occasion the German historian and journalist Professor Michael Freund from the University of Kiel traced his country's bad press in Britain back to the naval challenge of Wilhelm II. Discussion followed, and while the ex-PoWs deplored press distortions, they were ready not only to admit the errors and the crimes of their country's past but also to criticise aspects of its present.

A British journalist from the *Daily Telegraph* reported that, 'most impressive of all to the outsider was the sense of dedication that shone through everything that was said. The ex-prisoners were aware of the cynicism they were likely to meet in their task and were anxious to avoid a false idealism or sentimentality. Messages from patrons of the group were full of warm good wishes for its success. No reasonable observer would wish it less.'

When the journalist and broadcaster Bernard Levin spoke at the annual meeting a few years later, in 1969, he addressed the continuing gulf between Britain and Germany, concerned that such attitudes 'prevent understanding and friendship.'

But he, like Sulzbach, was encouraged when he looked to the younger members of his country:

> Young people are growing up now who seem to have no trace of the anti-German feelings with which their parents and grandparents grew up. If the young people in Britain today are no longer interested in the quarrels of their fathers and grandfathers, then it means that in time the hostility

towards Germany will die away completely. We have got to start thinking of ourselves, all of us, as Europeans.

Sulzbach was proud of the quality of speakers who addressed the meetings at Düsseldorf. He trawled through his contacts book to find sympathetic members of parliament from Britain, political representatives in Germany, prominent journalists and broadcasters from both countries, members of the legal profession and the armed forces, and other eminent personalities who were watching European events.

When Peter Hehn died in July 1964 as a result of a traffic accident, Kurt Schwedersky took over his role, and Hermann Ziock became a member of the committee. At that time, Schwedersky was greatly occupied as an investigating judge collecting witness statements against former SS guards accused of complicity in the murder of 700,000 Jews at Treblinka concentration camp.

Schwedersky's first task was to arrange the speaker for the annual meeting and that year he invited Terence Prittie who had been the *Guardian* correspondent in Bonn for sixteen years. Sulzbach and Schwedersky both assiduously cultivated their relationships with members of the press, who were always invited in large numbers to the meetings in Düsseldorf. They usually had a very positive response. A typical report in 1967 commented that in a world that longs for peace, there seemed little comfort in a reunion that had been arranged for a hundred former officers of Hitler's Wehrmacht. On the contrary, the journalist looked forward to the evening in Düsseldorf the following month as one of the most remarkable post-war reunions ever to be held: 'a meeting of hope and sanity.'

Those who attended the meetings – the ex-PoWs – were now judges, bankers and diplomats, and in many other positions to influence German thought. Whenever an anti-British letter appeared in a German newspaper, Sulzbach could be sure that one of them would immediately reply to it.

And Kurt Schwedersky was in no doubt about their motivation. He knew that for so many of the men who had been held captive at Featherstone Park, Herbert Sulzbach had left them 'with a deep impression of the meaning of freedom and the determination that the new Germany would incorporate that freedom.' In Germany they wanted to continue to meet to make sure that those lessons would never be forgotten. As he told a journalist, 'every one of us today is a firm friend of Britain.'

The speaker invited for 1967 was Desmond Donnelly, the Labour MP for Pembroke since 1950. He was also a personal friend of the German Ambassador in London at the time, Herbert Blankenhorn, whose son had both worked in a kibbutz in Israel and also stayed with the Donnellys in Wales. When Sulzbach wrote to Schwedersky with this information, he also asked him:

> Do you think that it would be a good idea or not if I invited Gunther d'Alquen to the meeting in October?

D'Alquen had been a prisoner at Featherstone Park for only a few weeks. He was an ex-SS *Standartenführer* – a senior member of the Nazi party – and the chief editor of *Das Schwarze Korps*, the SS weekly, to whom Sulzbach had written his barbed critique of their 'obituary' of Czechoslovakia in 1938. Sulzbach felt that he had subsequently been able to influence Gunther d'Alquen – even though his stay at Featherstone Park had been so brief – and afterwards d'Alquen had often written to him. When d'Alquen was being investigated for war crimes at Nuremberg he wrote to Sulzbach, thanking him because, 'in the bitter discrepancy between theory and practice you forced me to a real respect.'

During August 1948 – while he was working on the Berlin airlift – Sulzbach visited d'Alquen and his wife in Bremen, finding him 'probably one of the most interesting of all the PoW people whom I have come across.'

Aside from considerations of courtesy in discussing this with the secretary, it was unusual for Sulzbach to hesitate with his invitations to ex-PoWs to attend the association's meetings. History does not record whether or not this once powerful and still controversial personality was ever invited or attended.

Sulzbach and Schwedersky were not only firm friends but were also both utterly committed to the ideals of the Featherstone Park Association.

Kurt Schwedersky was very conscious of his personal need to be involved in post-war reconciliation work. On one visit to London he talked with a journalist about his work to bring war criminals to trial: 'It is justice, and it is a warning of what can happen when tolerance goes. I have listened to many Jewish witnesses who suffered, and it is impossible to describe what it feels like when one of them comes up to

DÜSSELDORF, GERMANY. STAYING FRIENDS

you and shakes your hand. It is wonderful that such feelings can survive something so terrible.'

Schwedersky encouraged his children to attend the annual Featherstone Park Association meetings, so that they became unusually conversant with aspects of the Second World War and its aftermath from an early age. His daughter, Regine, remembered that:

> When I was about 12 or 13, I was allowed to go to the meetings. We went to a hotel in Düsseldorf. At this camp [Featherstone Park], they were not all Nazis. They were all party members – but not tough Nazis. They were *Mitläufer* [hangers-on]. But within this group there were very different people. There were people like my father who never had any sympathy for the Nazis, but didn't do anything to resist them, and he suffered from this *Schuldgefühl* [feeling of guilt] for the rest of his life.

The annual meeting of the Featherstone Park Association was mainly for men. It was acknowledged by all involved that Kurt Schwedersky did much of the organising but 'Herbert was always the one who brought people together.' He was seen as a symbol of German-British relationships and as a natural focus – being halfway between Britain and Germany. Sulzbach gave optimism and inspiration to the association. The Schwedersky family were also generous hosts to the meeting, inviting the main speakers and guests to their home for breakfast on the morning afterwards.

Bernard Levin, at that time a columnist of the *Daily Mail*, was the main speaker at the 1969 meeting. In his speech he addressed the 'special dimension of misunderstanding' that he felt existed 'between Germany and Britain, between Britain and Germany'. This was at the height of the 'Cold War'.

Even though he saw 'a particular quality of mistrust that goes deeper and is more difficult to eradicate than the usual trivial prejudices that exist between all countries', he also saw 'hopeful tendencies. We are moving into an era when a higher loyalty than to our country is needed. A new partnership is needed. We must work together to build a peaceful, prosperous and united Europe, in which Germans and British will be equal partners.'

When Henry Faulk came to write his account of the re-education of German PoWs in Britain, he analysed the psychological effect of the experiences of men such as those who attended the Featherstone Park Association meetings. He recognised that there existed amongst repatriated PoWs 'a widespread sense of being a closed group with a group purpose.' Although they returned to Germany as individuals, they felt themselves to be members of a group that was 'better capable of rebuilding the homeland' – and, in comparison with the civilian population, were 'the spiritually stronger, the more hopeful, the keener to rebuild a new and better world.'

This was recognised as not altogether a good thing by some observers, such as Neal Ascherson, who was a journalist for the *Observer* in post-war Germany. He remarked on the Featherstone Park circle as being 'ferociously loyal to each other, and to Herbert, and fearfully proud of themselves – and this didn't make them terribly popular in Germany.'

Ascherson attended several of the annual meetings and remembered that a coach full of schoolchildren – who had had a four-hour journey – attended the one in 1974.

Considering Sulzbach's energetic pursuit of reconciliation in the face of noticeable opposition, Ascherson remarked that:

> He was up against the whole British establishment who said that he'd got it wrong, that these ex-PoWs were incorrigible. Yes, he was naïve. If he hadn't been naïve, he wouldn't have been able to do what he did. It is true that there was a certain type of scepticism among the experienced, hard-boiled correspondents about Sulzbach. He was absolutely tireless in picking one up, protesting about something the *Observer* had said, or hadn't said.
>
> At the meetings, he endlessly circulated, always immaculately dressed, with his charming smile and blue eyes. He was a great manipulator, but a manipulator for the good – a kind of malicious little saint. He was extraordinary.

Publicity from press coverage often put Sulzbach back in touch with ex-PoWs. In the late 1970s, he received a letter addressed to: 'Herbert Sulzbach, ex Army Officer, c/o the village cop (ex-PoW guard), Haltwhistle, on the South Tyne.'

DÜSSELDORF, GERMANY. STAYING FRIENDS

It was written in perfect English by an ex-prisoner from a different camp who had learned that a policeman at Haltwhistle had once been a German PoW who had afterwards chosen to remain in England. The letter was forwarded to the embassy by the post office in Newcastle. The writer wanted to know whether it was possible for him to join the association or whether membership was restricted to 'ex-inmates of Featherstone Park.'

The Düsseldorf meeting on 29 October 1980 was the twenty-first since the association's foundation. It was also the last meeting prior to Sulzbach's retirement from the embassy, which had been planned for the following April. Sir Oliver Wright, the British Ambassador to Bonn, and Dr Jürgen Ruhfus, the German Ambassador to London, were special guests. Two days earlier, on 27 October, the British Ambassador in Bonn had given a celebratory lunch in honour of Sulzbach, also inviting Staatssekretär van Well (himself an ex-PoW of Featherstone), Dr Ruhfus, and Karl-Günther von Hase, a previous ambassador to London.

The ex-PoWs who attended the annual meetings of the Featherstone Park Association understood how much they owed to Herbert Sulzbach. They recognised that it was unusual for officers who had been prisoners of war to meet again twelve years after their release to form an association that had the aim of continuing friendship between earlier enemies – out of gratitude towards the country that had kept them prisoner, and towards 'a hundred percent non-Aryan German', as Herbert Sulzbach described himself. It was an irony that he fully appreciated.

Members and friends of the association at this time were considering how they could best show this appreciation of Sulzbach with some permanence. Matthew Barry Sullivan, author of *Thresholds of Peace*, which includes an account of Sulzbach's work at Camp 18, wrote to Schwedersky suggesting 'a stone by the banks of the Tyne', which would have 'a few appropriate words about this seedbed of Anglo-German reconciliation.'

Schwedersky approved of the idea and discussed it with Sulzbach, who suggested Eric Henderson as a well-placed local contact to give help with practical details, since he was a resident of Northumberland. Both Schwedersky and Henderson liked the idea of commissioning a stone in memory of the beginning of reconciliation, instead of the more conventional memorial of a war or battle, but they needed the local Haltwhistle people's agreement. In this they were helped by the owner of Featherstone Castle, John Clark, who was sympathetic and helpful. Clark, and the owner of the neighbouring parkland on which Camp 18 had once stood, were unsure about the wisdom of a large monument but they suggested that a plaque could be built into one of the old stone pillars at the gate entrance to what had once been the camp. John Clark offered to be responsible for any maintenance to the pillar and plaque and noted how much recent interest (in 1981) there had been in the existence of the old PoW camp. The parish council gave its approval, and Eric Henderson set about finding a stone mason to create the plaque.

Kurt Schwedersky travelled to Northumberland at the end of April 1982 for a few days as ITV sent a film crew to report on the unveiling of the plaque and the story behind it. Herbert Sulzbach, Henry Faulk, Engelbert Hoppe and Eric Henderson were also there when the plaque was unveiled on 29 April 1982. The final wording on the plaque read:

> Here was the entrance to POW Camp 18 where thousands of German officers were held in the years 1945 – 48. The interpreter since January 1946 was Captain Herbert Sulzbach OBE who dedicated himself to making this camp a seedbed of British-German reconciliation. Our two nations owe him heartfelt thanks. The friends and members of the Featherstone Park Association of former inmates of Camp 18 1982

In a speech at the plaque, Schwedersky said of Sulzbach:

> It was a long journey that you began here more than thirty-six years ago, but every journey which will lead to reconciliation after years of war and animosity or even hate is a long one. In the same way it needs a great deal of time if you want to get a seedling out of a seedbed, and if you wish the seedling to grow up to a real tree. I think one can speak now of a real tree in connection with the idea of reconciliation.

Later that year, Eric Henderson was invited as a special guest to the October meeting of the Featherstone Park Association in Düsseldorf. The speaker was Dr J. Nimtz, chief editor of the *Frankfurter Neue Presse*

DÜSSELDORF, GERMANY. STAYING FRIENDS

who had earlier been the correspondent for that paper in London for twelve years. Henderson was particularly impressed by the participation of two men engaged in earnest conversation together. One was a short man, a Dutch Jew – Herr Weisbeker – who had survived three years in Auschwitz and had attended the association's meetings since their inception as an expression of reconciliation. The other was a tall man with a military bearing who bent low to converse with Weisbeker. This was one of Herbert Sulzbach's 'most trusted' PoWs – Major Herbert Christiansen of the SS.

By October 1983, numbers at the association's meetings had begun to dwindle as the members grew older. Sulzbach himself was nearly 90 years old, and the administration of the association was a huge job for Schwedersky, who had retired some years earlier from his work as a judge.

It was decided to close the Featherstone Park Association at its twenty-fourth meeting on 29 October 1983. About forty to fifty ex-PoWs attended from all parts of the republic, and there were also many friends, making altogether about ninety people. The guest speaker was Professor H. Koch, head of the history department at the University of York – the former leader of a Hitler youth patrol who had contacted Sulzbach in the 1970s when he had had the opportunity to continue reading Sulzbach's First World War published diaries.

While there was sadness at the closure, there was also a feeling of accomplishment. The association had achieved what it had set out to do.

Less than two years after the final meeting, and immediately after Sulzbach's death, the chairman of the Anglo-German Association wrote to the German Ambassador to London:

> Herbert Sulzbach's very life seemed devoted to the cause of Anglo-German friendship and his tireless efforts in this field are so well known and well chronicled that it would be difficult to pick out any one of his many accomplishments. Perhaps we may be allowed to highlight the Featherstone Park Association. It was special to him – something unique, so very successful, and always to be cherished in association with his name.

Chapter 11

Everywhere. Reconciliation

Many German officers who were PoWs at Featherstone Park between 1946 and 1948 gave gifts to local English people during their time there. These were given as tokens of a new friendship, with a wish for mutual understanding, as well as in thanks for hospitality shared with strangers in difficult times.

The Dixon family living at Featherstone Castle was given, 'a beautifully carved, very detailed, replica of the Holy Family. It was made from the bottom of a beer barrel and put together with potassium permanganate.' More than sixty years later, the 9-year-old great-grandson of the recipients took this plaque to school for a 'show and tell' session in his classroom. One young boy was keeping friendship alive – and celebrating that gesture of reconciliation – as he talked with his school friends.

Herbert Sulzbach was the man who was largely responsible for the creation of an environment at the PoW camp where ideals of enduring friendship and reconciliation could thrive. Working towards those ideals became Sulzbach's all-consuming passion during the second half of his life. He viewed it as his *Lebensaufgabe* – his 'life's mission'.

People who were caught up in any way with Sulzbach's work recognised that his success stemmed largely from his own character. A German ambassador referred to him as 'the man with a big heart.' A prisoner who had known him well at Featherstone Park realised that he 'gave us a perfect example of a humanitarian.' Terence Prittie, the journalist who had initially been very sceptical of Herbert's enthusiasm for reconciliation, described his great goodness of character as one where Herbert enjoyed devotion, faith, conviction, determination and comradeship.

But these do not convey the extraordinary vitality, even into old age, that Sulzbach displayed. 'There was his impish sense of humour, his boyish enthusiasm,' 'Herbert saturates himself with friendship and is instinctively understanding of all viewpoints,' were some observations from friends and colleagues.

Herbert Sulzbach knew intuitively how to facilitate reconciliation, and in this respect, he was perhaps a man ahead of his time. In his work in the PoW camps at Comrie and Featherstone Park, he had understood that a period of reconsideration and re-appraisal is necessary for everyone involved if reconciliation is the goal. He gave people time to do this themselves – while all the time providing the personal, material and emotional support that was required. He recognised that for post-war 're-education' to be successful, it had to come from within the German nation itself. Time and distance from wartime events would be necessary before anyone could engage critically with these events.

Trusting people and unfamiliar processes had not been easy for German PoWs immediately after the end of the Second World War. It had been a struggle for everyone, but with Sulzbach's help many had found that their initial despair, defiance and humiliation had been given a new direction. In one fairly routine interview with a prisoner at Camp 18, Sulzbach described how the man had been with him for over an hour. He had entered Sulzbach's office 'utterly defiant – but I found him to be a reasonable man.' By the end of the interview, the PoW 'went away relaxed and a changed person. He was no longer boastful or defiant but had become insightful and grateful – without being able to say so.' Afterwards Sulzbach 'wrote him a few lines', which he copied to General Heim. Heim was astounded: 'You've worked a masterpiece there!'

When Sulzbach later came to write about his experiences with German PoWs, he used the illustration that his friend, the poet Ernst Wiechert, had used to try to explain what he thought they faced initially. Wiechert had described how, at the end of the war, Germans had felt as though they were standing in front of a ruined house, seeing the stars above the ruins of the earth. Hearing the rain pouring on the graves of the dead and on the grave of an era, they had felt as lonely as ever a people have been on this earth, and branded much more than ever a nation has been branded.

Sulzbach saw that for reconciliation to be effective everybody involved needed to realise why they were lonely, why they felt branded. They had to face the truth of the situation. With the PoWs, this meant giving them the true facts about the final stages of the war, the truth about the realities of the concentration and extermination camps in Germany, and an objective explanation of the nature of National Socialism.

With the British people and members of the Jewish community, it meant encouraging them to acknowledge the humanity of most German people, and the courageous actions of those Germans who had attempted to resist the Nazis. Despite the barbarity of the National Socialist regime, Sulzbach wanted people to look towards the creative possibilities of reconciliation.

Trying to understand the truth, and actively take part in reconciliation, was a painful process. The truth had not only to be exposed, it had to be discussed and confronted, so that the terrible hurt and losses were brought into the open.

Bernhard Schlink, a German lawyer and author who was born immediately after the Second World War, has described how true understanding includes people putting themselves into another person's place, trying to put themselves into other people's thoughts and feelings, and doing their utmost to view the world through another person's eyes.

Herbert Sulzbach empathised with the German soldiers both intellectually and emotionally, and parts of his own life-history were shared by many of them. He vividly remembered his own days as a young, patriotic soldier during the First World War, so was fatherly towards the young men in his care – even though he disagreed strongly with their notions of patriotism. With the older PoWs he shared memories of a similar cultural heritage and education.

The education that Sulzbach and the older German officers had shared in schools before the First World War had been a product of eighteenth-century Enlightenment in Germany. Having its roots in classical ideas of education, it had laid emphasis on the nurturing of one's inner life and development. This, clearly, was at odds with the closed, authoritative nature of National Socialism and had meant that some of the older officers had struggled to identify with Hitler's ideology. For them, identification with this regime had been more difficult than it had been for the young men who had been brought up and educated solely under Nazi ideology.

His 'favourite Germans' were those who could say openly to him, 'Captain Sulzbach, I am still a Nazi: I have learnt nothing else. Show me something that is better.' Engelbert Hoppe remembered that Sulzbach taught them 'that this twelve-year period in German history was looking at a short period of time, but other periods had created people such as Goethe and Schiller, Beethoven and Haydn.'

He encouraged all the prisoners to not only acknowledge and lament the crimes of the Nazi regime, and their own part in it, but also balance their shame for the recent past with a pride in a previous Germany. Sulzbach's farewell message to them included the words: 'Contribute towards Germany regaining her name as the country of poets and philosophers.'

In mid-1946 Sulzbach was almost overwhelmed on his first reading of *Officers against Hitler*, Fabian von Schlabrendorff's account of wartime resistance amongst German officers towards Hitler – especially when he discovered the names of several fellow soldiers from the First World War whom he had known, and who had been involved in the July 1944 plot against Hitler. He was also awed by the hitherto unknown scale of the resistance.

He began to realise that there had been much more resistance than he had ever suspected – and that it had been activated without the involvement of Jews. He was much encouraged by the knowledge of the organised military resistance, which to him demonstrated the essential goodness of the German character, and therefore the likelihood that Anglo-German unity and reconciliation were achievable goals.

One aspect of Sulzbach's background that was different from that of the PoWs was his Jewishness. He never hid his racial origins, and this deeply impressed the prisoners. They recognised that at a time 'when hate would have been understandable', Sulzbach had instead given them help as well as new hope and confidence. 'He was for us the personification of humanity and tolerance.'

But Sulzbach never found it very easy to persuade other Jews that his view of reconciliation was right, possible or desirable. He tried frequently – and forcefully – to impress upon the members of his local Jewish community in London that they should refrain from generalisations about German people and their wartime behaviour, since he considered this to be as dangerous as the generalisations that had been levelled against the Jews. Many of his fellow Jews sometimes felt that he went too far in his defence but recognised that he was also equally committed to giving voice against anti-Semitic and neo-Nazi incidents in Germany.

Sulzbach was particularly perplexed – and angry – when his views were not accepted by members of his own family. In exasperation and non-comprehension, he reminded his wife of all the non-Jewish Germans they had once known and liked, and who had liked them. 'So, are they exceptions?' he demanded. 'When we lapse into the delusion of making generalisations, of hating, then we are Jewish Nazis!' But he wrote this in September 1946: many people needed much more time to come to terms with recent events.

He was outspoken against such generalisations that allowed people to avoid confronting reality. When he was working at Featherstone Park, he had told the PoWs repeatedly how he had changed his own understanding about Nazis only the previous year, whilst working at Comrie. The prisoners were grateful to him but puzzled. As Engelbert Hoppe said, 'Some people didn't understand him. We couldn't understand. I couldn't understand.'

It was especially difficult for people to embrace Herbert Sulzbach's attitude of empathy, friendship and reconciliation in the immediate post-war years. Other people who were engaged in similar work experienced a parallel response. For example, a few weeks after the bombing of Coventry, and the destruction of the city's cathedral, the provost had stood amongst the ruins and said in a live radio broadcast just before the king's speech on Christmas Day 1940:

> We are trying, hard as it may be, to banish all thoughts of revenge. We are going to try to make a kinder, simpler – a more Christ-like – sort of world in the days beyond this strife.

Very few of the people of Coventry agreed with him.

Sulzbach continued to try to convince people – and he was incredibly persuasive – that reconciliation was the crucial focus. This symbiosis of Jew and German, and of German and British, enabled Sulzbach to see more clearly those things that unite people – and helped him to concentrate on those – rather than the things that divide them. He understood essential connectivity between people as being a vital part of their humanity and he abhorred division. He was utterly convinced of the possibilities of rebuilding friendship between Britain and Germany, and saw this friendship as being redemptive, creative and restorative. 'Somehow these two countries belong together.'

But it was never easy for others to understand what Sulzbach did with his own hurt and anger. They frequently asked him not only how he was able to forgive those who had perpetrated such crimes under National Socialism, but also how he dealt with his own personal pain and anguish. His replies remained consistent: 'one should fight against evil, when another is affected, not oneself!' and as far as hatred was concerned, he had no part in it, frequently asserting that hatred leads to self-destruction.

However, he recognised the need for justice within the reconciliation process. When he was eventually able to renew letter contact with his sister in Germany after the war, he read of her desire for revenge but reminded her that if she wanted to hang all Nazi criminals, she would probably have to hang ten million – and then criminals all over the world. 'The murder of thirteen million civilians was not the deed of just a few.' Although he showed sensitivity and insight in his work with PoWs, he maintained that he was harsh towards anyone he suspected to be a criminal – and reported each one to his London office.

In German, the word *Versöhnung* (reconciliation), was originally related to *verurteilen* (to pass judgement), so being held responsible for a misdeed was also linked to the atonement required to prevent revenge and restore public order. This sense of justice had to permeate all aspects of the new relationships – including individual, group, and civic relationships. Such concepts were also familiar to Kurt Schwedersky, who had worked in legal circles before the war, and who returned to similar work once repatriated. During his time at Featherstone Park, he had come across a book about the extermination camp at Treblinka and wondered at the 'fantasy' of the story. Before long he discovered that the descriptions in the book were no fantasy, and – like many others – his personal shame and guilt were heavy.

He had not been in the Resistance and he had not saved Jewish friends' lives. At Featherstone Park he was able to come to grips with what had happened, with his personal situation and with his guilt. His professional life became dedicated to unravelling war crimes. On his return to Germany, Schwedersky became an investigating judge into wartime atrocities, and some years later it fell to him to interview witnesses all over the world as part of the trial against those responsible for Treblinka. He appreciated that although those responsible had to be brought to trial, this had to happen in a way that was humane and considerate. And this is what he had learned at Featherstone Park – 'that people should treat each other in a humane and considerate manner.'

For reconciliation to be successful and enduring, empathy and understanding need to be translated into concrete democratic terms. Sulzbach was not only idealistic, he was also intensely practical and well organised. At Featherstone Park, he was delighted with the uncensored newspaper that was written by the prisoners, circulated within the camp, and then sent around Britain, and all over Germany. On the anniversary of the paper's first edition, he wrote to the editors congratulating them on 'the spirit which is visible in every edition: the spirit of freedom, openness and honest criticism. Your paper visibly shows the will for positive work and reconstruction.'

At Featherstone Park, orchestras, theatre groups, marionette plays, and choirs travelled to nearby (and fairly distant) venues to meet local people, and to share their interests and hospitality. Such occasions were opportunities for promoting mutual understanding, and for sharing both practically and culturally. They also helped to consolidate and strengthen growing friendships that could lead to further reconciliation. One young observer was very impressed by those PoWs who had formed an orchestra and choir, and at Christmas 1946 been invited by the local Salvation Army to give a concert in Hexham, which she attended. Sixty years later, she remembered her 11-year-old self as being puzzled by these talented, refined men – not at all the jack-booted Nazis she had been expecting.

Groups of prisoners were also invited to visit the civic institutions at Newcastle to see the democratic process at work in the offices, chambers and courts of the city. The prisoners who took part in these excursions enjoyed their discussions with British lawyers and local politicians and they frequently continued the debate until late into the night back in their huts.

Visits to London were also arranged, such as an invitation for three PoWs and Sulzbach to participate in a conference in July 1947. This conference took place over three days and was attended by a cross-section of administrators, academics, politicians and others who were interested and involved in building up the new democratic Germany. There were delegates from both Britain and Germany.

Sulzbach persuaded his wife to meet him and the German PoWs when they arrived in London and suggested that she straight away invite them all to the Sulzbach home for tea and sandwiches. After the end of the conference, Sulzbach suggested another get-together in their home – this time with friends from their Jewish community (most of whom were refugees from Nazi Germany). He had already sent an urgent request to his wife before leaving Featherstone Park: 'call Otto John and invite him for Sunday.'

So, on the Sunday afternoon, three high-ranking German ex-officers met in the London home of Herbert Sulzbach – the Jewish refugee, now a British officer – with his family and their fellow refugee friends. Otto John, a man who had played an active part in the resistance against Hitler, and particularly with the July 1944 assassination plot, was their special guest.

Sulzbach was sure that this was the first time that these particular German officers – now PoWs – had come into contact with a resister. He also knew that it was not only the first time that his Jewish friends had met a German who had resisted Hitler, but it was also the first time that any of them had heard such a full account of the activities of the resistance movement.

This was a particularly ambitious reconciliation meeting. Sulzbach spent the rest of his life arranging formal and informal – and always hospitable – meetings between what sometimes appeared to be unlikely participants. As the editor of Sulzbach's local paper in London wrote to him many years later, 'there are a few rare people for whom life is an opportunity to become involved personally in the sometimes chaotic and tragic world in which we live.'

Sulzbach was glad that after the war he had been able to renew contact, and remain friends with, many of those non-Jewish Germans with whom he had always been on good terms. As he reminded his wife, it had been von Seebach who had first advised him to get out urgently. He understood that many of his friends from years before had felt as conflicted about wartime events in Germany, and their part in it, as did the PoWs he knew.

He clung tenaciously to what he saw as the painful but necessary path to Anglo-German friendship. Even with his celebrated sense of humour, everyone knew that he would never give up on the cause of reconciliation. As an ambassador said of him:

> In his gentlemanly way, he could be stubborn and persistent at times. But when he insisted, he was stubborn for a cause.

One formal expression of the reconciliation process was that of post-war town twinning between Germany and Britain. Engelbert Hoppe, who was so glad to have experienced his captivity in Featherstone Park that he always referred to himself as a 'Prisoner of Peace', initiated one of the first town twinnings. In 1952, he took a group of his adult education students from Germany to England for the town twinning meetings and made arrangements for them to stay with local people in the area. Not all British town councils were prepared to accept twinning with a German town. The list of possibilities in the early 1950s was quite short.

The Featherstone Park Association was not formally constituted until 1961, but Sulzbach had been instrumental in gathering together small groups of ex-PoWs in Germany as early as his first post-war visit to Germany in 1948.

Including children in the meetings of the Featherstone Park Association was welcomed as a sign that reconciliation was being passed down to future generations. Kurt Schwedersky recognised the benefits of his continuing contact with people in England, of being able to send his children to visit English friends, and the resulting more open-minded atmosphere that his children were able to experience.

Reconciliation is clearly 'an endeavour for the long term' and Sulzbach was determined that young people should become part of this endeavour. Schwedersky and Sulzbach wrote regular letters and articles to the children in Eric Henderson's Northumberland school, and sent cassette tapes to be used by the pupils. As late as March 1984, when Sulzbach was 90 years old, he was still in touch with the school and spoke to the senior pupils when he visited there.

Later in 1984, ex-PoW Herbert Schmitt and his wife also visited the school and afterwards revisited the site of the Featherstone Park camp. Schmitt, who had become a close friend of Herbert Sulzbach, was clear on the message that should be passed on to future generations:

> While others were bathing in their war adventures, I was telling my three children only about the senselessness of war, the blood-smeared back side of the shining war medals. I did not and do not feel personally guilty about the cruelties, the mass murder committed in the name of the German people – but I feel deeply ashamed about it. And that is the message that I have passed on to my children.

EVERYWHERE. RECONCILIATION

Schmitt's own contribution to reconciliation had been his involvement in the setting up and maintenance of a free and democratic press in Frankfurt. He was glad to support Eric Henderson's educational initiatives, recognising that they were 'so much more important to our two countries than all the books and TV shows which have been devoted to English-German relations. Telling children about other people living in other lands, having other manners and mores, is such a thrilling yet responsible task.'

Sulzbach had been confident that if he could successfully convince the PoWs of the imperative for reconciliation whilst they were at Featherstone Park, they would carry that message back to Germany on repatriation. But perhaps one of the most significant cases of 'healing' at Featherstone Park was that of Herbert Sulzbach himself. As he told a friend in 1981:

> For me, those years in Northumberland were the most gratifying of my life because my former compatriots gave me faith that there could be another Germany.

Many of the PoW German officers knew that Sulzbach had rediscovered his love of Germany, and the Germans, through his own time at Featherstone Park, and when Engelbert Hoppe gave a speech at the German Embassy in London on Sulzbach's retirement he referred to it:

> At the end of our PoW days in Britain, we left with what we called the Featherstone Park Spirit. Born out of this spirit is the most noble and touching confession of Herbert Sulzbach finding his way back to Germany by and through his prisoners of war.

After Sulzbach's death, Bernard Levin considered the exceptional achievement of his life and work for reconciliation:

> His was an extraordinary life, straddling two infinitely different worlds, with the same human qualities, the same courage, and the same integrity in both. He was a man of two nations, two faiths, two wars, two armies, two careers, and in every one of those categories, the soul of honour in both.

A JEW WHO DEFEATED NAZISM

Those involved in the post-war process of Anglo-German reconciliation recognised that there could be no easy or speedy way of achieving this, and on Sulzbach's death there were many people who voiced their wish that his work should continue to develop. As a journalist, and friend of Herbert Sulzbach, commented:

> The business of reconciliation is an active one. Thousands have been touched by his faith, his courage, and his determination that understanding and forgiveness should triumph in both our countries.

Acknowledgements

The most wonderful and extraordinary part of writing this book has been meeting with people who have wanted to encourage and participate in the telling of Herbert Sulzbach's story. And the more that I have discovered about this man, the more I have realised that this is totally in accordance with the way that he lived his own life – with openness, friendship, integrity, and conviviality.

Clearly, I owe a huge debt of gratitude to Sulzbach's niece, Yvonne Klemperer, who has been extremely generous in sharing her memories, family papers, and her insights. Although a biography of her uncle could have been written without these, it would have been a very different story – and a poorer one. I am extremely grateful to Yvonne for her generosity and friendship over the past few years. When someone struggles into the room with yet another cardboard box, saying, 'And these are his school reports,' dumps it on the floor and allows you to load it – and many other boxes – into the boot of your car and take them all away for as many weeks as it takes to read and note them, you know that you have encountered a real treasure of a friend and co-worker.

When researching Sulzbach's life, I walked in his footsteps as far as possible – wandering the streets of Frankfurt; exploring Neubabelsberg and Berlin; getting to know his London; immersing myself in Comrie, Featherstone Park and Northumberland; being welcomed to the German Embassy in London. It was a journey that opened up valuable friendships with so many people who had known Sulzbach, or who understood significant aspects of the time, or who offered expertise and practical help to make his story known.

In Germany, I am especially grateful to Ingrid Leifgen, her husband Tom Hoppe, and the rest of his family – as well as to Eduard Hoffman and Ingrid Schulte. They have all been most hospitable on my visits, and I learnt a lot from working with Ingrid Leifgen and Eduard for their radio programme from Northumberland. Ingrid's journalist skills have been invaluable in tracking down contacts in Germany when the language has defeated me, and she has been a constant inspiration. One of my earliest visits to Germany was to visit Tom's late father, Engelbert Hoppe, who spent several days sharing his papers and his memories of Herbert Sulzbach, 'my father figure'. I will always be grateful for his kind hospitality, stories, and advice. Through Engelbert and his family, I was able to begin to understand and appreciate the humanity of the people involved in this story, the complexity of the inter-weaving strands of historical events, people's personal beliefs and allegiances, and everyone's domestic turbulence.

Conversations in Brussels and Cologne with Regine Schwedersky-Sucker and her brother Thomas Schwedersky brought tremendously alive not only the presence of their father, Kurt, but also the atmosphere surrounding the people and meetings of the Featherstone Park Association during the 1970s. Regine's memory brought alive so many details of events and people that were a joy to hear. (I had no idea that Herbert's 'favourite expression' at one time was "I was flabbergasted!".) I very much appreciate the famed Schwedersky hospitality, and am grateful to Regine and her husband, Michael Sucker, and Thomas and his wife, Karola Block, for all the breakfast, coffee and cake. To Thomas, I particularly extend my gratitude for his trust and generosity in presenting me with family documents and photographs to take from Bonn to Brighton to study. Quite calmly, he asked me just to 'drop them off next time you are passing'.

Visiting beautiful Neubabelsberg for research was initially frustrating and confusing, mainly because most of the roads had been renamed at least twice during the previous hundred years. In fact, I became totally lost during my research there, and very nearly gave up trying to make sense of what I knew from history with what I could see on the ground – many years (and several different political regimes) later. Eventually, a librarian in Potsdam suggested a couple of names of local historians who might be able to help. Time had run out before my return journey, so once back in Brighton I immediately emailed them. Several disappointing days went by, and then came a long message, with accompanying photographs. One careful and friendly historian, Klaus Arlt, had spent the weekend walking some distance from his home, taking notes and photographs of Herbert Sulzbach's factory in Neubabelsberg. So many

ACKNOWLEDGEMENTS

details that I had known then fell into place, and the 1920s photos that I already knew matched perfectly. It was a delight to be invited to Klaus and Helga's home on a subsequent visit to share their knowledge, hear their memories, and be able to thank them in person.

I had been saved by that calm, efficient and kindly librarian in Potsdam who showed me records and eventually put me in touch with Klaus Arlt – and also pointed me towards the local bookshop, where I found so much of value. So, I wish to record my thanks to the librarian, Marlies Sell: I will always remember that she rescued an important part of my investigation and encouraged my perseverance (and then directed us towards a café with the best apple pie, custard, double cream – and coffee – that seemed necessary at the end of that hot and frustrating afternoon).

Herbert Sulzbach had so many friends, who typically became one immediately on meeting him. I am indebted to so many of them who have shared their memories and insights with me. In particular, Eric Henderson has lent me documents, hosted meals, introduced me to others who knew Sulzbach, and – essentially – talked at length over many years to help me to understand the character of the man, their shared friendships and values, and their commitment to a better future through the education and care of young people. Eric has been part of the writing of this story from its very early days and I am grateful to him.

When Sulzbach's First World War diaries were published in English translation, Ian Angus contacted him when he realised that his father had fought in the same battles – on the opposite side. I am grateful to Ian's later generous hospitality to me, and his fascinating conversations about the First World War, and Sulzbach's later interest in the German Resistance, as well as to Ian's son, Garry Angus, for permission to quote from his father and his family papers.

Ann Alston-Smith has given me an intriguing insight into the setting-up of town twinnings, such as that experienced by her father, Kenneth Cook, with help from Herbert Sulzbach and the German Embassy. I am grateful to Ann, her husband Ray, and her mother (the late Kathleen Cook), for their correspondence and sharing of information, photos and memories. It has all helped me to understand not only the process of town twinning, but also the consequent reconciliation at a very local level.

Herbert Sulzbach's address book was stuffed full of contacts with people in the press and media worlds, and I am glad to have been able to listen to recordings of some of his interviews and to read many of the press reports that were issued during the second half of his life. I am particularly grateful to Neal Ascherson for sharing his memories of Herbert, and for his vivid account of the Featherstone Park Association meetings that he attended. Neal has brought Herbert brilliantly to life for me, and what a joy it was to read his most recent postscript: 'I can see Herbert so clearly now, twinkling in his best suit.'

There was a considerable press presence at the final parade of the Old Contemptibles in August 1984 and I am grateful to Rosie Meikle, the widow of David (the then rector in Ipswich), for her memories of the occasion and her encouragement in the pursuit of reconciliation.

Alec Taylor interviewed Sulzbach for the Cologne-based *Deutschlandfunk* in the 1970s on the publication of *With the German Guns* – an interview that was heard throughout mainland Europe, including both parts of Germany. I am grateful to him as a source of inspiration for creative ways to promote the life and achievements of Herbert Sulzbach and his focus of reconciliation. I hope that some version of Alec's ideas of a drama, or film – that we have discussed so many times – will one day become reality, and I am glad of his insights.

So many people were inspired by Sulzbach, and I was delighted to discover the published diaries that Hermann Ziock dedicated to the man whom he had first met and admired at Featherstone Park. It is a book that is always on my desk, and I thank his family – Georgia-Maria Jebens, Cornelia Morrison, and Klaus-Hermann Ziock – for their generous permission to quote (in translation) from it.

Featherstone Park held a very special place in the heart of Herbert Sulzbach, and I am extremely grateful to the many people in Northumberland who have helped me in my research and understanding. John Clark, the current owner of Featherstone Castle, has been generous with sharing his memories and archive material – to say nothing of his hospitality at the castle. A unique place, with a unique history, this wonderful building has captivated me as much as it did many of the reluctant prisoners who were kept in captivity in its grounds.

The Clark, Clark-Lowes, and Dixon families – who have all been involved with the castle in recent years – have been magnanimous in sharing with me their knowledge, memories and experiences. Gill Dixon wrote to me many years ago about an incident of reconciliation – to do with the bottom of a beer barrel – that possibly neither of us fully recognised at the time for its significance in my story. Francis Clark-Lowes

ACKNOWLEDGEMENTS

(who also turned out to be my near neighbour) has been astonishingly conversant with background information of the more distant Sulzbach family history. I am grateful for their kind and open-hearted help.

Anthony Hellen has extensive knowledge of PoW camps and the people within them, especially the camps in Northumberland. For many years, he has given unstinting help and time to anybody – including myself – who shares that interest, and who wishes to know and understand more. His hospitality and kindness are much appreciated, and I am also grateful to his wife, Ingeborg Hellen, for her detailed research into PoW camp newspapers, which has helped me to appreciate the importance of *Die Zeit am Tyne*.

I lost count of the number of times that I encountered people around Featherstone who – when they knew about my interests – wanted to share family stories connected with the camp, or the PoWs, or the atmosphere in the area during the post-war 1940s. Many of these encounters were with people whom I met along local paths or in the pub (with a special thank you to the Wallace Arms). But the Haltwhistle Partnership – and particularly Ellen Walton – has been helpful in linking me to local people with stories to tell and enabling me to hear those stories. I am very glad of their local knowledge and help.

Many libraries and archives have made the writing of this book possible, but this story would never have got off the ground without the fortuitous work and generous help of Mark Benjamin and Hexham Library. When I discovered the plaque at Featherstone, I went first to the nearest library for help. Mark, who at that time was the librarian at Hexham, gave me access to all the material that he had quite recently acquired from ex-PoWs. So once a week – every Thursday, for several months – I drove from my then home in York to the library in Hexham. It was a treat and a privilege, which I still remember with pleasure and gratitude, to pore through the letters and other documents that Mark had gathered together as a local history resource and data base. They were an absolute gold mine.

The Wiener Library in London has been (and continues to be) a major source of information and reliable knowledge. I am glad of my membership there, and of the gentle, helpful, and professional guidance of the librarians.

The archivists at the Red Cross archives in Geneva have been outstanding in their efficient and helpful research on my behalf, and in their kindly responses to requests for information. I fully understand the rapport that Herbert Sulzbach had – way back in the 1940s – with the representatives from the Red Cross who investigated the PoW camps with which he was involved.

Researching Sulzbach's roots in Frankfurt, and the destiny of so many of his friends and colleagues in the city's Jewish community of the late nineteenth and early twentieth centuries, was made easier by the resources of the Jewish museums there. I would like to thank the staff at both the Jewish Museum and the Museum Judengasse for their guidance and patience, and to commend their database that enabled me to trace what had happened to so many of Sulzbach's family and friends during the Holocaust.

Tramping around the Isle of Man to discover the places where Herbert and Beate Sulzbach were interned was an eye-opener. Understanding the facts and their context was made much easier with the help of Wendy Thirkettle and staff at the Manx Library and Museum. The focused knowledge and specialist archive material was absolutely invaluable – and I so much enjoyed discovering the island. In different circumstances, I think that Sulzbach would have loved it.

Most people who want information about the twentieth century's wars and their effects on people and countries, will find themselves at the Imperial War Museum in London. I was so pleased to read Sulzbach's own documents that he had deposited there, and to listen to his recorded interviews. The museum's staff members were painstakingly generous with their time and advice over many months, and I am particularly grateful for permission to quote from their sources. Amongst those sources I discovered Hermann Ziock's diary, dedicated to Sulzbach – what a gem.

Herbert Sulzbach was, as his niece described him to me, 'the ultimate networker'. He cultivated friendships with people from all walks of life. One friendship that was important to him at a time when he particularly needed an understanding ear was that with Basil Liddell Hart. I thank the Liddell Hart Centre for Military Archives at King's College in London for the opportunity to read correspondence between the two men.

The archives at the BBC contain so many of the interviews and programmes with which Sulzbach was involved, and I am grateful to have been able to listen to many of these.

The Royal Logistical Museum, which holds many of the histories of the Royal Pioneer Corps that Sulzbach joined in 1940, has been

ACKNOWLEDGEMENTS

a welcoming place with helpful staff. I am very glad to have viewed Sulzbach's medals on display there, and to have had the opportunity to present an account of his life at an evening talk. I wish the museum well in its new premises.

It has been a long journey to publish this account of Herbert Sulzbach's life and I am indebted to the magnificent team at Pen and Sword Books that has made this possible. I will always be grateful to Lester Crook for his belief in the importance of the telling of the story, and to Harriet Fielding, Lori Jones and Diane Wordsworth for seeing it to completion. The preparation time for publication during a global pandemic has not been an easy period for them and I thank everyone involved at Pen and Sword Books for their cheerfulness, professionalism, encouragement, and optimism.

Prior to this book being published, I had written a couple of articles about Herbert Sulzbach and I am grateful to have had them published in *Humanitas* by the George Bell Institute and in *Kirchliche Zeitgeschichte/Contemporary Church History* by Vandenhoeck and Ruprecht. For this, I thank the editors, Andrew Chandler and Andrea Strübind.

The German Embassy in London has been extremely welcoming, and I am grateful to those who showed me around, invited me to receptions, and talked with me about their memories of working with Sulzbach. Margit Hosseini has been friendly and hospitable, and also helpful with background information, facts and memories. Ezio Le Donne, who worked there for so many years, has been a treasure trove of reminiscence and has given me a detailed appreciation of the changes at the embassy over the long period that he and Sulzbach worked there together – both as local employees. During preparations for publication, Ralf Teepe has been generous with his time in obtaining permission for me to quote from embassy sources and I am grateful to him for his patience.

Halina Hodi has been helpful and gracious in sharing memories of the time when she and Sulzbach both worked at the embassy, and friendly and encouraging in her enthusiasm for his story to be written. I am especially grateful to her for lending me the recording of the memorial event that took place after Sulzbach's death, and for entertaining me in her home.

I have been the grateful recipient of so much hospitality from those who once knew Sulzbach. Gerda and Rainer Dobbelstein have become friends and colleagues since my visit to their house in Bonn where a magnificent spread was provided as we talked about memories and history and discovered photographs and articles. I am grateful to them for their company and conversation on subsequent visits to Germany, for countless emails, and for their ongoing support and suggestions for this book.

Rita and Rolf Breitenstein have given me useful information about the press and cultural departments of the German Embassy of the 1970s – as well as a generous and lengthy lunch at their home. I thank them for their welcome and help.

It has been a joy to get to know Christine and Heinrich Evers through conversations with Christine, who worked for a short time at the embassy – again, in the 1970s – and was one of the young people who so impressed Sulzbach. I am grateful to her for her memories and insights, and to both of them for the happy time that I spent with them at their home.

When a manuscript is finished, it can be daunting to be contacted by someone with extra information. However, we broke off a family holiday in Germany to visit Heidi and Bertold Brandenstein and I am so grateful to him for his memories of working at the embassy, and for his staunch support of Sulzbach and his life-story. We intended to visit for a few hours and stayed all day, were treated to a meal by the castle in Würzburg, and came away with more gifts from them both than we could easily carry. Thank you.

This book might never have seen the light of day without the constant guidance of Andrew Chandler. He has known about it since its earliest days and has unstintingly offered his knowledge, authorial experience, and academic expertise to make sure that it would one day be published. I appreciate his gentle and direct interventions when needed, his empathy and continuing friendship. He has also helped me to understand the dynamics of reconciliation in Europe during the twentieth century, and I am very grateful to him for that.

I first talked about aspects of Herbert Sulzbach's life with students of the Workers' Educational Association in Leeds who attended my courses in social history. I thank all of them for their interest, their engagement, and their encouragement. Some of those students invited me to tell Sulzbach's story to members of the local Jewish community and I am very glad of their welcome and interest.

ACKNOWLEDGEMENTS

I am also grateful to the Jewish community in London, especially to Anthony Grenville who has been generous in sharing with me his knowledge and understanding of Herbert Sulzbach's life and times. The Association of Jewish Refugees has helped with its archives and the opportunity to trace those who knew Sulzbach.

My research into Sulzbach's work at Cultybraggan PoW camp near Comrie would have been impossible without the assistance and generosity of the late Eunice Cartwright and of Grant Carstairs, and their colleagues and friends at Comrie Development Trust. My visits to Comrie were always a delight and I am grateful for the friendship, hospitality and accommodation given to me by Eunice and her husband, Bill. Fran Loots helped to organise my visits to Cultybraggan, and arrange for the Comrie chapter of this book to be written in a Nissen hut in the old PoW camp and I am glad to have been allowed to do this – it was a salutary experience.

I am extremely grateful to everyone mentioned above for so willingly giving me permission to quote from our conversations, from letters and diaries, and recorded memories. You have allowed Herbert Sulzbach to come alive for me.

Permission to quote from other publications has also been given from several other sources. I am grateful to them all: to the Imperial War Museum for permission to quote from documents that Sulzbach had deposited with the museum, and from extracts in recordings that he made in 1963 and 1979; to the Foreign Office in Berlin for permission to quote from previous ambassadors from Germany to the Court of St James in London; to *The Guardian* for allowing quotes from that paper and from The *Manchester Guardian* of 1891, the 1940s, and 1960; to Orion Books for permission to quote from *The Diaries of Victor Klemperer 1945 – 59. The Lesser Evil*; to the *Hampstead and Highgate Press* (one of Sulzbach's local papers, known colloquially as the *Ham and High*) to quote from an article from 1968; to the letters editor at the *Daily Telegraph* for permission to use words from letters and articles published in the paper in 1940, 1942 and 1960; to Immediate Media Company for permission to quote from *The Listener Magazine* of November 1975; to Associated Newspapers Ltd for allowing a quote from the *News Chronicle* of 1943; to the BBC for permission to use material from an interview of Sulzbach with Jack de Manio on Radio 4 in 1978; to Haydon Bridge High School for the use of translations of

Die Zeit am Tyne that were completed by former students of the school – Sulzbach would no doubt have been delighted that they were involved in reading the camp newspaper and making it accessible in English.

I have been unable to contact anyone who can give me permission to have quoted from Bernard Levin's speech at the Featherstone Park meeting in 1969, a copy of which is amongst Herbert Sulzbach's papers. Likewise, for his words at the memorial event for Sulzbach in November 1985. I shall be pleased to rectify this if contacted.

On that day in the summer of 1996 when we first wandered along the River South Tyne and discovered the plaque on the gatepost to the remains of the Featherstone Park PoW camp, my sons were young teenagers. I very much appreciate their ongoing interest in my work and research over the past many years, and their encouragement in my telling of this story. To them, their partners and children, I am indebted for not only keeping me going but cheering me on the way.

It was my husband, Peter Hepburn, who first suggested exploring the mysteries that we puzzled over in the wording on that plaque. A German name with an OBE decoration? A PoW camp here, in the middle of nowhere? Until 1948 – which was after I had been born, and thus definitely post-war? And – most intriguing of all – 'a seedbed of reconciliation'? Peter's emotional, financial, and all-encompassing support has enabled the writing of this book and the telling of Herbert Sulzbach's story. I am grateful to him for travelling this journey with me.

Bibliography

Books

Adam, Hans-Christian, *Berlin: portrait of a city* (Taschen 2007)
Adler, Gerhard, *Ich, Bartosch – Kriegsgefangener Nr. 915051* (Bastei Lübbe 1985)
Aldington, Regine, *The German Ambassador's Residence in London* (John Adamson, Cambridge, 1993)
Angell, Norman, with Buxton, Dorothy, *You and the Refugee* (Penguin Books 1939)
Baker, Nicholson, *Human Smoke. The Beginnings of World War II. The End of Civilization* (Simon & Schuster 2009)
Barron, Stephanie, *Exiles and Emigrés. The Flight of European Artists from Hitler* (Los Angeles County Museum of Art and Harry N. Abrams, Inc. 1997)
Beer, Gillian, *Arguing with the past. Essays in narrative from Woolf to Sidney* (Routledge 1989)
Berghahn, Marion, *Continental Britons: German-Jewish Refugees from Nazi Germany* (Berg 1984)
Biddiscombe, Alexander, *The De-Nazification of Germany: a history 1945 – 1950* (Tempus 2007)
Bienert, Michael and Buchholz, Elke Linda, *Die Zwanziger Jahre in Berlin* (Berlin Story Verlag 2006)
Böll, Heinrich, *Der Zug war pünktlich* (Deutscher Taschenbuch Verlag 1972)
Bonhoeffer, Dietrich, *Letters and Papers from Prison* (Fontana 1959)
Bourke, Joanna, *An Intimate History of Killing* (Granta 2000)
Bourke, Joanna, *Fear. A Cultural History* (Virago 2006)
Bravati, Brian, and Jones, Harriet (eds), *From Reconstruction to Integration. Britain and Europe since 1945* (Leicester University Press 1993)

Breitenstein, Rolf (ed.), *Pillars of Partnership* (Wolff 1978)
Breitenstein, Rolf (ed.), *Total War to Total Trust. Personal accounts of 30 years of Anglo-German relations* (Wolff 1976)
Breitenstein, Rolf (ed.), *Twinning. Partnerschaften* (Wolff 1974)
Burleigh, Michael, *Moral Combat. A History of World War II* (Harper Press 2010)
Bush, Kate and Sladen, Mark (eds.), *In the Face of History. European Photographers in the 20th Century at the Barbican Art Gallery, London* (Black Dog Publishing 2006)
Ebsworth, Raymond, *Restoring Democracy in Germany. The British Contribution* (Stevens and Sons Ltd. 1960)
Ehlers, Hella and Crick, Joyce (eds), *The Trauma of the Past. Remembering and Working Through. Lecture series organised by the Goethe-Institut London in January 1993* (Goethe Institut 1994)
Faulk, Henry, *Group Captives. The Re-education of German Prisoners of War in Britain 1945 – 1948* (Chatto and Windus 1977)
Fehrenbach, Heide, *Cinema in Democratizing Germany* (University of North Carolina Press 1995)
Fischer, S, *Hinaus aus dem Ghetto. Juden in Frankfurt am Main 1800 – 1950* (S. Fischer Verlag 1988)
Foss, Brian, *War Paint. Art, War, State and Identity in Britain 1939 – 1945* (Yale University Press 2007)
Foster, Paul (ed.), *Bell of Chichester (1883 – 1958). A Prophetic Bishop* (Otto Memorial Paper, University of Chichester 2004)
France, Peter and St Clair, William (eds), *Mapping lives. The uses of Biography* (Oxford University Press for the British Academy 2002)
Francis, David J (ed.), *Peace and Conflict in Africa* (Zed Books 2008)
Friedenthal, Richard, *Goethe: his life and times* (Weidenfeld and Nicolson 1965)
Fry, Helen, *Churchill's German Army* (The History Press 2007)
Garfield, Simon, *Our Hidden Lives: the everyday diaries of a forgotten Britain 1945 – 1948* (Ebury 2004)
Garfield, Simon, *Private Battles: our intimate diaries – how the war almost defeated us* (Mass Observation Archive, Ebury 2006)
Gay, Peter, *My German Question* (Yale University Press 1998)
Gay, Peter, *Schnitzler's Century. The Making of Middle-Class Culture 1815 – 1914* (W.W. Norton & Co. 2002)
Geheran, Michael, *Comrades Betrayed. Jewish World War I Veterans under Hitler* (Cornell University Press 2020)

BIBLIOGRAPHY

Geiger-Verlag, *Neuendorf-Nowawes-Babelsberg: Stationen eines Stadtteils* (Geiger-Verlag 2000)

Gilbert, Martin, *Churchill. A Life* (Pimlico 2000)

Gill, Anton, *A Dance Between Flames. Berlin between the Wars* (John Murray 1993)

Gollancz, Victor, *In Darkest Germany* (Gollancz 1947)

Gollwitzer, Helmut, Kuhn, Käthe, and Schneider, Reinhold (eds.), *Dying We Live* (Pantheon 1956)

Grenville, Anthony, *Continental Britons. Jewish Refugees from Nazi Europe* (Association of Jewish Refugees and the Jewish Museum, London, 2002)

Hannam, Charles, *A Boy in your Situation* (Deutsch 1977)

Hattersley, Roy, *The Edwardians* (Abacus 2004)

Hart, B.H. Liddell, *The Other Side of the Hill. Germany's Generals. Their Rise and Fall, with their Own Account of Military Events 1939 – 1945* (Cassell 1948)

Hennessy, Peter, *Never Again: Britain 1945 – 1952* (Penguin 2006)

Hill, Roland, *An Embassy in Belgrave Square* (The Embassy of the Federal Republic of Germany 1991)

Hoffman, Eva, *Lost in Translation. A Life in a New Language* (Vintage 1998)

Hoffman, Eva, *After Such Knowledge. Memory, History and the Legacy of the Holocaust* (Secker and Warburg 2004)

Holmes, Richard, *Footsteps. Adventures of a Romantic Biographer* (Harper Perennial 2005)

Holroyd, Michael, *Works on Paper* (Abacus 2002)

Horseman, Grace, *Growing Up in the Forties* (Constable 1997)

Howe Taylor, Pamela, *The Germans We Trusted* (Lutterworth Press 2003)

Howe Taylor, Pamela, *Enemies become Friends* (The Book Guild 1997)

Jasper, Ronald, *George Bell, Bishop of Chichester* (OUP 1967)

Kaplan, Marion A., *Between Dignity and Despair: Jewish Life in Nazi Germany* (OUP 1998)

Kielinger, Thomas, *Crossroads and Roundabouts. Junctions in German-British Relations* (Bouvier 1997)

Klemperer, Victor, *I Shall Bear Witness: the diaries of Victor Klemperer 1933 – 41* (Weidenfeld and Nicolson 1998)

Klemperer, Victor, *To the Bitter End: the diaries of Victor Klemperer 1942 – 45* (Weidenfeld and Nicolson 1999)

Klemperer, Victor, *The Lesser Evil: the diaries of Victor Klemperer 1945 – 1959* (Weidenfeld and Nicolson 2003)

Klemperer, Victor, *The Language of the Third Reich. LTI – Lingua Tertii Imperii. A Philologist's Notebook* (Continuum 2006)
Kochan, Miriam, *Prisoners of England* (Macmillan 1980)
Laqueur, Walter, *The Changing Face of Anti-Semitism, from ancient times to the present day* (OUP 2006)
Laqueur, Walter, *Weimar: a cultural history 1918 – 1933* (Phoenix 2000)
Last, Nella, *Nella Last's War* (Profile Books Ltd. 2006)
Last, Nella, *Nella Last's Peace: the post-war diaries of Housewife 49* (Profile Books Ltd. 2008)
Lee, Hermione, *Body Parts* (Chatto and Windus 2005)
Lerner, Franz, *Bestand im Wandel* (Gerd Ammelburg 1956)
Litvinoff, Barnet, *A Very British Subject: telling tales* (Vallentine Mitchell 1996)
MacDonogh, Giles, *A Good German: Adam von Trott zu Solz* (Quartet Books 1989)
Malet, Marian and Grenville, Anthony (eds), *Changing countries. The Experience and Achievement of German-speaking Exiles from Hitler in Britain from 1933 to Today* (Libris 2002)
Marwick, Arthur, *Britain in the Century of Total War. War, Peace and Social Change 1900 – 1967* (Bodley Head 1968)
Marwick, Arthur, Emsley, Clive, and Simpson, Wendy (eds.), *Total War and Historical Change. Europe 1914 – 1955* (Open University Press 2001)
Mather, Carol, *Aftermath of war. Everyone must go home* (Brassey's 1992)
Maxtone Graham, Ysenda, *The Real Mrs Miniver* (John Murray 2001)
Mayer, Eugen, *The Jews of Frankfurt* (Waldemar Kramer 1990)
Meehan, Patricia, *A Strange Enemy People. Germans Under the British 1945 – 50* (Peter Owen Publishers 2001)
Mendes-Flohr, Paul, *German Jews. A Dual Identity* (Yale University Press 1999)
Moeller, Robert G., *War Stories. The Search for a Usable Past in the Federal Republic of Germany* (University of California Press 2001)
Neave, Airey, *Nuremberg. A Personal Record of the Trial of the Major Nazi War Criminals in 1945 – 6* (Hodder and Stoughton 1978)
de Normann, Roderick, *For Führer and Fatherland. SS Murder and Mayhem in Wartime Britain* (Sutton Publishing 1997)

BIBLIOGRAPHY

Nicholson, Virginia, *Millions Like Us. Women's Lives in War and Peace 1939 – 1949* (Viking 2011)

Nicolson, Harold, *Why Britain is at War* (Penguin Books Ltd 1939)

Nicolson, Harold, *Diaries and Letters 1907 – 1964* (Weidenfeld and Nicolson 2004)

Oltermann, Philip, *Keeping Up with the Germans. A History of Anglo-German Encounters* (Faber and Faber 2012)

Patterson, Michael, *The Revolution in German Theatre 1900 – 1933* (Routledge and Kegan Paul 1981)

Powell, Jennifer and Vinzent, Jutta, *Visual Journeys: Art in Exile in Britain* (George Bell Institute at the University of Chichester 2008)

Pressler, Mirjam, *Treasures from the Attic. The Extraordinary Story of Anne Frank's Family* (Phoenix 2011)

Prittie, Terence, *Germans Against Hitler* (Hutchinson 1964)

Prittie, Terence, *My Germans 1933 – 1983* (Wolff 1983)

Prittie, Terence, *The Velvet Chancellors. A History of Post-War Germany* (Muller 1979)

Pronay, Nicholas and Wilson, Keith (eds), *The Political Re-education of Germany and her Allies after World War II* (Croom Helm 1985)

Ramsden, John, *Don't Mention the War. The British and the Germans since 1890* (Abacus 2007)

Remarque, Erich Maria, *All Quiet on the Western Front* (Vintage 1996. First published in German 1929)

Roberts, J.M., *Europe 1880 – 1945. A General History of Europe* (Pearson Education Ltd 2001)

Robertson, Edwin, *Unshakeable Friend: George Bell and the German Churches* (CCBI 1995)

Ross, Alan, *Colours of War. War Art 1939 – 45* (Jonathan Cape 1983)

Roth, Joseph, *What I saw. Reports from Berlin 1920 – 33* (Granta Books, London 2003)

Schlingensiepen, Ferdinand, *Dietrich Bonhoeffer 1906 – 1945. Martyr, Thinker, Man of Resistance* (T&T Clark International 2010)

Schneider, Helga, *Let Me Go. My Mother and the SS* (Vintage 1995)

Schneider, Helga, *The Bonfire of Berlin* (Translated from the Italian by Shaun Whiteside. Heinemann 2005)

Schraeder, Helena P, *The Blockade Breakers. The Berlin Air Lift* (The History Press 2008)

Seiffert, Rachel, *The Dark Room* (Vintage 2002)

Seller, Maxine Schwartz, *We Built up our Lives; education and community among Jewish refugees interned by Britain in World War II* (Greenwood Press 2001)
Sereny, Gitta, *The German Trauma. Experiences and Reflections 1938 – 2000* (Allen Lane. The Penguin Press 2000)
Shah, Shabibi, *Where do I Belong? From Kabul to London. A Refugee's Life* (Longstone Books 2001)
Shawcross, Hartley, *Life Sentence* (Constable 1995)
Sherriff, R. C., *Journey's End* (Penguin Books 2000. First published 1929)
Schlink, Bernhard, *Guilt about the Past* (Beautiful Books 2010)
Shirer, William L., *The Rise and Fall of the Third Reich* (Hamlyn 1987)
Shirer, William L., *This is Berlin: a narrative history, 1938 – 40* (Hutchinson 1999)
Shirer, William L., *The Nightmare Years, 1930 – 1940* (Birlinn 2001)
Shirer, William L., *End of a Berlin Diary* (Hamilton 1947)
Simmons, Michael, *Berlin: the dispossessed city* (Hamilton 1988)
Sissons, Michael and French, Philip (eds.), *Age of Austerity* (OUP 1986)
Smith, Arthur L. (Jr), *The War for the German Mind. Re-educating Hitler's Soldiers* (Berghahn Books 1996)
Smyser, W.R., *From Yalta to Berlin. The Cold War Struggle over Germany* (Macmillan Press Ltd 1999)
Snowman, Daniel, *The Hitler Émigrés. The Cultural Impact on Britain of Refugees from Nazism* (Chatto and Windus 2002)
Stent, Ronald, *A Bespattered Page? The Internment of 'His Majesty's most Loyal Enemy Aliens'* (Deutsch 1980)
Struther, Jan (Maxton Graham, Joyce), *Mrs Miniver* (Virago 1989).
Sullivan, Matthew Barry, *Thresholds of Peace. German Prisoners and the People of Britain 1944 – 1948* (Hamish Hamilton 1979)
Sulzbach, Herbert, *With the German Guns: Four years on the Western Front* (Leo Cooper 1998)
Tutu, Desmond, *No Future Without Forgiveness* (Rider 1999)
Uhlman, F., *The Making of an Englishman* (Gollancz 1960)
Vogt, Hannah, *The Burden of Guilt. A Short History of Germany 1914 – 1945* (OUP 1965)
von Mises, Ludwig, *Omnipotent Government* (YUP 1944)
von Schlabrendorff, Fabian, *The Secret War Against Hitler* (Hodder and Stoughton 1966)
Wasserstein, Bernard, *Barbarism and Civilization: a history of Europe in our time* (OUP 2007)

BIBLIOGRAPHY

Waterman, Ruth, *When Swan Lake Comes to Sarajevo* (Canterbury Press 2008)
Wawro, Geoffrey, *The Franco-Prussian War: the German conquest of France in 1870 – 1871* (CUP 2003)
Weitz, Eric D, *Weimar Germany. Promise and Tragedy* (Princeton University Press 2007)
Woolf, Virginia, *The Crowded Dance of Modern Life. Selected Essays Volume 2* (Penguin 1993)
Ziock, Hermann, *Jeder geht seinen Weg allein* (Bläschke Verlag 1981)

Pamphlets

Political Intelligence Department, *Re-education of German POW* (Foreign Office 1945)

Articles

Brailsford, H.N., *Psychological Disarmament, or the Re-education of Germany*. Edgar G. Dunstan and Co. originally printed in *The New Statesman and Nation* 16 January 1943. Reprinted by Friends Committee for Refugees and Aliens, London.
Hellen, Ingeborg, *The Boys' Own Papers: the case of German PoW camp newspapers in Britain, 1946 – 8*. German Historical Institute, December 2008.
Hoppe, Engelbert, *A Prisoner of Peace*, in Channel Islands Occupation Review No. 37 (Channel Islands Occupation Society 2009)

Exhibitions

Kitaj, R. B., Obsessions. *The Art of Identity* (Jewish Museum, London, and Pallant House Gallery, Chichester, 2013)

Films

Müller, Herms, *Der Richter und sein Freund* (Westdeutsche Rundfunk 1984)

Index

Adenauer, Chancellor Konrad, 149, 152–3
Adler car, Emil Sulzbach's, 3, 14
Airlift, Berlin, 118–24, 133–4, 141
D'Alquen, Gunter (SS newspaper editor), 41, 174
Amsterdam, 118
Anglo-German Association, 150, 179
Anglo-German Circles, 149–50
Angus, Ian (correspondent of HS), 157, 161–2
Arandora Star, SS, 49
Ariadne, SMS, 14
Ascherson, Neal (journalist), 176
Auxiliary Military Pioneer Corps, 56–8

Bad Oeynhausen, 119–20
Barcelona, 135–7
Bartlett, Colonel (Featherstone Park camp commandant), 114
Basel, Switzerland, 38, 42, 137
Bauer, Captain (Comrie camp interpreter officer), 83–5
Baumgarten (Featherstone Park clerk), 112–13
Beaulieu, Hampshire, 71
Bell, George (Bishop of Chichester), 53, 55–6, 107–8

Beneš, President Edvard, of Czechoslovakia, 39–40
Bergen-Belsen concentration camp, 90–1, 103, 148
Bergenthals (old friends of HS), 118
Berlin, 121–34
Bitker, Heinz (ex-Featherstone Park PoW), 156
The Black and the Grey (radio programme), 163
Blank, Herr (chauffeur), 3
Blind Eye to Murder (TV programme), 159
Blüth, Julius (business contact of HS), 34
Böhner, Siegfried (ex-Featherstone Park PoW), 111
Booker, Mrs
    see Stone, Gertrude 'Nini' (HS's governess)
Boxberger, Georg von (HS's brother-in-law), 9, 14
    see also Sulzbach, Lili (HS's sister)
Boxberger, Herbert von (HS's nephew), 12
Brandt, Chancellor Willy, 150, 154–5
Bückner, Dr (family friend), 13

INDEX

Bultmann (Comrie camp PoW), 86–7
Buxton, Dorothy (friend of HS), 145, 148
Bystock Court convalescent home, 68

Camp 18, PoW
  see Featherstone Park camp, Northumberland
Cardinal, Martha von (HS's former secretary), 106
Chamberlain, Prime Minister Neville, 40, 44, 46
Chichester, Bishop of (George Bell), 53, 55–6
Christiansen, Major Herbert (ex-Featherstone Park PoW), 179
Ciolina, J. B. (photographer), 5
Cirencester, Gloucestershire, 64
Clark, John (owner of Featherstone Park), 177–8
Codford, Wiltshire, 64–5
Comrie PoW camp, Perthshire, 78–97
Consulate, post-war German
  see Embassy, post-war German
Cook, Kenneth (newspaper editor), 151–2
Cooper MP, Duff, 40, 42–3
Coventry, bombing of, 184
Currency, post-War German, 121–2
Czechoslovakia, 39–43

D-Day, June 1944, 73–4
Dempsey, Major (HS's superior in Berlin), 122–3
Devizes, Wiltshire, 76–7
Dirnall Camp, Didcot, 60, 64

Dobbelstein, Rainer (Embassy friend of HS), 146, 160
Le Donne, Ezio (German embassy butler), 155
Donnelly MP, Desmond, 174
Donniford Camp, Somerset, 66
Dora (HS's nurse), 3
Drabich-Wächter, Generalleutnant Viktor von (contemporary of HS), 76–7
Dürrenmatt, Peter (newspaper editor), 137

Edward VII, King, 5
Ehrlich, Mr (HS's benefactor), 44, 63–4
Elizabeth II, Queen, 149, 153
Embassy, post-war German, 144–65
Enlightenment, German, 8

Falmouth, Cornwall, 68–9
Faulk, Colonel Henry (in charge of PoW re-education), 94–5, 98, 101, 113, 157–8, 176
Featherstone Park Association, 153, 165, 169–79, 188
Featherstone Park camp, Northumberland, 98–116, 165
Ferdinand, Archduke Franz, 13
First World War, 14–18
Flying bombs, 74–5
Frank, Anne, 150
Frankfurt, 2–21, 138–42
Fraternisation with PoWs, 107, 112
Freund, Professor Michael (historian), 172

Gatow airfield, Berlin, 121–4
Gauck, President Joachim, 153

209

Gebrüder Sulzbach bank, 7–8, 36
Gewirtz, Dr Jacob (London Jew), 146
Gifts from PoWs, 180
Goebbels, Joseph, 31, 41
Goltz, Joachim (Comrie camp PoW), 88
Grüneburgpark, Frankfurt, 4

Hasenclever, Walter (playwright), 26, 31, 51
Hehn, Peter (ex-Featherstone Park PoW), 169, 172
Heim, Generalleutnant Ferdinand (Featherstone Park PoW spokesman), 105, 112–13, 181
Heimann, Major (ex-Featherstone Park PoW), 120
Henderson, Eric (headteacher), 158, 162, 177, 179
Herzog, Wilhelm (writer friend of HS), 38
Hessen, Friedrich and Max von (Kaiser Wilhelm's nephews), 4
Heuss, President Theodor, 148–9
Hilsea Camp, Portsmouth, 71
Hitler, Adolf, 29–30, 32, 76, 88
Hohnholz, Helmut (ex-Featherstone Park PoW), 167
Holloway Prison, 50–2
Holocaust (TV programme), 159
Hoppe, Engelbert (ex-Featherstone Park PoW), 104, 113–14, 116, 151, 160–1, 183–4, 189
Horlitz, Herr (ex-Featherstone Park PoW), 139
Hoven, Franz von (architect), 2

In Flanders Fields (John McCrae), 95–6, 163

Inflation in Germany, 27
Internment, debate on, 52

Jagdhaus, Das (Sulzbach hunting lodge), 13
Jailed by the British (TV documentary), 162–3
Jedermann (Hugo von Hofmannsthal), 102
John, Otto (Hitler assassination conspirator), 110, 154, 187
Josty, Café, Berlin, 33, 129

Kaula, Nellie and Frederic (family friends), 68, 74–5
Keiper, Hermann (HS's violin teacher), 6
Kennedy, Ludovic (broadcaster), 159
Kindervatter, Mieze (girlfriend of HS), 9–10, 12, 138
Kirchholtes, Heinrich (HS's cousin by marriage), 8, 36, 139
Klemperer, Victor (writer), 122, 131
Koch, Professor H. (historian), 179
Köhler, Hermann (colleague of HS), 5
Kokoschka, Oskar (painter), 26, 31
Konservatorium, Frankfurt, 6
Kristallnacht, 37, 42

Levin, Bernard (journalist), 172–3, 175, 189
Liddell-Hart, Basil (author), 68, 90
Lindeiner-Wildau, Colonel von (ex-Featherstone Park PoW), 167–8
Löffler, Dr Bernhard (HS's tutor), 8–10, 139
Looking back without anger (newspaper article by HS), 159–60
Lucky numbers, HS's (14 and 19), 5

INDEX

McBain, Colonel Hubert (Featherstone Park camp commandant), 110–12
Macmillan, Prime Minister Harold, 149
Market Lavington, Wiltshire, 76–7
Martha (HS's friend), 9, 14
Masaryk, Jan (Czech foreign minister), 72
Memorial pillar at Featherstone Park, 177–8
Menuhin, Yehudi (violinist), 116
Merkel, Colonel (Featherstone Park PoW spokesman), 115
Mohn (ex-Featherstone Park PoW), 132
Mosler Swimming Institute, 4
Muller, Alfred (business associate of HS), 135
Munich agreement 1938, 39–40

Neubabelsberg, 20–1
Neumann, Dr (Featherstone Park PoW doctor), 132
Neustadt, West Germany, 120–2
Nicolson, Harold (British diplomat), 40–1, 117
'Nini'
see Stone, Gertrude 'Nini' (HS's governess)

Officers against Hitler (Fabian von Schlabrendorff), 110, 154, 183
Old Contemptibles' Parade, Ipswich (1984), 163
Olympic Games 1936, 35
Onchan internment camp, 48–9, 54

Palmengarten, Frankfurt, 4–5
Peace Pledge Union, 47

The Plain House, Chipstead, 68–9, 74–5
Plainfare, Operation
see Airlift, Berlin
Pless, Herr (HS's tennis partner), 3
Plymouth, Devon, 66
Poland, 44
'Popular University,' Onchan Camp, 54
Potsdam Conference for post-war peace, 92
Prittie, Terence (journalist), 147, 170–1, 173, 180

Radio in the American Sector [of Berlin] (RIAS), 128
Red Cross, International, 101, 104
Regional Advisory Committee, 47–8
Reichmann, Eva (friend of HS), 156
Reichsfluchtsteuer, (Reich Flight Tax), 34
Reise, Professor Otto (friend of HS), 37
Reitzenstein, Irene von (Berlin guide), 124–7, 130
Remembrance Days 1945/46, 95–6, 110
Reuter, Ernst (mayor of Berlin), 133
Rocholl, Margot (HS's first wife), 18–25, 27
Rocholl, Meta (née Eichengrün) (HS's first mother-in-law), 18
Rosterg, Wolfgang (PoW), 81
Ruhr, French and Belgian troops occupy the, 27

Salcombe, Devon, 66
Salomons, Professor (Margot Rocholl's stepfather), 18, 20, 70

Sanders, Henry (HS's business agent), 33–5
Scheel, Walter (German foreign minister), 155
Schenk, Leutnant (ex-Featherstone Park PoW), 124
Scherk, Beate (HS's second wife):
  early life, 25–6
  meets and marries HS, 25–7
  interned, 47–62
  carries out fire-watching duties, 73
  in shock at Chipstead, 74–5
  death, 161–2
Scherk, Frau (Beate's mother), 70
Scherk, Herr (HS's rowing partner), 3
Scherk, Ruth (Beate's sister), 25, 29, 31, 33–8, 50, 59–60
Scherk, Walter and Alice (Beate's cousins), 135–6
Schlabrendorff, Fabian von (Hitler opposer), 110, 153–4
Schlange-Schöningen, Dr Hans (post-war German Consulate leader), 144–7
Schlink, Bernhard (author), 182
Schmitt, Herbert (ex-Featherstone Park PoW), 103, 166, 188–9
Schmitz, Sybille (tenant of Frau Scherk), 33–8
Schneider, Friedl (girlfriend of HS), 10, 12
Schulz, Major (ex-Featherstone Park PoW), 106
Schwänke, Sergeant (Comrie camp PoW), 85
Schwedersky, Kurt (ex-Featherstone Park PoW), 112–13, 149–55, 158, 164–5, 173–8, 185
Screening, PoW, 93–5, 109, 111–12
Second World War, 44, 88–90
Seebach, Hans Ado von (friend of HS), 32–3, 141, 144, 148, 156
Seligmann, Caesar (family friend), 5
Smith, George (HS's son-in-law), 47
Sorensen MP, Reginald, 168
Soviet occupation of Berlin, 117
Stock, Colonel (ex-Featherstone Park PoW), 105–6
Stoke Military Hospital, 67
Stokes MP, Richard, 107
Stone, Gertrude 'Nini' (HS's governess), 8–9, 14, 32, 59, 89–90
Strikes in Germany (1922), 25
Sudetenland, 43
Sullivan, Matthew Barry (author), 163, 177
Sulzbach, Dorothee 'Dodo' (HS's daughter), 18–21
Sulzbach, Emil (HS's father), 2, 5–7, 30–2
Sulzbach, Ernst (HS's brother), 2, 14, 33, 37, 90, 123
Sulzbach, Herbert:
  birth and early childhood, 2–5
  reveres grandfather, 5
  lucky numbers (14 and 19), 5
  and music, 6
  on his father, 6–7
  attends Goethe Gymnasium, 8
  fails *Abitur*, 9–10
  and romantic involvements, 9–10
  trip abroad with tutor, 10–11
  works at family bank, 12
  accepted into 2nd Bavarian Field Artillery Regiment, 13
  enlists with 63rd Artillery Regiment, 14

INDEX

service in First World War, 14–18
attitude to the French, 15–17, 28–9
marries Margot Rocholl, 18–19
awarded Iron Crosses, 18, 32
daughter 'Dodo' born, 18–21
stays at St Blaise Sanitorium, 19
paper factory in Neubabelsberg, 20–4, 29–30, 35
divorced from Margot, 24–5, 27
meets and marries Beate Scherk, 25–7
corresponds with French families, 28–9
Zwei lebende Mauern (First World War diaries), 32, 38, 155–6
paper factory in Slough, 33, 36
emigrates to England with Beate and Ruth, 34–7
writes to Duff Cooper, 40, 42–3
writes to Neville Chamberlain, 40
appears before 'friendly alien' tribunal with Beate, 45
applies to join British Army, 45
offers military service to several allies, 46
interned, 47–57
joins Auxiliary Military Pioneer Corps, 56–8
posted to Dirnall Camp, Didcot, 60, 64
reconsiders overseas service, 65–6
treated for infected appendix, 66–7
granted compassionate leave 1944, 74–6
appointed as interpreter 1944, 78–80
at Comrie PoW camp, Perthshire, 78–97
appearance, 81
temporarily changes name to Salbrook, 83
interprets at Comrie camp enquiries, 84–8
commissioned in British Army, 96
at Featherstone Park camp, 98–116
promoted Captain in British Army, 98
writes final letter in *Die Zeit am Tyne,* 107
concerns about his post-war future, 114–15, 134
posted to Berlin, 118
and Berlin airlift, 118–24, 133–4
in Neustadt, West Germany, 122–3
in Berlin, 124–30
tensions with Beate, 129, 131
demobilised from British Army, 133–4
as negotiator in Beate's cousin's cork business, 136–8, 140–1
has German nationality returned, 144
in German Consulate, 144–65
concerns about Embassy salary, 148
on negative British press, 149–50
estranged from daughter and granddaughter, 154
awarded German Grand Cross of Merit, 155
awarded European Cross of Peace, 159
criticises TV programmes, 159

writes *Looking back without anger* newspaper article, 159–60
retires, 160–1
awarded Order of the British Empire, 161
desolated by Beate's death, 161–2
reaction to *Jailed by the British* (TV documentary), 162–3
reads in *The Black and the Grey* (radio programme), 163
takes part in Old Contemptibles' Parade, Ipswich (1984), 163
holds ex-PoW meeting in 1950, 168–9
arranges reconciliation meeting in London, 186–7
death and funeral, 163–5
Sulzbach, Julie (HS's mother), 2, 31–2
Sulzbach, Karl (HS's uncle), 5, 8
Sulzbach, Lili (HS's sister), 2, 6, 9
Sulzbach, Rudolph (HS's grandfather), 5, 7
Sutherland, Graham (artist), 152
Synagogue, Frankfurt, 2

Thame, Oxfordshire, 71
Tidworth, Hampshire, 72–3, 77–8
Tunbridge Wells/Wiesbaden twinning, 151
Twinning, town, 151, 188

Vaughan, Keith (artist), 65
Vickers, Colonel (Featherstone Park camp commandant), 98–100, 108–9

Wechmar, Ambassador Baron Rüdiger von, 164
Weisbeker, Herr (Auschwitz survivor), 179
Weymouth, Dorset, 69
Wiechert, Ernst (HS's poet friend), 181
Wiesbaden/Tunbridge Wells twinning, 151
Wilson, Colonel Archibald (Comrie camp commandant), 82
Winter, Bridget (filmmaker), 157
With the German Guns
see *Zwei lebende Mauern* (HS's First World War diaries)
Wunstorf airfield, West Germany, 120–4, 133

Young Men's Christian Association (YMCA), 101

Zandvoort, 4
Die Zeit am Tyne (Featherstone Park newspaper), 106–7, 186
Ziock, Hermann (ex-Featherstone Park PoW), 99, 101–3, 106, 116, 173
Zwei lebende Mauern (HS's First World War diaries), 32, 38, 155–6